LONG HAMMERING

LONG HAMMERING

ESSAYS ON THE FORGING OF AN AFRICAN AMERICAN PRESENCE IN THE HUDSON RIVER VALLEY TO THE EARLY TWENTIETH CENTURY

A. J. Williams-Myers

Africa World Press, Inc.

P.O. Box 1892
Trenton, New Jersey 08607

Africa World Press, Inc.
P.O. Box 1892
Trenton, NJ 08607

Book and Cover design: Jonathan Gullery
The cover shows a detail from *Kitchen Ball at White Sulpher Springs, Virginia,* 1838, Christian Mayr c. 1805–1851, The North Carolina Museum of Art, Raleigh, purchased with funds from the State of North Carolina.

Library of Congress Cataloging-in-Publication Data

Williams-Myers, Albert James, 1939—
  Long Hammering : essays on the forging of an African American presence in the Hudson River Valley to the early twentieth century / A. J. Williams-Myers.
      p.   cm.
  Includes bibliographical references and index.
  ISBN 0-86543-302-X (HB). - - ISBN 0-86543-303-8 (PB)
  1. Afro-Americans - - Hudson River Valley (N.Y. and N.J.) - - History. 2. Hudson River Valley (N.Y. and N.J.) - - History. I. Title.
F127.H8W57 1994
974.7 '300496073 - - dc20

                                                    93-43528
                                                    CIP

CONTENTS

Preface

The history of the African presence in the Hudson River Valley has been, and is, an arduous journey—"a long hammering" to forge its image on the land. That history is an unfortunate tale of man's inhumanity to man and the incredible perseverance, preservation, and triumph of a people over tremendous odds. When Africans were first brought to the region they were not intended to become permanent, long-range residents. They were to be temporary sojourners in what would eventually become a region designated for whites. Africans were to observe, learn, and serve. In due time they were expected to die out because of their small number or to be absorbed by the general white population. This arduous journey, this "long hammering," encompassed the transformation from being to nonbeing, from human to inhuman, from civilized to uncivilized, and from religious believer to infidel. It was a journey from light into darkness, from dream into nightmare, and from purgatory into hell and damnation. It was a tale never intended to be told as it deserved, one touted by the teller of tales as "full of sound and fury yet signifying nothing." But the perseverance and the will to live of the African people has meant their triumph against enormous odds in the struggle for ultimate inclusion in a more equitable and humane society.

The journey continues to be arduous with much disappointment, disillusion, disbelief, and disgust. But those first Africans who arrived in the Hudson River valley were determined to see the journey through to the end. They knew they would not reach the mountain of their reward but laid the basis for the ongoing fight their progeny would assume in the ensuing months, years, decades, and centuries. Theirs was truly an heroic epic of "long hammering."

ACKNOWLEDGEMENTS

The author wishes to thank the editor of the journal, *Afro-Americans in New York Life and History* for permission to publish chapters 1, 2, 3, and 5, which originally appeared in volumes 1 (January 1983), 9 (January 1985), 11 (July 1987), and 12 (January 1988), respectively. Research for chapter 4 was made possible through two summer Faculty Research Grants (1986 and 1987) from the New York African American Institute in Albany, New York; the research was completed at Rhodes House Library, Oxford University. Parts of chapters 6, 7, 8, 9, 10, and 11 were abstracted from this work and appear in *The African American Presence in New York State History: Four Regional History Surveys* (Albany, N.Y.: New York African American Institute, 1989).

Chapter 1
Introduction

THE AFRICAN PRESENCE IN THE MID-HUDSON VALLEY BEFORE 1800: A PRELIMINARY HISTORICAL SKETCH

The reconstruction of the African presence in the Mid-Hudson Valley poses a difficult but interesting and fascinating challenge for the would-be historian. The difficulty arises from the fact that, although it is a given that the African was brought to the valley first by the Dutch and later by the British and American revolutionists, more concrete evidence of his cultural and economic contributions have yet to be researched.[1] Most of the available published material approaches the study of the African presence in the state of New York on a macroscopic level, and, as a result, a more personal and realistic look at the day-to-day life style of the African is lost.[2] Besides, at this level of writing there is a tendency to place the role of the African on the periphery and to deny him historical substance.[3] To rectify this situation and to create thereby a more historically accurate picture of the African presence, the task of the would-be historian is to develop a methodology which examines the historical roots of that presence in a microcosm. This approach would insure a more personal look at a topic which heretofore has historically been short on evidence and has been much too broad.

What is of interest and lends fascination to this challenge is the potential richness of the primary sources to allow for a more substantive historical reconstruction of the African presence. Further, the possible historiographical contributions such a study could make to the history of African Americans and that of the state of New York would go far towards filling in the so-called "historical gaps." Fascinated by these possibilities, this author has already begun such a research project by making a preliminary, cursory examination of sources and by pursuing leads through personal contacts. The results thus far have been both revealing and inspiring, giving hope of the project's feasibility, and, at the same time, somewhat frustrating. The frustration arises because prior to the mid-twentieth century writers simply refused to acknowledge the significant role of the African in the economic development of the region. For example, in one work which cites the 1714 census returns for three towns in Columbia County (Claverack, Kinderhook, and Coxsackie), the number of male and female slaves over sixteen and under sixteen years of age are given, but a more tangible, substantive image of these people and the identities of their owners are noticeably absent.[4] Even when this work rather extensively discusses the manufacturing, whaling, and sealing industries between 1786 and 1825, the reader gets no sense of the general composition of the work force or whether free and enslaved Africans were employed.[5] This very form of written history necessitates a more in-depth examination of the primary sources.

History is the story of the past: what happened, what people and events were involved, and the manner in which what happened was resolved. In history there is the idea of interdependence between man and nature, man and animal, and animal and nature. But in some of the published material on the African in New York, especially those sources which were published before the mid-twentieth century, there is no evidence of the interdependent relationship between African slaves and their white owners.[6] The African became marginalized and almost nonexistent other than to appear as a statistic when counting material possessions.[7] Before the turn of the nineteenth century, travellers crisscrossed the Mid-Hudson Valley region almost completely without once mentioning the presence of the Africans in the accounts of their travels.[8] There is ample statistical data on the presence of Africans in such towns as Hurley, Kingston, Poughkeepsie, Pawling, Newburgh, and New Paltz, but apparently they were of little importance to those early travellers. Yet according to the data, in 1790 there were 12,303 Africans, both free and slave, in the counties of Columbia, Albany, Orange, Ulster, and Dutchess, as compared to 184,491 whites.[9] In 1746, Africans in Ulster County alone accounted for one of every five inhabitants.[10]

Those Africans who were enslaved to whites in the Mid-Hudson prior to the beginning of the nineteenth century, pursued a life-style different only in degree from that of their counterparts in the southern regions of the eastern seaboard. Plantation-type farms were nonexistent. Most farms were small homesteads, some having been parceled out of larger grants.[11] The number of African slaves per homestead varied, from as few as one to as many as ten or more. The largest number alleged in the Dutchess County area during the eighteenth century was forty held by a German settler, Jacob Evarston.[12] Also in Dutchess County, Martinus Hoffman was the owner of ten African slaves.[13] In New Paltz town, Solomon Dubois and Abraham Hardenburgh each owned seven slaves, while Simon Dubois was the owner of six.[14] Because the growing season was short, farm work was complemented with domestic duties and with an array of work tasks on the land, including the hiring out of Africans to meet the cost of upkeep.[15]

Traditionally the African resided in the same household with the owner's family. Most basements were arranged to accommodate African servants, and they appear to have been quite spacious and well lighted.[16] On many occasions the children of the white owners and those of the African servants gathered together in the basements for play and, at times, mischievous acts were committed against the Blacks. The Vanderburgh mansion which was located northwest of present-day Poughquag in Dutchess County

[was] constructed partly of stone and partly of wood, with a broad cornered piazza extending the whole length in front, and a roomy, well lighted basement, which was set apart for the use of the slaves. One of his boys is reputed to have pointed an old musket at a slave boy [apparently not knowing that it was loaded], while playing with the slave in the basement, and shot him to death. He cried out before firing: "See me shoot a black crow."[17]

Such attitudes on the part of white children only mirrored the outlooks and opinions adults held about Blacks. Throughout the eighteenth century a climate of fear and hate prevailed among the whites of the Mid-Hudson region. Many were fearful that their own African slaves would repeat the bloody acts of violence against them which had been committed or alleged to have been committed against whites on Manhattan Island in 1712 and again in the conspiracy of 1741.[18] As a result of these real possibilities, it is believed that one of the reasons for many of the inaccuracies or "missing figures" in census data for Blacks had to do with security. Wherever there were large concentrations of Africans, these figures were never published. This was particularly true for the period after the early slave revolts, during the French and Indian War, and during the American Revolution.[19]

The punishment meted out to suspected perpetrators of violent acts and/or the accused was swift, at times corporal, and appropriately described as, "quite diabolic." For example, in 1735 an African slave who resided in Dutchess County named Quacko was sentenced to thirty-nine lashes at Poughkeepsie and an additional forty-eight at Rhinebeck for attempted rape.[20] Another African, "Negro Jack," was burned alive in Ulster County in October 1732 for "burning a barne and a barrack of wheat."[21] And in the town of Kingston a slave known only as Tom was executed for attempted rape and the murder of a white woman.[22] Yet in spite of the climate of hate and violence that existed toward the African, he did prevail; by 1790 in four Mid-Hudson counties, Albany, Dutchess, Orange, and Ulster, the African population was estimated to have been 5.2, 4.1, 5.4, and 9.9 percent, respectively, of the total populations.[23]

In the mountains south of Poughquag, around what is

today Mt. Storm and/or Stormville, there sprang up in the second half of the eighteenth century Freemanville, a community considered to have been settled entirely by free Africans. These Africans sought to maintain their distinctiveness and African heritage by also referring to their community as Guinea, after that region in West Africa from which many may have been taken as slaves. Among them was a mulatto named Freeman (perhaps after whom the town was named). He appears to have been the largest landholder in the community; in the last quarter of the nineteenth century there were older white citizens who still remembered him as the most important individual among the African Americans who resided in Guinea.[24]

South of Freemanville lived another free African called Tone, who, after his manumission from John Warring because of his enlistment in the Revolutionary Army, developed two prosperous businesses: boat rentals to fishermen and a tavern on a pond named after him. He married a woman of both African and Indian ancestry, and one of his grandsons is remembered as having married a beautiful young white girl. Her love for him appears to have been centered more in what he would be worth as a slave than as a spouse. She eventually induced him to go south with her where she succeeded in selling him into slavery.[25] Without a doubt there were other notable Africans on the Mid-Hudson like Charles Freeman and Tone; they must have been very much an integral part of the economic structure as were the first African pioneer settlers on the lower Hudson around Tappan in the 1680's.[26] But these have yet to be researched from the primary sources.

For most of the eighteenth century, the Mid-Hudson region was part of what was then considered the hostile frontier populated by bloodthirsty savages and Frenchmen. Albany (Fort Orange), which had been established on the "far frontier" in the early seventeenth century, initially failed, like some of its eighteenth century counterparts, to attract white settlers because of frontier conditions. As a result of this, many homesteaders on the Hudson were dependent upon slave labor. In order to insure that African slaves remained with their owners, measures had to be taken to prevent them from escaping their bondage on the frontier and from joining with the Indian tribes. In 1705, one of the many laws which were to go before the colonial legislature to control the movement of Blacks was passed, prohibiting Africans from traveling forty miles north of Saratoga, present-day Schuylerville.[27]

Frontier conditions were such that the whites were dependent upon the Africans for more than simply clearing and working the farms and various forms of domestic work. Many were used as auxiliaries in the campaign against Indian tribes and played significant roles in the French and Indian War.[28] The African was first used in 1660 on the Mid-Hudson by the then Dutch Governor of New Amsterdam, Peter Stuyvesant, against the Esopus Indians who lived in the region in and around the towns of New Paltz and Kingston. In February of that year he wrote to Dutch officials on the Caribbean Island of Curaçao, requesting "clever and strong" African slaves to "pursue the Indians," adding that it is "evident that in order to possess this country in peace and revenge affronts and murders we shall be forced into a lawful offensive war against them [the Indians]."[29] Despite the fact that the African was used to fight against the Esopus, this tribe was one of the many among whom escaped slaves sought refuge. Today on the Mid-Hudson it is possible to hear rumors of the past existence of "Black and White Esopus," an apparent reference to those of mixed African and Indian ancestry and those of predominately Esopus blood. In the Poughkeepsie militia, African slaves and free Blacks were used as scouts against what was referred to as "rebel slaves of Poughkeepsie," undoubtedly escaped slaves whose positions of resistance to the institution had become that of maroons.[30]

As has been evident in this essay, the African presence on the Mid-Hudson developed as a result of the institution of slavery. It was a presence which continued to grow in response to an ever-existent demand for labor. Therefore, contrary to the beliefs that slavery as an institution declined rapidly after the Revolutionary War and that by the end of the first decade of the nineteenth century was almost non-existent, African slavery in New York actually showed an increase in certain areas.[31] In both Dutchess and Ulster counties there were marked increases in their slave populations between 1723 and 1790, with each gaining 1,813 and 2,340 additional slaves, respectively. Between 1771 and 1790, the Revolutionary period, both had respective gains of 496 and 952, small but significant increases for the region and for an institution considered to have been in decline at the time.[32]

It probably could be surmised that a significant number of African slaves imported into the Mid-Hudson region were trans-shipped from points in the Caribbean and South America such as Cuba, Santo Domingo, Curaçao, Barbados, Brazil, and even the Guinea Coast of Africa.[33] In support of this it is recorded that a consignment of African slaves that had apparently disem-barked at either the ports of Hudson or Albany from "Havannah" were later transported further north up the river to Whitehall (then known as Skenesborough) where they were sold to prospective buyers.[34] Directly following the Revolutionary War and with the growth and/or expansion of both industry and commerce in and around the Hudson River towns of Claverack and Hudson, it is even possible to speculate that many of the slaves which were shipped to this region also came from Charleston, South Carolina.[35]

It has been argued elsewhere that the majority of African laborers "performed a large part of the unskilled and menial labor in colonial [New Amsterdam and] New York where they probably comprised the major portion of household servants, field hands and workers of little or no training." But unfortu-nately this view fails to take into consideration the number of apparently skilled craftsmen, either those trained in the colony or those imported as skilled laborers.[36] Such numbers have to be considered, because, if the initial need was for farm laborers, then it goes without saying that, whether the average African was either from the West Indies, Brazil, or Africa, he was, neverthe-less, from an agricultural society.[37] It is even probable that many possessed skills of the best craftsmen and that, with masonry, it was simply a matter of adapting to Western architectural styles. Until the influx of large numbers of whites from Europe, skilled Africans worked at many of the crafts. Responding to such a need and to the appeal for the use of Black craftsman, Peter Stuyvesant, following instructions from the directors at Amsterdam (Holland), proceeded, as early as 1657, to use African slaves as caulkers, blacksmiths, bricklayers, and carpenters to fill an acute void among whites in such crafts.[38]

Even though the data are yet unpublished, it is more than likely that key points on the Hudson River, such as Newburgh, Poughkeepsie, Hudson-Claverack, and Albany, were major areas where the largest concentration of Blacks were to be found. In the Hudson-Claverack region alone, as a result of the growth of industry and commerce (whaling, sealing, iron and leather industries) in the second half of the eighteenth century, on board many of the ships which sailed down the river to the sea probably were Black sailors who filled many of the important skilled positions. It is likely that free and enslaved Africans were employed in the towns in the leather, iron, and building trades. Thus, if all or most of this can be substantiated through a closer examination of the primary sources (as will be demonstrated in successive chapters), perhaps there may be a need to qualify the belief that African laborers were mainly limited to "unskilled and menial labor in New York."[39]

Manumission in the Mid-Hudson, as throughout all New York, was both a joyous and traumatic event for Africans and whites, although perhaps more joyous for the Africans. It was traumatic because, despite the New York legislature's passage of the gradual emancipation acts of 1799 and 1817,[40] many slave holders were reluctant to relinquish their human property without compensation and, therefore, sought to remove their slaves clandestinely from the state to be sold in the south.[41] In 1717, apparently in support of supporters of slavery, the legislature moved to make the manumission of slaves a difficult act by stipulating that an owner had to put up a two-hundred-pound security bond to guarantee that the former slave would not become a charge to the city or town. After the final manumission act was passed on 4 July 1827, it was still possible to find legally enslaved Africans in the Mid-Hudson.

NOTES

1. E. B. O'Callaghan, ed., *Documentary History of the State of New York*, 4 vols. (Albany, N. Y.: Weed, Parsons and Company 1850); E. B. O'Callaghan, ed., *Voyages of the Slavers "St. John" and "Arms of Amsterdam"* (Albany, N. Y.: J. Munsel, 1867); Berthold Fernow and E. B. O'Callaghan, eds., *Documents Relative to the Colonial History of the State of New York*, 15 vols. (Albany, N. Y.: Weed, Parsons and Company, 1856-1887); Elizabeth

Donnan, ed., *Documents Illustrative of the History of the Slave Trade to America*, 4 vols. (Washington, D. C.: Carnegie Institute, 1932), 3:424; E. Olson, "Negro Slavery in New York, 1626-1827," (Ph.D. diss., New York University, 1939); Huguenot Duzine Collection, New Paltz Elting Public Library.

2. Cf. Edgar J. McManus, *A History of Negro Slavery in New York* (Syracuse, N. Y.: 1966); E. J. McManus, *Black Bondage in the North* (Syracuse, N. Y.: 1973); Samuel McKee, Jr., *Labor in Colonial New York, 1667-1776* (Port Washington, N. Y.: 1963).

3. Cf. Edwin V. Morgan, *Slavery in New York* (New York: 1896); A. Judd Northrup, *Slavery in New York* (Albany, N. Y.: State Library, 1900).

4. *History of Columbia County*, New York (Philadelphia, Pa.: Everts and Ensign, 1878), 135, 162.

5. *Ibid.*, 162-205.

6. Cf. Ralph Le Fevre, *History of New Paltz 1678-1820*, 2d ed. (Albany, N. Y.: Fort Orange Press, 1909).

7. *Ibid.*, 92-93; Philip H. Smith, *General History of Dutchess County from 1609 to 1876, Inclusive* (Pawling, N. Y.: Published by author, 1871), 469.

8. Barlett Burleigh James and J. Franklin Jameson, eds., *Journal of Jaspher Danckaerts 1679-1680* (New York: Barnes and Nobles, 1946). This book mentions an African who could converse in the Dutch language owned by a Mr. Theumis outside of Albany (193), J. Lossing, *The Hudson from the Wilderness to the Sea* (New York: Virtue and Yorston, 1866); Philip H. Smith, *Legends of the Shawangunk and its Environs* (Syracuse, N. Y.: reprint of 1822 Syracuse University Press, 1965). An African occasionally appears in some of the legends aiding whites in their fights against Indians, allies of the French. There appears to have been an accepted American mind set among historians which "required that Blacks (and Native Americans) assume an anonymous image bereft of fully human capacities for thought, feeling and the comprehension of social experience." (Cedric J. Robinson, "Class Antagonisms and Black Migrations: A Review Article," *Race and Class* 24, no. 1 [1982]: 49-50). But according to the American historian Wesley Frank Craven it was a mind set that was constantly confronted with the truth. He wrote: "We tend to preserve or restore only that which by some artistic or other standard seems worth preserving, and so the picture can be distorted. Who among us can wander down the street of Williamsburg, with promptings on every side to remember Washington and Jefferson, and still remember that it all rested originally on the back of a Negro?" (*The Legend of the Founding Fathers* [Ithaca, N. Y.: Cornell University Press, 1965], 121, 131).

9. McManus, *Negro Slavery*, 97-100; Thomas J. Davis, "New York's Long Black Line: A Note on the Growing Slave Population, 1626-1790," *Afro-Americans in New York Life and History*, 2 (January 1978): 46-51.

10. Davis, 46-51.

11. Carl Nordstrom, "Slavery in a New York County: Rockland County 1686-1827," *Afro-Americans in New York Life and History*, 1 (July 1977): 149.

12. Smith, *General History of Dutchess County,* 141.
13. Davis, 51.
14. Le Fevre, 93.
15. Nordstrom, 156.
16. Ibid., 151-152; Smith, *General History of Dutchess County,* 140-41.
17. Smith, *General History of Dutchess County,* 141.
18. Kenneth Scott, "The Slave Insurrection in New York in 1712," *New York Historical Society Quarterly,* 45 (January 1961): 43-74; Daniel Horsmanden, *The New York Conspiracy, or A History of The Negro Plot* quoted in Roi Ottley and William J. Weatherby, eds., *The Negro in New York: An Informal Social History* (Dobbs Ferry, N. Y.: Oceana Publications, 1967), 22-24, 27-30.
19. Cf. Davis, 42-43; Howard Pecham, *The Colonial Wars 1689-1762* (Chicago, Ill.: University of Chicago Press, 1964).
20. Julius Goebel, Jr., and T. Raymond Naughton, *Law Enforcement in Colonial New York* (New York: Columbia University Press, 1944), 627.
21. E. B. O'Callaghan, ed., *Colonial Laws of New York,* 5 vols. (Albany, N. Y.: 1896), 2:763.
22. Leo Hershkowitz, "Tom's Case: An Incident, 1741," *New York History* 52, no. 1 (1971): 63-71.
23. Davis, 45-51.
24. Smith, *General History of Dutchess County,* 134.
25. *Ibid.,* 470.
26. George H. Budke, "The History of the Tappan Patent," quoted in Nordstrom, 145-147.
27. Ottley and Weatherby, 22.
28. Cf. Laura E. Wilkes, *Missing Pages in American History* (Washington, D. C.: Laura E. Wilkes, 1919), 20.
29. Ottley and Weatherby, 12. Cf. Smith, *Legends of Shawangunk.*
30. Smith, *General History of Dutchess County,* 346-347. Cf. Herbert Aptheker, "Maroons Within the Present Limits of the United States," *Journal of Negro History* 32 (October 1947): 453-60.
31. Davis, 55-57.
32. *Ibid.,* 48-49. In 1771 the white populations in Dutchess and Ulster counties were 21,044 and 11,996, respectively (O'Callaghan, *Documentary History of New York,* 1:697).
33. *History of Columbia County,* 162; Ottley and Weatherby, 5. Based on estimates from Rockland County, it is probable that the average male slave in good health sold for about one hundred pounds sterling or $250, and a female for sixty-five pounds sterling (Nordstrom, 147).
34. Personal correspondence with Ms. Doris B. Morton, *Philip Skene of Skenesborough* (Gransville, N. Y.: Grastorf Press, 1959), 23, 32.
35. *History of Columbia County,* 162-170; Nordstrom, 154-55.
36. McKee, 114.
37. Cf. Perter H. Wood, *Black Majority, Negroes in Colonial South Carolina from 1670 through the Stono Rebellion* (New York: W. W. Norton and Company, 1974), 30-31, 62; R. L. Watson, "American Scholars and the Continuity

of African Culture in the United States," *Journal of Negro History* 39 (1954): 8-26.

38. Ottley and Weatherby, 7.
39. McKee, 114.
40. Davis, 57.
41. Ottley and Weatherby, 59-60; Nordstrom, 157.

page 12 prints blank

Chapter 2

HANDS THAT PICKED NO COTTON:
AFRICAN SLAVE LABOR IN THE
COLONIAL ECONOMY OF THE HUDSON
RIVER VALLEY TO 1800

In a recent article Gary Nash reminds us that a large majority of those who crossed the Atlantic in the centuries prior to the American Revolution to take up life in the New World were Africans. Because historians have concentrated more on the institution of slavery rather than on the slave, the social history of those Africans has been neglected. As a result, we continue to depict "some one million Africans brought to or born in America before the revolution as mindless and cultureless drones, without realizing that the slaves themselves [were] active participants in a social process."[1] To paraphrase Douglas Greenberg, slaves were in the history of the colonies without being of that history.[2] Such a situation can be rectified by creating a new corpus of scholarship on African American social history and subsequently incorporating that new scholarship "into an overall analysis of colonial social development."[3]

For New York, a social history of the African American presence still awaits the would-be historian. This is not to slight some of the earlier perceptive monographs that have been written on slavery throughout the state.[4] But because these studies concentrate mainly on describing the kind of institution established, they fall short of giving us any idea of the social history of Africans imported to or born in New York State. Yet there does appear to be an incipient corpus of scholarship (some published, some unpublished) for the African on the lower Hudson River—on Manhattan and adjacent areas to the east—in the making.[5] Unfortunately, much of it focuses on the system of slavery, too. But the work of Jessica Kross, Thomas J. Davis, and Vivienne Kruger appears to be on the cutting edge of African social history because it acknowledges the significant participatory and social role of the Africans in the development of New York history around the mouth of the Hudson River.

There is a dearth of published information on the African presence in the Hudson River Valley; the history of white penetration and settlement contains numerous histories of early families, towns, and counties as well as general studies of an economic, political, and social nature.[6] But most of these histories mirror Gary Nash's position in that they paint a picture of Hudson Valley society almost completely devoid of Africans as active participants in the social process.

In spite of this dearth of information, there has been an attempt within the last decade to fill the gap in the historiography of the Hudson River Valley region.[7] I include in this attempt my own two recent preliminary articles which tend to complement the earlier material.[8] My initial approach has been a personalization of the African, which is unlike the earlier perceptive works of McManus and McKee whose emphases are more impersonal.[9] But the one thing that my writings, and the works of others as well, lack is a more analytic historical framework in which to view the social development of the African over time. This paper, therefore, is an attempt to address a serious and evident historiographical gap in the writing of the so-called "new history of the early modern era" for colonial New York.[10] The paper's focus is the African presence in the Hudson River Valley of eastern New York, a region that can be conveniently described as the embryo of New York history. In this paper, the process of filling the gap in the historiography as well as the enhancement of the personalization of the African will center around the creation of a functional analytical framework which attempts to answer a number of questions. First, why would there have been such a demand placed on the use of slave labor when New York was so unlike the British colonies of Virginia, South Carolina, and Georgia, and the Leeward Islands of the Caribbean which had developed staple crop economies? Was the immigration of indentured servants and tenants sufficiently low to warrant the importation of African laborers in the valley? Could forms of established land tenure or holding patterns have been obstacles to white settlement, and thus there was the need for slave labor to exploit the natural resources of the valley? In what capacities were African slaves utilized, and did they ever reach significantly high numbers? One final question, which undoubtedly has bearing on all the other questions, to what extent are the sources for such a study readily known, reliable, and accessible to the researcher?

Sources

The lack of a corpus of scholarship on the African presence in the Hudson River Valley requires that the historian carefully and painstakingly cull the appropriate data from the primary documents which are stored/housed in various depositories in both Albany and New York City and in the towns and counties along the Hudson. Some of the archival material is now available in published form, having been either translated and edited from Dutch or simply compiled and edited from English documents.[11] Among this primary material are data from the Federal Census of 1790 and earlier tabulations of the Hudson Valley's colonial population; court records, wills, and death certificates; and the records of local churches and the Society for the Propagation of the Gospel in Foreign Parts.[12] Much of this is complemented by secondary sources and/or little-known, not too readily available, material such as personal correspondence, travellers' accounts (journals), reminiscences, and biographies.[13]

The newness of this field of study and the fact that a great deal of the primary material has yet to be tapped, without a doubt, have built a degree of speculation or hypothesis into it, but it is speculation within the realm of probability. For example, we will probably never know the exact number and origins of Africans imported into the Hudson region from Africa, Barbados, and Jamaica. But this should not deter us from saying something about relative numbers concerned with a particular place in time.

Source material for creating a functional framework in which to view the African presence is fairly good.[14] Kim's *Landlord and Tenant,* although it falls short on African involvement, does offer a solid foundation for examining the manorial structure in the valley, its consequences for settler tenancy, and its role in the economic exploitation of the region. The articles of both Richard B. Sheridan and Douglas Greenberg on the Middle Colonies are supportive of and complement Kim.[15] The essential point, though, is that the use of this material not only makes allowances for a larger angle of vision in which to view the social development of the African, but it affords the historian the opportunity to integrate and incorporate pertinent historical data into an overall analysis of colonial social development.

Economic Viability or Unprofitable Colonialism: New York Under the Dutch and British

There is no dearth of information on the topography of the Hudson River Valley.[16] The region is mountainous. The Catskill and Taconic ranges parallel the Hudson River west and east, respectively, and the towering, precipitous Shawangunk Ridge, about mid-valley, stretches west to the south of the Catskills. (See map #1.) Further south, there are the Bear and Ramapo mountains. It is a region of lush, fertile valleys which are heavily forested and watered by a number of meandering minor rivers and, at times, swiftly flowing streams. Most of the minor rivers are tributaries of the Hudson, which itself was a vital artery both for early trade from the interior to its entrepôts of Albany and New York and for settlement along its banks and the immediate hinterland. Settled throughout the valley were scattered indigenous lineages of the Minisinks, Delawares, Esopus, and Wappingers Indians on the middle Hudson and of the Manhattans on the lower river, all apparently remnants of larger groups around the watersheds of the Hudson-Mohawk-Delaware and Connecticut rivers (Algonquin speakers). (See map #2.)

It was into this region that the Dutch and the British introduced the institution of African slavery as an alternative and supplementary labor force to that of yeomen and indentured servants. Although the numbers of Africans imported into the valley never totalled the numbers of Africans imported into the Chesapeake and lower south, they existed in sufficient numbers and were involved in viable economic pursuits so that their labor roles were many on a profit-oriented continuum stretching from New York, through the Chesapeake, Georgia, and South Carolina to the Caribbean.[17] By the end of the seventeenth century, slaves had become an important staple of the region's economy. But what motivated this importation of African slave labor rather than making a concerted effort to attract white indentured servants and yeomen?

Despite the region's apparent idyllic setting and enormous potential for economic success, until the turn of the eighteenth century both the Dutch and the British found it difficult to populate the area with a sufficient number of white, industrious settlers to make it a worthwhile venture. In fact, the Dutch developers of New Netherlands had determined by 1628 that the Dutch West India Company's efforts were a financial failure.[18] An alternative approach for the company was the encouragement of private initiative and less company interference in some areas of economic pursuits, outside the fur trade north of Fort Orange (Albany). The outcome was a "grandiose plan" to establish a series of fiefdoms up and down the valley. These so-called fiefdoms, referred to as patroonships, were to be "autonomous legal entities within the colony" with the Patroons obligated to settle the estates with white settles in order to make them economically viable.[19]

Unfortunately, the only patroonship established in the Hudson Valley was Rensselaerswyck which straddled the upper Hudson and encompassed Fort Orange, the result of the private financial efforts of one of the company's directors, Kiliaen van Rensselaer.[20] By the end of the 1630s, New Netherlands lacked a population significantly large enough to make it financially solvent. Possible reasons for this included the company's monopoly on the fur trade and/or the possibility of the "imposition of a feudal order upon free soil" which acted as a deterrent to settlement.[21] When the British assumed control of the region in 1664, the Dutch were diligently involved in an alternative labor source—African slaves.

Following in the wake of the Dutch, the British proceeded to establish large manors—initially with a feudal base—in order to attract tenants and indentured servants as a potential labor force for exploiting the land. During the tenure of Governor Dongan in the late 1680s, Rensselaerswyck and a series of manorial estates and royal patents were given to wealthy New York families and merchants in the lower and upper valley. (Rensselaerswyck was simply reconfirmed as a private holding of the van Rensselaer family.)[22] Most of the grants were quite liberal. For example, in addition to Rensselaerswyck Manor with a total of 850,000 acres, including the lower manor east of the Hudson at Claverack, there were the Livingston Manor, with its lower manor of Clermont of 160,000 acres just south of Rensselaerswyck, and both the Cortlandt and Philipsburg Manors on the lower Hudson with the latter's acreage approximately 92,000.[23] (See map #3.) Among some of the patents there was the Hardenbergh Patent of 1,500,000 acres, which comprised most of the present counties of Ulster, Delaware, Sullivan, and Greene and in which Robert Livingston, Jr., had a substantial interest. Others included the two mid-Hudson patents of Henry Beekman, Jr., Rhinebeck (21,766 acres) and Beekman (approximately 84,000 acres), and the 85,000-acre Rombout Patent in southern Dutchess, purchased from the Wappingers Indians by Francis Rombout and Gulian Verplanck, both New York City merchants.[24]

The grantees had the designated task of making a bad economic situation more viable. In the decades immediately after 1664, immigration from Holland virtually stopped; English immigrants trickled into the colony with an "average of three English, Scottish, or Irish families a year from 1678 to 1685." By 1686, the profitable fur trade was hit by a serious depression. The one item that was to make the colony economically viable, the undergirding of Dongan's idea for the manorial system, was grain. The need for large quantities of flour both in the West Indies and Europe was one of the incentives which attracted business-minded people like Frederick Philipse, Staphanus van

Cortlandt, Robert Livingston, and others to Governor Dongan's idea. Basically merchants, they nevertheless lost no time in diversifying their business activities beyond being landlords and producers of flour and lumber to establishing gristmills and sawmills on their estates.[25]

The business acumen of the manor lords and the patentees was the necessary panacea for the economic ills which plagued the Hudson River Valley. Through diversification of their economic pursuits, most estate owners appear to have fared rather well economically. In addition to maintaining a monopoly over the construction of all mills and lumbering, they also "claimed exclusive jurisdiction over all rivers and streams within [their estates] suitable for mill sites" as well as venturing into the manufacturing of iron.[26] Men like Frederick Philipse and his son Adolph were able to diversify to such an extent that by 1690 they had set up a "commercial network" with ten of their own ships in interlocking trade with Europe, Africa, the lower south, and the West Indies. Others like the Livingstons, van Rensselaers, and Schuylers were either involved as individual ship owners or with a holding interest.[27]

By the third decade of the eighteenth century, the economy of the valley was vibrant, and there was an apparent division of labor between the lower and upper valley. With Albany as its most profitable focal point, the upper valley concentrated on the production of wheat and corn and some manufacturing, while the lower valley, adjacent to New York City, responded to that city's needs for foodstuffs by combining its production of wheat and corn with a venture into commercial livestock and dairy husbandry.[28] Tenants on the various estates adjusted or strengthened their efforts in the production of these items both as rent payment and for the provincial markets.

Although by the third decade of the eighteenth century the plight of New York as a colony had moved from a position of unprofitable colonialism to that of economic viability, the economy remained on a somewhat precarious footing because of a constant shortage of labor—tenants as well as indentured servants. The French and Indian "menace" on the frontier did not help matters with respect to attracting settlers. As a result, by the end of the first decade of the eighteenth century, manor lords in the lower valley bemoaned the fact that their estates were sparsely settled. At Cortlandt and Philipsburg there were only eighty-seven and 309 white inhabitants, respectively. On the upper Hudson, Rensselaerswyck Manor and Livingston Manor were experiencing a similar sluggishness in settlement. By 1714, Rensselaerswyck had only eighty-two tenants and a total population of 427, "an average increase of only one tenant family a year," while Livingston Manor had thirty-three tenants and approximately 170 whites.[29] In addition to the disturbing frontier condition, it has been argued elsewhere that in reality the manorial system in the Hudson Valley was an obstacle to white settlement. Driven by the psychology of the yeomen who came to America, the immigrants viewed the system as a version of the feudalism they had experienced in Europe. For them the "manorial system was an instrument of oppression and exploitation, which offered only marginal security from abject poverty."[30] They much preferred to be freeholders. What all of this meant to the British in New York was that they had to find a remedy for the labor shortage. Like the Dutch before them, they soon developed a great reliance on African slave labor.

The African Nexus

The British resort to slave labor can be interpreted as an acknowledged acceptance of the utility of their predecessors' labor system which was indispensable prior to 1664.[31] Unwilling to invest in the cost of bringing servants to New Netherlands, whose supply by no means ever equaled the demand, the Dutch, as early as 1629, found it cheaper and more convenient to import African slaves to perform the labor needs of the colony.[32] English manor lords and patentees, finding themselves in a similar predicament with regard to tenants and servants, simply plugged into a preexisting labor system and supply, making it reflect the needs of a colonial economy geared towards export and import.

The immediate source of slaves for the valley was New York, itself an important port of call for slaving vessels as well as the site of a lucrative slave market (at the foot of Wall Street on the East River).[33] Prior to 1748 the bulk of African slaves imported into the colony came primarily from the British Caribbean colonies—such as Barbados, Jamaica, and Antigua—and from the mainland colonies of South Carolina and Virginia. After 1748 there was an appreciable increase in the trafficking in slaves from Africa, a remarkable seventy percent reversal in terms of point of embarkation. An appropriate estimate for the total imports of Africans into New York (from American and African sources) between 1700 and 1774 is 6,800. Even by 1723, the African slave population, as a result of natural increases and importations, had already reached the figure of 6,171 (with 2,395 of that total alone having been imported between 1701 and 1726 from Africa and the West Indies).[34] By 1790 the African slave population had increased to approximately 21,324.[35] In reaching that figure, New York's slave population went through a phenomenal growth period for a mainland colony quite unlike those of the Chesapeake and lower south. For example, Jessica Kross's microstudy of Newtown (part of Queens) indicates that by 1790 the slave population was five times what it had been in 1698, making it one-third the total population, while the figure for whites had fallen short of actually doubling.[36] In the colony as a whole, the Black population fluctuated between twelve and twenty-four percent of the total during the first half of the eighteenth century. At the time of the Federal Census of 1790, that percentage was more like ten to fifteen.[37] What much of this tells us is that, for a colony which lacked an economy geared towards the production of a staple crop, New York, by the end of the colonial period, "possessed the largest Black population north of Maryland." New York's slave population in 1790 far outdistanced its nearest competitors in the Middle and New England Colonies and was only seven thousand below Georgia's total of 29,264.[38] It is even possible to speculate that if New York could have generated enormous profits from her exports, similar to the exports of rice and naval stores from South Carolina and Georgia, then perhaps her merchants might have made the African population in the Hudson Valley mirror those numbers in the colonies of the Chesapeake and lower south.[39]

In the Hudson Valley, the African population varied from county to county depending upon economic exploits and degree of wealth. By the end of the first quarter of the eighteenth century, the largest holdings appear to have been in the lower and upper valley where much of the growing of grains, the lumbering, the manufacturing, and the rearing of commercial livestock took place. Between 1723 and 1771, Albany and Westchester counties had slave populations (and the figures might also include some free Blacks) of as low as 808 and 448, respectively, in 1723 to as high as 3,877 and 3,430, respectively, in 1771.[40] In 1790 the slave figures increased for Albany whose slave population then stood at 3,929 of a total population of 75,921. The city of Albany alone had 572 slaves in 1790 out of a total population of 3,491.[41] On the middle Hudson, Dutchess and Ulster counties held their own in terms of numbers. By 1771 their slave populations were 1,360 and 1,954, respectively, but in 1790 they had jumped to 1,856 and 2,906, a sizable increase for the Revolutionary period and for an institution considered to have been in decline in the region at the time.[42] Yet, in examining the figures further, we find that, in 1746, Africans in Ulster County alone accounted for one of every five inhabitants. In the counties of Albany, Dutchess, Orange, and Ulster, by the end of the Revolutionary period the African populations of these counties were estimated to have been 5.2, 4.1, 5.4, and 9.9 percent, respectively, of the total population.[43]

Throughout the valley, slaves were constantly bought and sold. The importation of slaves into individual counties required a payment of three to five pounds on each slave.[44] Agents for prospective buyers in the valley either purchased Africans in New York at a certain price and with a desirable personality trait as prearranged with clients, or they acted as independent businessmen and resold their purchases at Albany, Kingston, Newburgh, or Poughkeepsie. For example, on 17 October 1748, Gerard G. Beekman of New York City, acting as agent for his brother, James, and others who resided in Kingston, wrote an agent of his in Rhode Island inquiring of slaves. "I received yours of the 10 instant and observe you have for sale one young negro wench and child of 9 months. If she is likely brisk and no bad quality the two will fetch fifty pounds or more."[45] Cadwallader Colden who had an estate in Newburgh, as well as a residence in New York, wrote to a Doctor Home of New York in December 1721 with a request to purchase for him three slaves to be used at the Newburgh estate. He wanted two males to be about eighteen years of age and of good temper, and an African girl of about thirteen years of age. "My wife desires her chiefly to keep the children and to sow . . . one that appears to be good natured."[46] Before the turn of the eighteenth century, Africans around Albany were sold outright by agents and owners or rented out for a number of years at prices established in marketable goods (winter wheat, beaver pelts, lumber, or peas) or Dutch guilders. On 1 July 1665, an African slave named Augustynus was sold by Cornelis Martensen Potter for 150 guilders. Apparently a slave dealer at Albany, Amadoor Vopie sold to Claes van Pettern on 27 May 1682, an African male named Jan for "the sum of 50 good, whole deliverable beaver skins, but failing of beavers . . . good, marketable winter wheat, or peas, as the market price thereof shall be in beavers."[47] Skilled Africans went for considerably more. In October 1778, Gerard W. Beekman purchased an African coachman for 200 pounds and, in August 1779, acquired an African "cuper" [cooper], who could also "shave and dress haire," for 1000 [100?] pounds.[48]

Aside from Beekman and Colden, who were some of the other owners of these slaves? And in what capacity of work were they employed? First, most white families in the valley did not own slaves, and those who did, on the average, had one or two slaves. It could be argued that the majority of slaves were held by families who owned one or two. Perhaps the largest slave owners were manor lords, some patentees as well as some tenant farmers and freeholders.[49] An Englishman on a trip through the valley remarked in the 1790s that "many of the old Dutch farmers . . . have 20 to 30 slaves [and] to their care and management every thing is left."[50] When Frederick Philipse died at the turn of the eighteenth century, he left to his son Adolph and his grandson Frederick, Jr., thirty or more slaves on his upper and lower manors—Philipsburg and Yonkers. A total of twenty can be counted in his will.[51] A German settler, Jacob Evarston, who resided in the town of Amenia in eastern Dutchess County, held forty slaves, while Martinus Hoffman of the same county was the owner of ten slaves.[52] Both Herman Knickerback of Albany and Jacob D. van der Heyden of Troy are remembered for their large retinue of slaves. But the individuals holding in bondage the largest number of Africans in the colony during the period between the end of the seventeenth century and the mid-eighteenth century were Sir William Johnson, Indian Agent above Albany and owner of a large part of the Mohawk Valley region, and Lewis Morris of Morrisania on the lower Hudson in Westchester County. Sir William Johnson's slaves are said to have exceeded sixty, and he is alleged to have lived in "regal splendor" (the assets in his will verify this), while those of Lewis Morris totaled fifty-five.[53] He was the largest slaveholder in the county.[54] Even as late as the time of the Federal Census of 1790, thirteen individuals in the town of Kinderhook held nine or more slaves. The van Alstines, Philip and Abraham J., held the largest, sixteen and eighteen, respectively.[55]

Labor and Economy: the African World of Work

Work regimes of Africans ran the gamut from unskilled and menial tasks to those requiring a command of certain technical skills. Undoubtedly a large percentage of slaves were employed in agricultural and domestic tasks. From the writings of Hector St. John de Crevecoeur, whose estate, Pine Hill, was in Orange County near Newburgh, we get the impression that the African was an indispensable element in the efficient operation of a farm. He was that "essential cog in the wheel" that kept the farm solvent. He was instrumental in the care of the oxen, cows, colts, sheep, horses, and ducks, as well as farming the land.[56] During the second half of the seventeenth century Jeremias van Rensselaer corresponded with his brother Jan Baptist in Holland about the expertise of an African slave.

> Your negro, Andries, has this winter taken care of the horses alone and has done it so well that during my time [there] the horses have never looked so fine.

> [Jan Baptist responded] Please send him [Andries] over on the first ship and contract for his passage at the lowest price possible. I need him very much at Carlo to take care of my horse [which is full of worms].[57]

Those slaves who were owned by tenants, such as the five of Joseph Vail (or Veal) of Fishkill on the Beekman Patent in

Dutchess County, as well as those attached to manors and owned by Patentees, probably joined with indentured servants in performing obligatory services called the "riding" for the manorial lords as part of rent payments.[58] Under the "riding" system, tenant farmers got their slaves and servants to maintain the roads on the manor as well as the adjacent King's Highway (Albany Post Road) and to cut and to cart firewood, timber, stones, and coals as desired by the lord.[59] Africans had to mesh these obligatory services of their tenant owners with those normally required of them by tenant and manor lord. Slaves were involved in the production of almost every item used or consumed on the farm: from such simple items as brooms, ladles, and cords of firewood for use year-round to more elaborate ones such as barns and Dutch cellars in which roots, vegetables, cider, milk, butter, and meat were stored for preservation.

As with farm work, males and females shared domestic chores but with a clear division of labor by gender. Women were often found in the kitchen cooking, cleaning house, washing, and caring for their owners' children as well as being integrally involved in the production of linens and woolens for home consumption and the colonial markets.[60] One condition of the 1682 lease of a young female slave of Captain Johannes Clute to Arnout Carnelissen Viele was that, in addition to providing the young woman with proper clothing, he was also required "to teach her to sew, knit and spin according to her capacity."[61] Men were waiters, butlers, coachmen, and skilled craftsmen such as carpenters, masons, and wheelwrights. William Strickland, who visited the Livingstons in the 1790s, wrote of domestic roles he observed at the homes of Chancellor Robert Livingston and his mother, Margaret Beekman Livingston, with both of whom he took meals.

> four black boys, eldest about 11 or 12, the youngest about 5 or 6 years old, clean and well dressed but barefooted in a livery green turned up with red, waited about the table [during breakfast]. . . . Three black men in livery waited at dinner and the boys before mentioned, their children. It is not unusual for female blacks to wait; an instance of which we met with yesterday at Mrs. Livingston's, the mother of the Chancellor.[62]

Mary Humphreys, biographer of Catherine Schuyler, described a scene which complements that of the Livingstons: in many of the big houses in and around Albany, it was the job of the Africans to visit each room in the cold of winter and in the cool of autumn to start the fires in the fireplaces "at stated hours, making the house sparkle with dancing flames."[63] Echoing Crevecoeur, she wrote about similar tasks for the Africans attached to the wealthier families in the upper valley.

> For every department of the household there was a slave allotted. They hoed, drilled, shod horses, made cider, raised hemp and tobacco, looked after the horses and the garden, made and mended the shoes, spun, wove, made nets, canoes, attended to fishing, carpentering, each household sufficient unto itself.[64]

There was also more prestigious work in which Africans were engaged. For example, some of the wealthy Dutch families made a tradition of travelling in an open carriage pulled by exquisite stallions and manned by African coachmen who sat on elevated seats decked out in fine livery. Some slaves of Madam Brett, wife of Roger Brett of Fishkill Landing (Beacon in Dutchess County), held such an enviable position. During the decades of the mid-eighteenth century, these African coachmen handled Mrs. Brett's coach-in-four as she rode about Fishkill Landing on church and gala days.[65] There is also the story of Caesar, an African slave in the Rensselaer Nicoll family of Bethlehem estate, eight miles below Albany. Caesar handled the large sleigh pulled by horses over the frozen Hudson when the family made its annual winter trip to and from New York.[66] A further "prestigious" work role was that held by Quam, a slave of Martin Wiltse and son, of Fishkill Landing. During the second half of the eighteenth century, Quam captained a ferry service belonging to the Wiltses which served Fishkill Landing and Newburgh. He conducted the service between the towns on the Hudson by "means of a row boat and a piraqua, a two masted vessel without a jib."[67]

Although something has already been said about African work roles with respect to animal husbandry, with the rise of commercial livestock rearing in the lower valley, slave labor probably was used because of a shortage of white labor.[68] Kim describes the perceptible increase in white settlers between 1716 and 1776 on the manors. One thousand Palatines (German soldiers, released from Queen Anne's army, and their families) settled on Livingston Manor between 1710 and 1718 and thus contributed to that manor's twelvefold rise in population between 1716 and 1766. The population of Rensselaerswyck reached a thousand by 1779. Despite the most dramatic expansion in population which occurred throughout the valley after 1763, "when the northern and northwestern frontiers were at last freed from persistent French-Indian menace," a definite labor shortage continued to plague the colony.[69] Therefore, it seems logical that African labor was brought in to bolster and sustain the colony's economic investments in the production of foodstuffs, especially meat and dairy products, produced in the lower and upper parts of the mid-Hudson Valley, particularly Dutchess County.

The population figures for Africans between 1723 and 1771 in these areas tend to support this; towards the end of this time span, in 1756 and 1771, the figures for Dutchess County stood at 859 and 1,360, respectively, and for Westchester County 1,156 and 3,430 respectively.[70] Along with the towns in Westchester, those of Dutchess County—Fishkill, Poughkeepsie, Amenia, Pawling, and Rhinebeck—had high concentrations of sheep, cattle, and horses.[71] The assumption, therefore, is that the moderately high Black population figures (excluding the small percentage of free Blacks) tend to point to an aggregation of Africans as laborers in the foodstuff industry in those areas in addition to their work in other sectors of the economy and as domestics.

The other sector of the economy in which Africans appeared to have been used to sustain economic growth was manufacturing: grain, flour, lumber, and iron. Again, African labor was used extensively in both unskilled and menial capacities, as well as in those areas where a degree of skill was required.

In the areas of grain and lumber milling, manor lords and patentees retained a monopoly on the construction of such mills. Mills were constructed because they could attract tenants and could produce profits if operated. One of the reasons why Robert

Livingston acquiesced to the establishment of a Palatine community on his manor was because of its potential market for his flour and lumber.[72] Another incentive was production for export in order to earn coveted hard cash or bills of exchange for foreign goods.[73] One result of what has been called the "scramble" for wheat and lumber profits was the carefully planned growth of gristmills and sawmills on the manors throughout the valley, with heavier concentration on the upper Hudson.

Some of the earliest mills were established at Rensselaerswyck and Philipsburg manors. Milling had already begun on Rensselaerswyck before the British colonial period, but, with the succession of Kiliaen van Rensselaer (the grandson) as lord of the manor proper in 1687 and of his brother Henry at Claverack, milling for export assumed a high priority. Initially, Kiliaen permitted Henry to erect one gristmill on the Claverack Manor but, because of the demanding nature of the business, subsequently allowed him to put up an additional gristmill and one sawmill.[74] When Kiliaen acquired Rensselaerswyck, along with several other gristmills and sawmills, "it had all the necessary agricultural-processing industries." Content with these, he simply proceeded to dole out sparingly manorial grants for the construction of mills elsewhere within the confines of the manor. In the early 1700s, he granted permission to some entrepreneurs to build a sawmill at Greenbush.[75] By 1764, Rensselaerswyck had a number of gristmills and sawmills within its boundaries, either managed directly by the van Rensselaers or on lease.[76]

During the last two decades of the seventeenth century, Frederick Philipse constructed two gristmills, each with a pair of grindstones, at Philipsburg on the Pocantico stream and at the "Lower Mills" at Yonkers. By 1750 two more pairs of stones were added at these mills, and another sawmill was erected at Philipsburg. As such, Philipsburg and the "Lower Mills" were "equipped to handle grinding, bolting and the packing of flour."[77]

The distribution of mills on the Livingston Manor proper and at Clermont mirror that of Philipsburg and Rensselaerswyck. At the manor proper, Robert Livingston constructed, along with his mansion, a sawmill with twelve saws and a gristmill. When the Palatines settled in the southwest corner of the manor, he added an additional gristmill to meet their needs. In the 1730s in response to the developing iron industry, Robert's son, Philip, erected a sawmill and a gristmill at Ancram. In the 1750s, Robert Livingston, Jr., operated two gristmills at Clermont.[78] There were also gristmills and sawmills in other parts of the valley operated by both patentees and private businessmen, for example, those of the French Huguenots on the Wallkill River at New Paltz and in adjacent vallyes of Shawangunk, Esopus, and Plattekill.

Before discussing milling as it existed on some of the manors, a little should be said of those mills operated by patentees and private businessmen. Henry Beekman of Kingston is alleged to have operated sawmills and gristmills on his eastern Rhinebeck patent in Dutchess County with the use of slave labor.[79] Andries DeWitt, also of Kingston and Hurley, operated both gristmills and sawmills on the tributaries of the Esopus, Plattekill (Fish Creek), and the Binnewater along with his sons, Isaac and Tjerck. A sawmill of theirs, the first in the Kingston area, was established on the Plattekill in 1669 and operated by Tjerck DeWitt and a partner, William de la Montagne, through a grant obtained from Governor Lovelace.[80] It was probably at the Kingston sawmill and, later in 1686, at their Greenkill gristmill in Hurley (famous for its "Green Kill" superfine wheat flour that was preferred above all others and sought after by Mrs. George Washington from her husband's headquarters in Newburgh) where the DeWitts employed a number of their slaves in the milling business.[81] In 1686, William West, a Kingston miller, was deeded a part of "the mill upon the Green Kill in Hurley" by Tjerck DeWitt and undoubtedly used African labor to operate his gristmill.[82] His gratitude to them is shown in his will of 28 May 1738, in which he made his slave Saser and his wife "heirs of all my estate."[83] The male slaves of the Schuyler brothers in Albany cut trees in the winter and, at an adjoining sawmill, milled them into planks, staves, and other lumber articles for the West Indian marker, where they were shipped along with the year's production of flour.[84] Madam Brett of Fishkill Landing operated that town's only gristmill, attracting grain producers from both sides of the Hudson River.[85] The large contingent of Africans, retained by Sir William Johnson on the frontier above Albany, was probably engaged not only in the flour business but also in the lumber industry. This industry produced boards, staves, and masts which, like flour and wheat, were commodities in a very profitable export trade to the West Indies and the New York market. Johnson's sawmill at Amsterdam in Montgomery County was the first in the region in 1742.[86]

In the census data slightly beyond the colonial period slaves are enumerated in moderately high numbers, mainly in the upper valley and in regions where milling was quite evident. If the gradual emancipation acts had not been passed towards the end of the eighteenth century, the number of slaves would have been even higher. It seems likely that those slaves were engaged in the milling industry as a work force either on lease or directly owned by mill operators. With respect to the manors, in three of the sawmills leased by Kiliaen van Rensselaer around the mid-eighteenth century, entrepreneurs operated them "with the assistance of black slaves."[87] Kiliaen's gristmills and sawmills at Watervliet and Schodack may have employed slave labor. When Adolph Philipse died in 1750, *The New York Gazette* and *The Weekly Post-Boy* carried advertisements indicating that one of the Africans to be sold, either alone or with the mills at Philipsburg, was a "Miller" or "negro man that understands grinding."[88] In fact, under both Adolph and his father, Frederick, and perhaps later under his nephew, Frederick, Jr., the gristmills and sawmills at Philipsburg were managed exclusively by their African slaves.[89] In the will of Robert Livingston, there is an occupational epithet for one of his slaves, "Jo Ye Miller," evidently pointing to the slave's expertise in the milling business of the manor.[90]

Another sector of the manufacturing business in which African labor was employed was the iron industry. This industry stretched from the lower reaches of the valley and included the Sterling iron foundries which were established in 1736 in Orange County. Iron manufacturing reached as far north as the ironworks at Ancram on the Livingston Manor, begun in the 1730s and 1740s.[91] The ironworks at Ancram were part of Philip Livingston's further diversification of his growing commercial, agricultural, and manufacturing empire. It is alleged that most of his laborers were wage earners from Connecticut who were housed at Ancram during the iron-making season and were at times highly unreliable. There is also evidence that slaves, as they were trained, became a complementary, skilled labor force.[92] In some of his correspondence with his son, Robert, Philip Livingston expressed his desire to rely on skilled Africans in the ironworks like his competitors throughout the valley and in the adjacent colonies of New Jersey and Pennsylvania.[93] In a letter to Robert (30 January 1774), he confided that he wanted one of Robert's slaves, Dane, to work closely with the blacksmith to teach him that trade. "I hope you can spare him . . . I must continue to have a negro to learn somewhat about ye iron works. I have now 5 at Ancram and want 10 more with a good over-seer."[94] On another occasion he wrote that he wanted "to buy two negro boys of 16 and 18 years to put to a smith hammer-man."[95] The ironworks at Livingston Manor, a 6,000-pound-ster-ling initial investment, had access to an abundance of iron ore and were highly productive. Robert Livingston, Jr., reported that, between 1750 and 1756, Ancram's total output of pig iron was 3,318 tons, of which 1,302 tons were made into bars.[96]

In an annual report on "Iron Rolling Mills in the Providence of New York," Governor George Clinton indicated the existence of an iron mill in Orange County which belonged to a Lawrence Scrauley, a blacksmith. The mill was six miles from the Hudson and was a "plating forge to work with a tilt hammer."[97] On the Cortlandt Manor in the lower valley, James De Lancey of the New York Board of Trade reported in 1757, there "were two furnaces and several blommeries."[98]

To get a glimpse of what the African labor force may have been like during the colonial period, the *Gazetteer of the State of New York* pinpoints townships in which industries were located and lists the number of slaves in those towns. The industries included textiles, linens and woolens produced in homes, undoubtedly, with the use of slave labor.[99] For example, the town of Bethlehem, Albany County, in 1810 had a total population of 4,430 of which 137 were slaves; the town had eight grist-mills, eleven sawmills, three fulling mills, two carding machines, five tanning works, 185 looms in family homes for weaving, and 6,480 head of sheep. The town of Greenbush in Rensselaer County had a population of 4,454 of which 145 were slaves.

Some or most of them apparently were employed in the lumber business, since a great deal of the town's business with Albany was in cordwood and other wood products. Claverack town, originally a part of Albany County, had a population of 3,593 of which 154 were slaves; it had fourteen gristmills and sawmills, four fulling mills, four carding machines, and 163 looms in family homes. Kinderhook (also originally in Albany County), whose total population by 1810 was 3,709 (302 slaves), was heavily involved in the textile industry. It had ten gristmills, eight sawmills, one textile mill, two paper mills, four carding machines, and one plaster mill.[100] Once the data are fully tapped on these industries, we will begin to see that Africans were integrally involved in the production process as skilled and unskilled laborers. They were employed in the grinding of grain, the bolting and casking of flour, and the making of bread for export. They were also involved in the manufacturing of pig iron, castings, and iron bars; the digging of iron ore; the making of charcoal; and the preparation of the finished products for shipping to foreign markets or for home consumption.[101]

If African labor could be used conveniently and efficiently within homes, on farms, and in industry, then why not employ that same source of labor as a substitute for wage earners or engage that labor alongside wage earners in mercantile river commerce? Despite the paucity of available data on African involvement in this industry, it is possible, based on census data which pinpoint aggregations of slaves in and around river ports, to speculate on their employment in some aspects of mercantile river commerce (sailors, cooks, dock workers, carpenters in shipyards). Before the Revolution, river ports like Albany, Lansingburgh, Hudson, and Troy were a part of Albany County. The African population in 1771 for the county was 3,877.[102] Therefore, it is highly probable that a significant portion of that number, similar to slaves in towns further south like Poughkeepsie, Beacon, and Newburgh, may have been employed in the mercantile industry.

The undergirding for such a notion lies in the economic importance of the valley. The Hudson River Valley can be described as the heartbeat of colonial economic activity, its marketable produce the sinews of that economy. So long as the farmers and entrepreneurs continued to reap good harvests of grain, raise good breeds of livestock, and exploit the lumber, manufacturing, and foodstuff industries, the sustaining force of the economy was assured. The Hudson River was the lifeline on whose currents hundreds of one-masted and two-masted sloops ferried the riches of the interior to the river's major entrepôt at New York. Along the banks of the river sprang up an assortment of feeder entrepôts: Albany at the confluence of the Hudson and Mohawk rivers, Poughkeepsie, Beacon, and Newburgh. Towards the end of the Revolutionary period, the resources garnered from the rich soils of the valley were funneled into cities like Troy, Lansingburgh, and Hudson for transport down the Hudson. These entrepôts and sloops were part of a thriving mercantile industry on the Hudson River, an industry which linked the valley and its produce to a larger world economy.[103]

Travellers through the valley and to New York constantly remarked on the quantity of goods involved in the river commerce as well as the extensive commercial network of which it was a part. Between 1759 and 1760, Burnaby remarked that "the people carry on an extensive trade. . . . They export chiefly grain, flour, skins, furs, pig iron, lumber, and staves [as well as] the manufacture of a small quantity of cloth."[104] William Strickland observed that from "New York, many parts of the continent are supplied with grain, and from the city of New York, and the ports of the river Hudson, more grain and flour are exported than from any other port . . . except, perhaps Philadelphia."[105] The Marquis De Chastelleux was impressed by the trade in horses from Canada conducted by a Mr. Thomas of Rhinebeck and by the shipping trade with that region and with the West Indies in horses, flour, and other goods.[106]

Pre-Revolutionary river ports like Albany, Poughkeepsie, Newburgh, and, perhaps, Fishkill Landing were major points for receiving, storing, and shipping of goods to New York and for ship building. Undoubtedly, Albany, for a long time, was the primary market for wheat and other grain crops from producers on both sides of the upper Hudson, as well as from the Mohawk Valley and along the shores of Lake Champlain.[107]

African slaves were introduced or may have been an ever-present labor force in the growth of the river commerce. When

Troy rose to challenge Albany and Lansingburgh as the prime entrepôt on the east bank of the river, one might speculate that African labor was used to store the bags of wheat in the spacious lofts of the warehouses fronting the river and drive the wagons and sleighs that brought the wheat to market. Africans operated the tackles that hoisted the bags and other items to be weighed and probably manned and directed the spouts that conveyed the grain to waiting vessels at dockside.[108] When these sloops edged their way out into the river, African slaves were, without a doubt, part of the crews that manned the ships down to New York and even on to foreign ports. When one of Frederick Philipse's vessels, the *Margaret*, set sail for Madagascar in June 1698, it had among its crew at least two known Africans: "Frank, Mr. Cortlands Negro, [a] cooper [and] Maramitta . . . cook."[109] On board the ship *Experiment* in 1785 when it sailed down the Hudson from Albany on its way to China was a young Black Albany native named Prince, who, upon his return, had amazing tales to tell of a larger world far beyond the Hudson River Valley.[110] It is already a known fact that, between 1720 and 1762, five Blacks, John Dego, John (Portugee), Theodo Twawoolshed, Peter Calumpoe, and Peter Jamey were among many others who served as sailors aboard colonial ships out of New York during the French and Indian War.[111] Just before the official demise of slavery in New York, the brig *Holkar* sailed from the port of "New York under Captain Brown, and a colored crew."[112]

Conclusion

The colony of New York, along with adjacent colonies, confronted a severe labor shortage for most of the eighteenth century. Such a shortage was rectified through the importation of African slaves, who subsequently became an integral, and indispensable, part of the colonial economy. Before the passage of the gradual emancipation act of 1799, the institution of slavery was on the verge of becoming entrenched in New York on proportions similar to the slave states of the Chesapeake and lower south. The 21,324 slaves in the state enumerated in the Federal Census of 1790 indicates such a trend. If New York merchants had been able to generate larger profits enabling them to purchase a larger volume of slaves, then, perhaps, the figure might have been higher.

This essay attempts to establish a base for a new corpus of scholarship on the social history of African Americans, one of the largest of the early groups of American immigrants, who for too long have remained in the shadows of American historiography. In the written history of the Hudson Valley, those shadows are fading and will continue to dissipate as historians cull from the data evidence of more positive and substantial participatory roles for Africans in the development of Hudson Valley society. Before those shadows are totally obliterated, historians must examine the documentation of manufacturing and river commerce to find evidence of that aspect of African involvement. They need to determine what percentage of the work force Africans composed and the extent and degree of work skills among them. They need to examine evidence of Africans engaged in other categories of work: coopers, blacksmiths, cobblers, and mariners. Other topics for exploration include lodging for the slaves and their ability to maintain families. African origins are of importance—for example, the gang of Africans from the Guinea Coast which disembarked at Rye, New York, and was taken overland to Philipsburg Manor.[113] The exact or relative number of Africans brought into the valley should be established. Finally, a study should be made of the institution of slavery as an instrument of race control and the responses of the slaves to that system and the people who fashioned it. If the historians can assume these challenges and succeed, then, clearly, they will have made a significant breakthrough to a more *integrated* approach to "the new history of the early modern era."

NOTES

1. Gary B. Nash, "Social Development," in Jack P. Greene and J. R. Pole, eds., *Colonial British America: Essays on Colonial and Revolutionary America,* (Baltimore, MD.: The John Hopkins University Press, 1984), 254–256.
2. Douglas Greenberg, "The Middle Colonies in Recent American Historiography," *William and Mary Quarterly,* 3d ser., 36 (1979); 414.
3. Nash, 254.
4. Cf. Edgar J. McManus, *A History of Negro Slavery in New York* (Syracuse, N. Y.: Syracuse University Press, 1966); Samuel McKee, Jr., *Labor in Colonial New York, 1667-1776* (Port Washington, N. Y.: Oceana Publications, 1967).

5.   Thomas J. Davis, "Slavery in Colonial New York City," (Ph.D. diss.,
     Columbia University, 1974); Jessica Kross, *The Evolution of an American
     Town: Newtown, New York, 1642-1775* (Philadelphia, Pa.: Temple
     University Press, 1983); Joyce D. Goodfriend, "Burghers and Blacks:
     The Evolution of a Slave Society at New Amsterdam," *New York History*
     59 (April 1978): 124-43; Morton Wagman, "Corporate Slavery in New
     Netherland," *Journal of Negro History* 65 (Winter 1980): 34-42; Vivienne
     L. Krugwe, "Born to Run: The Slave Family in Early New York, 1626 to
     1827." (Ph. D. diss., Columbia University, 1985).

6.   Cf. Ralph Le Fevre, *History of New Paltz 1678-1820,* 2d ed. (Albany, N. Y.:
     Fort Orange Press, 1909); Philip H. Smith, *General History of Dutchess
     County from 1609-1876, Inclusive* (Pawling, N. Y.: Published by author,
     1871); *History of Columbia County New York* (Philadelphia, Pa.: Everts and
     Ensign, 1876).

7.   Cf. Thomas J. Davis, "New York's Long Black Line: A Note on the
     Growing Slave Population, 1626-1790," *Afro-Americans in New York Life
     and History* 2 (January 1978): 46-51; H. W. Reynolds, "The Negro in
     Dutchess County in the Eighteenth Century," *Yearbook: Dutchess County
     Historical Society* 26 (1941): 89; Roberta Singer, "Slaveholding on
     Livingston Manor and Clermont, 1680-1800," *Yearbook: Dutchess County
     Historical Society* 69 (1984): 46-69; Carl Nordstrom, "Slavery in a New
     York County: Rockland County 1688-1827," *Afro-Americans in New York
     Life and History* 2 (January 1978): 46-51.

8.   A. J. Williams-Myers, "Introduction: The African Presence in the Mid-
     Hudson Valley Before 1800: A Preliminary Historiographical Sketch,"
     and "Pinkster Carnival: Africanisms in the Hudson River Valley," in this
     volume.

9.   McManus; McKee.

10. Jack P. Greene and J. R. Pole, eds., cited in note 1 above, 1-16.

11. Cf. P. R. Christoph K. Scott and K. Stryker-Rodda, eds., *New York
     Manuscripts: Dutch Kingston Papers,* trans. Dingman Versteeg, 2 vols.
     (Baltimore, Md.: Genealogical Publishing, 1976); *Book of Supervisors of
     Dutchess County, New York, A.D. 1718-1722* (Poughkeepsie, N. Y.: Vassar
     Brothers' Institute, 1908); A. J. P. van Laer, ed., "Early Records of the
     City and County of Albany and the Colony of Rensselaerswyck," trans.
     Jonathan Pearson, *New York Public Library History Bulletin* 10 (1918); E.
     B. O'Callaghan, ed., *Documents Relative to the Colonial History of the State of
     New York* (Albany, N. Y.: Weed, Parson and Company, 1856).

12. *Heads of Families at the First Census of the United States taken in the Year
     1790, New York* .(Washington, D. C.: Government Printing Office,
     1908); *Free Black Heads of Households in the New York State Federal Census of
     1790-1830;* E. B. O'Callaghan, ed., *The Documentary History of the State of
     New York,* 3 vols. (Albany, N. Y.: 1849); Frank J. Klingberg, *Anglican
     Humanitarianism in Colonial New York* (Philadelphia, Pa.: Church
     Historical Society, 1942); Sheldon S. Cohen, "Elias Neau, Instructor to
     New York's Slaves," *New York Historical Society Quarterly* 60 (January
     1971): 7-27.

13. Cf. Rufus Rockwell Wilson, *Burnaby's Travels Through North America* (New York: A. Wessels Company, 1904); Jasper Dankers and Peter Sluyter, *Journal of a Voyage to New York, 1679-80* (Brooklyn, N.Y.: Long Island Historical Society, 1867); John Woodworth, *Reminiscences of Troy from its Settlement in 1790 to 1807* (Albany, N. Y.: J. Munsell, 1860); Anne MacVicar Grant, *Memoirs of an American Lady: With Sketches of Manners and Scenery in America, as They Existed Previous to the Revolution* (London: Jack Munsell, 1808); James Fenimore Cooper, *Satanstoe or the Littlepage Manuscripts* (New York: W. A. Townsend and Company, 1890).

14. Sung Bok Kim, *Landlord and Tenant in Colonial New York* (Chapel Hill, N. C.: University of North Carolina Press, 1978); Oliver A. Rink, "Company Management of Private Trade: The Two Patroonship Plans for New Netherland," *New York History 69* (January 1978): 1.

15. Richard B. Sheridan, "The Domestic Economy," in Greene and Pole; Greenberg; Ira Berlin, "Time, Space, and the Evolution of Afro-American Society on British Mainland North America," *American Historical Review* 85 (1980): 44-78.

16. Cf. J. Lossing, *The Hudson from the Wilderness to the Sea* (New York: Virtur and Yorston, 1866); Richard H. Smith, *Legends of the Shawangunk* (Syracuse, N. Y.: Syracuse University, 1965); Richard Smith and F. W. Holsey, eds., *A Tour of Four Great Rivers* (New York: 1906); Henri and Barbara van der Zee, *A Sweet and Alien Land* (New York: Viking Press, 1978).

17. It was the reliance on slave labor that made these colonies so similar until the end of the Revolutionary period.

18. Rink, 7.

19. *Ibid.*, 17.

20. *Ibid.*, 25.

21. *Ibid.*, 25.

22. Kim, 28-29.

23. *Ibid.*, 36-39, 42. Cf. O'Callaghan, *Documentary History*, 3: 179-80; David M. Ellis, et al., *The History of New York State* (Ithaca, N. Y.: New York State Historical Association, Cornell University Press, 1973); Alexander C. Flick, ed., *History of the State of New York* (New York: New York State Historical Association, Columbia University Press, 1933).

24. Kim, 150-54, 362; O'Callaghan, *Documentary History*, 3: 611-835; *Madam Brett Homestead*, (Beacon, N. Y.: Melzingah Chapter, National Society, Daughters of the American Revolution). The Rombout Patent stretched eastward from the city of Beacon on the Hudson for fifteen miles and turned northeast along the Wappingers Creek behind Poughkeepsie to the present town of Pleasant Valley.

25. Kim, 28.

26. Ibid., 229-30.

27. Ibid., 43-46. Cf. Elizabeth Donnan, ed., *Documents Illustrative of the History of the Slave Trade to America*, 4 vols. (Washington, D. C.: Carnegie Institute, 1932); Jacob Judd, "Frederick Philipse and the Madagascar Trade," *New York Historical Quarterly* (October 1971): 354-74, 55. In

1750, Gerhard G. Beekman of New York complained to an agent in London of "'at least 300 pounds loser of my one-sixth part' of the brig *Revenge*, James Holmes Master, after 20 months voyage on 45 slaves, 79 ounzes of gold dust, 3 1/2 tuns of Camwood" (Philip L. White, *The Beekman Mercantile Papers 1746-1799* [New York: New York Historical Society, 1956]), 1: 122.

28. Kim, 112, 191.
29. *Ibid.*, 235. By comparison, and because it offered settlers military protection from the French and Indians Albany, just before the turn of the eighteenth century, had a population of 662 men and 340 women.
30. Kim, 130, 237.
31. Goodfriend, 144.
32. *Ibid.*, 127; E. B. O'Callaghan, *History of New Netherland, or New York Under the Dutch* (New York: D. Appleton & Company, 1855), 384-85; *Ecclesiastical Records: State of New York* (Albany, N. Y.: James B. Lyon, State Printer, 1901), 1: 229; George W. Williams, *History of the Negro Race in America from 1619 to 1880* (New York: G. P. Putnam's Sons, 1883), 2: 134-35. The Dutch, and later the British, bemoaned the fact that "the province being thus poorly inhabited, the price of labor became so enormously enhanced, that we have been [forced] to import negroes .. . who are employed in all kinds of servitude and trades" (*History of New York from the First Discovery to the year MDCCXXXII* [Albany, New York: Ryer Schermerhorn, 1814], 323).
33. Goodfriend, 129, 140.
34. "Account of Negroes Imported into New York from 1700 to 1726," in *Ecclesiastical Records,* 4: 2336; O'Callaghan, *Documentary History,* 1: 693. Cf. James G. Lydon, "New York and the Slave Trade, 1700 to 1774," *William and Mary Quarterly*, 3d Ser., 35 (April 1978): 357-94; E. B. O'Callaghan, ed., *Calendar of Historical Manuscripts in the Office of the Secretary of State* (Albany, N. Y.: Weed, Parsons and Company, 1866), 7: 426; O'Callaghan, *Documents Relative to the Colonial History of New York,* 5: 419; Philip L. White, *The Beekmans of New York in Politics and Commerce 1647-1877* (New York: New York Historical Society, 1956), 116.
35. Williams, 2: 436; Helen Tunnicliff Cotteral and James J. Hayden, eds., *Judicial Cases Concerning American Slavery and the Negro* (New York: Octagon Books, 1968), 351.
36. Kross, 248. It could be argued that New York's reliance on slave labor made it more like the Chesapeake and lower southern colonies than other northern ones.
37. Cotteral and Hayden, 351. The editors' figure one-seventh of the total population.
38. Williams, 2: 134-35.
39. For an example of a colony's heavy reliance on slave imports, see Peter H. Wood, *Black Majority, Negroes in Colonial South Carolina from 1690 through the Stono Rebellion* (New York: W. W. Norton and Company, 1974).
40. O'Callaghan, *Documentary History,* 1: 693, 697.

41. Evarts B. Greene and Virginia D. Harrington, *American Population before the Federal Census of 1790* (1932; reprint, Gloucester, Mass.: Peter Smith, 1966), 105, 111.

42. O'Callaghan, *Documentary History,* 1: 697; Greene and Harrington, 105. Ulster's Black population was approximately ten percent of the total of 29,397 in 1790, while Dutchess's total population was 45,266, thus making its Black population less than five percent of that total.

43. Davis, "New York's Long Black Line," 48-49.

44. "Act of 1740 to support taxes/duties on intercounty imports." New York Paper, Board of Trade Acts, vol. 115, chap. DCCIII, 281, on deposit (New York: New York Historical Society).

45. White, *Beekman Mercantile Papers,* 1: 64.

46. *Letters and Papers of Cadwallader Colden, 1711-1775* (New York: New York Historical Society, 1918), 1: 51.

47. A. J. P. van Laer, 539.

48. White, *Beekman Mercantile Papers,* 1316, 1334.

49. Cf. O'Callaghan, *Documentary History,* 3: 843-68.

50. William Strickland, *Journal of a Tour of the United States of America 1794-1795,* ed. J. E. Strickland (New York: New York Historical Society, 1971), 163-64.

51. Last Will and Testament of Frederick Felipe, 26 October 1700, Sleepy Hollow Restorations, Tarrytown, New York. Cf. Edward Hagaman Hall, *Philipse Manor Hall at Yonkers, N.Y.* (New York: American Scenic and Historical Preservation Society, 1925), 66, 97.

52. Davis, "New York's Long Black Line," 51; Woodworth, 49, 92.

53. Will of Sir William Johnson, 25 July 1774, "Abstracts of Wills," *Collections* (New York: New York Historical Society, 1919), 8: 185-91; E. Olson, "Negro Slavery in New York, 1626-1827" (Ph.D. diss., New York University, 1939), 42.

54. Ernest Freeland Griffin, ed., *Westchester County and its People* (New York: Lewis Historical Publishing Company, 1917), 1: 240. Cf. George Scott, *Model of Government of East New Jersey* (1865), reprinted in *Collections* (New York: New York Historical Society, 1919), 1: 239-43. This volume indicates that in 1685 a Colonel Morris (perhaps related to Lewis Morris, if not the same individual) employed sixty to seventy "negroes" on his manor in East New Jersey.

55. Edward A. Collier, *A History of Old Kinderhook* (New York: G. P. Putnam's Sons, 1914), 145, 553-59.

56. Hector St. John de Crevecoeur, *Sketches of Eighteenth Century America,* ed. H. L. Borndin, R. H. Gabriel, and S. T. Williams (New Haven: Yale University Press, 1925), 140-43.

57. J. E. van Laer, ed. *Correspondence of Jeremias van Rensselaer, 1651-1674* (Albany: University of the State of New York, 1932), 159, 197.

58. Kim, 203-7.

59. *Ibid.,* 207-8.

60. Cf. Grant, 53-54; Mary Humphreys, *Women of Colonial and Revolutionary Times: Catherine Schuyler* (New York: Charles Scribner's Sons, 1897), 37-

38.

61. A. J. P. van Laer, 545-46.

62. Strickland, 163.

63. Humphreys, 83-84.

64. *Ibid.*, 38.

65. *Dutchess County,* (Philadelphia, Pa.: William Penn, Federal Writers Project, 1937), 75; cf. *Manuscripts,* Sleepy Hollow Restoration.

66. Dunkin H. Gill, "Biography of a Slave 1737-1825, Caesar," New York Historical Society, New York.

67. Frank Hasbrouck, *The History of Dutchess County, New York* (Poughkeepsie, N. Y.: S. A. Matthieu, 1909), 347.

68. *Manuscripts,* Sleepy Hollow Restorations. The van Cortlandt family of Westchester County and the Philipses of Philipsburg used slave labor to tend their cows. Some of the slaves might have come from South Carolina or directly from Africa, two areas from which they may have obtained training in cattle-keeping. For South Carolina's use of African expertise in the art of cattle-keeping, see Wood.

69. Kim, 26, 238.

70. O'Callaghan, *Documentary History,* 1: 696-97.

71. Cf. Haration Gates Spafford, *A Gazetter of the State of New York* (Albany, N. Y.: H. C. Southwick, 1813), 124, 187, 273, 281, 266.

72. Kim, 165, 226. Kim indicates that the gristmill at Watervliet in Rensselaerswyck returned a net profit of from 225 to 400 pounds sterling between 1771 and 1775.

73. *Ibid.*, 156.

74. *Ibid.*, 159.

75. *Ibid.*, 159, 167-68.

76. *Ibid.*, 168.

77. *Ibid.*, 166.

78. *Ibid.*, 167; Cf. O'Callaghan, *Documentary History,* 3: 611-42; Singer.

79. Kim, 154-55.

80. Louise Seymour Zimm et al., *Southeastern New York* (New York: Lewis Historical Publishing Company, 1946), 1: 36-37.

81. For a genealogy of DeWitt's slaves see "Ages of the Black Gentry," Kingston, N. Y., *Argus* 17 April 1878.

82. Zimm et al., 1: 36.

83. Gustave Anjou, *Ulster County, New York Probate Records from 1665* (New York: Anjou, 1906), 2: 124.

84. Grant, 314.

85. *Madam Brett Homestead.*

86. Olson, 42; William F. Fox, *History of the Lumber Industry in the State of New York* (Harrison, N. Y.: Harbor Hill Books, 1976), 24-25.

87. Kim, 168.

88. *New York Gazette Revived in the Weekly Post-Boy,* 9 April 1750 and 6 January 1752.

89. Cf. Last Will and Testament of Frederick Felipe, in Manuscripts of Sleepy Hollow Restorations.

90. Cited in Singer, 55. During the French and Indian War, Joseph Scustile, a Black man, enlisted in the Albany Company of Captain Christopher Yate in March 1760 as a miller. "Muster Rolls of New York Provincial Troops 1755-1764," *Collections* (New York: New York Historical Society, 1892), 24: 288.

91. Kim, 167; O'Callaghan, *Documentary History,* 3: 611-842. Cf. Irene D. Neu, "The Iron Plantations of Colonial New York," *New York History 33* (1952); James M. Ransom, *Vanishing Ironworks of the Ramapos* (New Brunswick, N. J.: Rutgers University Press, 1966), 177-214.

92. Singer, 59.

93. Ibid., 60. Cf. Arthur Cecil Bening, *Pennsylvania Iron Manufacturing in the Eighteenth Century* (Harrisburg: Pennsylvania Historical Commission, 1938); Charles S. Boyer, *Early Forges and Furnaces in New Jersey* (Philadelphia: University of Pennsylvania Press, 1931). According to Bening, Blacks were used in the ironworks from the time of the establishment of the Pennsylvania industry. "In 1727 the shortage of [white] labor [similar to New York] was so acute that the iron masters in the colony petitioned the Assembly for permission to import Negroes free of duty to labor at their works. . . . The skilled workers on the iron plantations were usually English, Welsh, Irish, and German, although quite often freed Negroes and Negro slaves filled such positions at the forges" (112, 114). Boyer remarks that "in the early days, many of the furnaces and forges were operated largely by Negro slave labor, especially in the northern parts of New Jersey [adjacent to Orange and Rockland Counties] where slavery was more general than in the lower end of the state" (7).

94. Quoted in Singer, 60.

95. Quoted in Singer, 60.

96. Kim, 148; O'Callaghan, *Documentary History,* 1: 730.

97. O'Callaghan, *Documentary History,* 1: 729-30. The mill was located at a place called "Wawaganda" [Wawayanda, southeastern Orange County].

98. Ibid., 1: 730.

99. Spafford. At the time of the French and Indian War, Blacks who enlisted (or were enlisted by their owners) in the colonial forces had expertise in the textile trade. James Tradwell of Queens County, Nicholas Manuel of Orange County, and John Johnson of Albany County were all weavers. James Walters of Westchester County, John London of Ulster County, and Samuel Tarvis of Orange County were tailors. In related industries, James Sands of New York was a tanner; John Murray of Ulster County and Francie Mattyie of Orange County were cordwainers (shoes), and David Sampson of Suffolk County was listed as a shoemaker ("Muster Rolls of New York Provincial Troops 1755-1764," 60, 312, 332, 284, 394, 402, 426, 446).

100. Spafford, 134, 163, 197, 218-19.

101. Cf. Berlin. Berlin's section on the northern colonies, especially the Middle Colonies, is very supportive of my position on African labor in manufacturing, particularly with respect to iron. I can also draw paral-

lels from Pennsylvania's iron industry as demonstrated in Donald D. Wax's "The Demand for Slave Labor in Colonial Pennsylvania," *Pennsylvania History* 39 (1967): 334-35, cited in Berlin.

102. O'Callaghan, *Documentary History*, 1: 697.

103. Cf. Joel Munsell, *The Annals of Albany* (Albany, N. Y.: J. Munsell, 1850), 1: 258-61. At Fishkill Landing, Madam Brett "was a prime mover in establishing a cooperative storehouse on the [Hudson] river for produce going to New York City" (*Madam Brett Homestead*).

104. Wilson, 114-15.

105. W. Strickland, *Journal of a Tour of the United States of America 1794-1795* (London: W. Bilmer Col, 1801), 8-9.

106. Marquis De Chastelleux, *Travels in North America in the Years 1780, 1781 and 1782*, trans. and introd. Howard C. Rice, Jr., (Chapel Hill: University of North Carolina Press, 1963), 1: 194, 341n.23; Grant, 314; Munsell, 1: 256-61.

107. Woodworth, 23; Duke De La Rochefoucault-Liancourt, *Travels Through the United States of America, the Country of the Iroquois, and Upper Canada in the Years, 1795, 1796, 1797* (London: 1801).

108. Woodworth, 24. Cf. Berlin. Again, in his article, Berlin supports the hypothesis that African slaves played an important role in the mercantile industry.

109. Judd, 364.

110. Carl Carmer, *The Hudson* (New York, Toronto: Farrar & Rinehart, 1939), 32; Munsell, 1: 261.

111. "Muster Rolls of New York Provincial Troops," 306, 338, 420, 442.

112. Coterall and Hayden, 380.

113. J. Thomas Scharf, ed., *History of Westchester County, Including Morrisania, KingsBridge, and West Farms* (Philadelphia: William Penn, 1886), 667. Cf. O'Callaghan, *Calendar of Historical Manuscripts*, 7: 158.

Chapter 3

THE TIES THAT BIND:
THE DEFINING OF RELATIONSHIPS
BETWEEN THE MASTERS AND THE SLAVES

Introduction

In many ways, the dependence on African slave labor which developed in colonial New York paralleled that of the Chesapeake and lower South.[1] Content to import slaves and cognizant of the very tenuous modus vivendi of a slave society, especially the potential for violent retribution by the slaves, the British, at the turn of the eighteenth century, began the swift but deliberate process of defining socioeconomic boundaries for the African by drafting New York's slave codes.[2]

Some of the earliest proscriptions on Africans appeared in what came to be known as the Duke's Laws published in March 1664. In 1674 those laws were amended to read that "no Christian shall be kept in bond-slavery." This clause was aimed at protecting indentured servants. The amendment further stated that this law "shall not set at liberty any Negro or Indian slave, who shall have turned Christian after they had been bought by any person."[3] The amendment was enacted to allay the fears of slave owners on the question of freedom for slaves after conversion. Approximately thirty years later, on 21 October 1706, the colonial legislature, fearful that the "children of the devil" might practice evil among whites, passed the "Act to Encourage the Baptizing of Negro, Indian and Mulatto slaves."[4] The act went further than simply baptism; it established the condition for who would be defined as a slave as well as who could be a witness in criminal proceedings. The act read in part that all Negro, Indian and Mulatto children "born of Negro, Indian, Mulatto or Mestee, shall follow ye state and condition of the mother . . . [and no slave can be] a witness for, or against, any freeman, in any case, matter of cause, civil or criminal whatsoever."[5]

Elaborating on and enlarging the scope of an ordinance passed on 15 March 1684 by the corporation which governed the city of New York, the colonial legislation, on 26 November 1702, passed "An Act for the Regulation of Slaves." The 1708 murder of William Hallet, Jr., his wife, and children by an Indian slave and female accomplice in Newtown (Queens County) and the "Negro plot" of 1712 led to the passage of "An Act for Preventing, Suppressing and Punishing the Conspiracy and Insurrection of Negroes and other Slaves."[6] A very detailed and sweeping piece of legislation (fourteen points in all), this 12 December 1712 Act states:

> (3) that because slave numbers increase daily and they federate for purpose of running away or other ill-practices, no more than three to gather together other than in employ of masters on penalty of being whipped with forty lashes at the discretion of a Justice of the Peace; (4) Each town, city or manor to lawfully appoint a common whipper, who upon agreement of Common Council or town-meeting to pay whipper 3 shillings per head; 5) corporal punishment (to exclude life and limb) to he/she [slaves] who strike a freeman or woman, professing Christianity . . . (10) slaves shall be put to death for murder of whites, rape, or willfully burn any dwelling-house, barn, stable, out-house, states of corn or hay, or shall willfully murder any Negro, Indian or Mulatto within this colony.[7]

To prevent slaves from escaping to Canada, especially those slaves in the Hudson River Valley, on 4 August 1705 the colonial legislature passed "An Act to prevent the running away of Negro slaves out of the City and County of Albany to the French at Canada."[8] Earlier, on pain of death, the City of Albany "had forbidden any Negro slave, unaccompanied by master, or some one [who employed him], to travel forty miles above the city."[9] As the French and Indian War got under way in the colony, an amended version of the 1705 act was passed on 14 May 1755. It proscribed severe punishment for slaves who escaped to Canada. It stated that "those convicted of such an act shall be put to death, county to bear charge [cost] of execution; owners to be paid for the execution of slave, sum not to exceed 34 pounds. If owners wish, slaves to be tryed [sic] by 12 men, [and owners pay cost, not exceeding 9 shillings.]"[10]

Finally, in order to discourage owners from manumitting their slaves, on 2 November 1717, the legislature strengthened the act of 1712 mentioned above. The 1717 law stated that any owner intending to manumit his or her slave had to put up two hundred pounds sterling security and twenty pounds yearly as maintenance for the freeman. The act was later amended on 27 October 1730 so not to appear "very inconvenient, prejudicial, and in a manner, a prohibition to liberty . . . and [discourage] Negro, Indian or Mulatto slaves serving their masters and mistresses freely and faithfully."[11]

These legislative acts and many others which came to comprise New York's slave codes were enacted not only to maintain social and economic stability within the colony but also to "make them stand in fear."

The Making of a Slave Society: To Make Them Stand in Fear

The desires to have a hearty, obedient, docile, but dependable labor force and to make the African stand in fear were incentives that led the New York Colonial Assembly to enact some of the legislation described above. This legislation has been characterized as savage because of the summary acts of punishment meted out to the suspected or accused violators of the slave codes. These summary acts of punishment by whites against African slaves have also been described elsewhere as diabolic because of the inhumane, cruel, and unusual manner in which punishment was administered.[12]

Both the legislation and the punishment were the consequence of a continuous atmosphere of fear and violence that engulfed the institution of slavery. There was fear on the part of whites because of the potential destructive power of humans whom they held in bondage against their will. Because of the oppressive and dehumanizing nature of slavery, whites feared the possibility that Africans would strike back with violent acts of retribution. During the colonial period particularly in the eighteenth century, much of this fear and the resultant savagery against slaves was exacerbated by the reverberations emanating from the murder of the Hallet family in Newtown, the slave rebellion of 1712, and the Negro Plot of 1741. Thomas J. Davis in his recent book on the Negro Plot of 1741, *A Rumor of Revolt*, reconstructed the events surrounding the alleged plot and the summary acts of punishment administered to the accused. Based on Davis's reconstruction, the term savage, as used here, accurately defines the consequences of the atmosphere of fear in a slave society.[13] As Davis recounts in his preface, "Thirteen black men burned to death at the stake. Seventeen black men hanged. Two white men and two white women also hanged."[14]

In the Hudson River Valley, punishment decreed for suspected African perpetrators of violent acts was swift and often times corporal. For example, in 1677 George Hall of Esopus (Kingston) petitioned the government for indemnification in the "loss of his negro slave who had been executed for the murder of the two [white] women in the summer of 1676."[15] The punishment for a Hurley slave who killed a fellow slave in 1693 "was that he be suspended in chains hung by the neck until dead, and then that his throat be cut."[16] In 1735 an African named "Negroe Jack" was burned alive in Ulster County for "burning a barne and a barrack of wheat."[17] Forty years later, an African met a similar fate for setting fire to the house and barn of Jacob Van Benchaten of Poughkeepsie.[18] In the town of Kingston, a slave known only as Tom was executed for attempted rape and murder of a white woman.[19] And, in the city of Albany, two African females, Bet and Deane, along with an African male, Pomp, were executed after having been tried and convicted of setting the famous fire of 1793 in that city.[20]

A common form of punishment throughout the valley was whipping. On 10 April 1710 an African slave of Hermnase Fisher of Albany was found guilty of stealing sixpence and "sentence to be whipped around the city, at every corner receiving nine lashes on the bare back."[21] Crevecoeur referred to one means of punishment in the Newburgh area which involved tying the African naked to a stake situated in a salt meadow. Kept there for a long period of time, the African was "attacked and bitten by green and blue flies." As a result, the body swelled to a prodigious size, with the consequence being either death or some severe trauma to the body.[22]

During the Revolutionary period in the valley, the fear of African retribution also precipitated the enactment of laws by town governing boards in order to hold the slaves in check and to prevent any attempts to escape to British lines. Such a resolution was enacted by the governing council of the town of Newburgh in May 1775. Gathering at the home of Martin Weigand, men of the town council resolved:

> That any person owning Negroes in this precinct shall not, on any account whatever, suffer them to be absent from his dwelling. . . The daytime off their farm without a pass; and in case any house or farm after sundown, or send them out in case any Negroes be found abroad, contrary to the above resolve, they shall be apprehended and caused to receive thirty-five lashes, or any number less, as the said committee shall deem proper.[23]

Similar resolutions and laws were passed in other towns and cities across the Hudson Valley region. In Albany, as indicated in the *Minutes of the Albany Committee of Correspondence* for 22 October 1776, it was resolved "that any black found away from his/her residence after 6 P.M. without a permit in writing from master or mistress, he/she shall be immediately apprehended and receive corporal punishment."[24] During the late spring of 1775 whites were very suspicious of Blacks as a result of a great deal of meetings "of late . . . in disregard for a law of this colony passed the 24th of October 1730." Because these meetings took place at the time British forces were advancing against the colonies from Canada, it was recommended that people in the city of Albany and throughout the county be more "vigilant and strict in putting in execution the 4th and 20th sections of said Act [of October 24, 1730].[25] Throughout the eighteenth century, the colonists, fearful for their lives and property and concerned for the continued stability of their vibrant and viable economy, legislated into existence harsh but explicit measures to define the parameters of slavery within which the African was bound. Any unlawful traversing of those parameters was dealt with summarily.

Masters and Slaves:
The Defining of Relationships

Although summary acts of punishment were parts of a vigilant campaign to make African slaves stand in fear, they were not the last variable of the slavery equation in colonial New York. In addition to African work roles, there were also African social roles, both within the African slave community and with whites, which contributed to that equation. Those social roles not only defined the slave as African, and culturally distinct from the master class,[26] they also were important in defining the Africans' degree of maneuverability within the institution of slavery.

The ability of the Africans to maneuver points out the degree of openness of the system of slavery, but, more importantly, it addresses black and white relationships within the institution and the choices which were possible for a slave without having to transgress prescribed boundaries. By 1771 the slave population of the Hudson Valley was a little over one-third that of the entire slave population of the colony, which then stood around 17,500.[27] By 1790 the valley's slave population was 15,000.

We know very little about the development and nature of interpersonal relationships between slave and master in the Hudson Valley slave society. Where the number of Africans held as slaves by a particular household was small, close functional relationships could develop. The typical slaveholder who owned a small farm, was usually involved in the overall operation of his self-contained farm on the frontier. He worked right alongside his slaves. The smallness the of setting tended to enhance the possibility of functional closeness between the slave and master. No doubt a similar sense of functional closeness was harder to establish on the plantation-type farms in the valley where slaves could total as many as thirty or more.[28]

On smaller farms, African slaves lived in the home with the

owners, either in the basement prepared for that purpose or in the attic. There are references to slaves bedding down in the kitchen, which was normally built adjacent to the main house. On the large estates or manors, Africans could be housed in "slave quarters" appropriately constructed a short distance from the manor house and at times directly behind it. The Albany estate of Phillip Schuyler and the New Paltz estate of colonel Josiah Hasbrouck are two examples where slave quarters were either in the owner's home or a short distance from the main house.[29] On the Livingston Manor of Robert Livingston, Sr., slaves not only resided in or near the manor house but were scattered across the estate, perhaps at work stations or rented out to tenants. In 1689/90, Robert referred to one of his male slaves as "the Negro man of mine that lives by Towis Abraham."[30] Another slave, Anna, who probably was rented by one of his Palatine (German) tenants, is listed in his "Debts Due by the Palatines Living Alone in the Four Villages In the Manor of Livingston," as living alone and with a personal debt.[31]

In a frontier setting, the lack of other whites perhaps aided the development of a functional closeness between slave and master as the two pursued their work tasks together both in the home and in the exploitation of the land's natural resources. The lack of a high concentration of slaves as in urban areas was an added variable. The writings of Crèvecoeur, although somewhat paternalistic, lend support to this. While at his Pine Hill estate near Newburgh, he wrote that "the few Negroes we have are at best our friends and companions."[32] With respect to the composition of the household he wrote, "Thus the industrious family, all gathered to gether [sic] under one roof, eat . . . drink . . . and grow imperceptibly less talkative."[33]

An important factor that lent itself to the development of a functionally close relationship between some owners and their slaves was the Dutch custom of giving a child his or her own personal slave. Writing of this custom in his book *Satanstoe,* James Fenimore Cooper asserted

When a child of the family reached the age of six, or eight, a young slave of the same age and sex, was given to him, or her, with some formality, and from that moment the fortunes of the two were considered to be, within the limits of their respective

pursuits and positions, as those of man and wife. It is true,
divorces [separations] do occur, but it is only in cases of gross
misconduct . . . but this particular negro remains with him
[her] as long as any thing remains. . . . The day I was six, a boy
was given to me, in the manner I have mentioned; and he
remained not only my property, but my factotum to this
moment.[34]

The African slave Caesar, of the Rensselaer Nicoll family of the
Bethlehem estate eight miles below Albany, was involved in such
a relationship. Before his death in 1852 at the age of 115, Caesar
had belonged to three masters in the Rensselaer Nicoll family:
The first to whom he originally belonged, the second with whom
he grew to adulthood, and the third, the son of the second, to
whom he was a constant companion.[35]

Recent revelations about the van Cortlandt family at both
Peekskill and Croton at the southern end of the valley not only
support the existence of the Dutch custom but also offer an
insight into the concerns masters had for their chattel. Receipts
and references to medical care slaves received ranged "from
inoculations for the children, tooth extractions for Sal, vial
drops for Sibby, to visits from Dr. Nathanial Drake to care for
Tom and Titus."[36] Because Pierre van Cortlandt, Jr., had grown
up and lived with slaves at the Peekskill estate, letters in the family papers reveal his personal attachments to the African slaves.
In a response to his brother, Phillip, in 1814, about the sickness
of a female slave, he wrote: "I am very sorry to learn that poor
Abby is so ill. . . . I will be really distressed if she does not recover.
Let Abby know how uneasy I am about her.[37] Earlier, in 1813,
Pierre, Sr., expressed his despondency over the impending
death of his slave, Titus, with the remark: "I am sorry for him and
shall miss him."[38]

In some households where there was more than one slave
family (if such families were allowed to remain intact), rivalries
developed between families. For the slaves the rivalries acted as
a pressure valve, undoubtedly releasing built-up tensions that
could have been diverted inwardly at self and other slaves or at
the system of slavery.In this fashion rivalries were more con-
structive than destructive in terms of work efficiency. A good
example of this rivalry was that which existed in the Catherine

Schuyler household in Albany between the offsprings of Diana and Maria, two women who had been brought directly from Africa while they were still youngsters. According to Catherine Schuyler's biographer,

> In the Schuyler household the slaves all descended from two old women brought from Africa. . . . Diana was determined that in no respect of excellence would Maria's children surpass hers. If Maria's son Prince cut down wood with more dexterity and dispatch than anyone in the province, the mighty Caesar, son of Diana, cut down wheat and thrashed it better than he. His sister Betty, who to her misfortune was a beauty of her kind, and possessed wit equal to her beauty, was the best seamstress and laundress . . . and plain unpretending Rachel, a sister of Prince, wife of Tytus, alas Tyte, and head cook, dressed dinners that might have pleased Apicius.[39]

Within a household an African slave mother's influence was not only evident in the rearing of her own children, but she was able "sometimes [to] exert fully as much authority over children of the [white] family as the parent."[40] Some of these black mothers had not only raised their own children, while rearing those of their owners, but in fact had even been reared or grew up with their owners. And for these slave mothers, it was "astonishing . . . what liberty of speech was allowed to those [of] them who were active and prudent. They [could] chide, reprove, and impostulate in a manner that we would not endure from our hired [white] servants."[41]

As we begin to learn more about the interpersonal relations between masters and slaves, so, too, are we beginning to become knowledgable about the wearing apparel of Hudson Valley slaves. But other than what was written in colonial newspapers to described what runaway slaves wore, it has been difficult to ferret out primary sources that could shed light on what African slaves wore and on the quality and quantity of clothes distributed to them. Undoubtedly, the quantity and quality varied with the social and economic status of slave owners. Also, the wearing apparel of slave women, unlike that of men, was fashioned from among cottons consumed in the home by the white females. Male slaves, like their free white counterparts, had their wearing apparel tailored by skilled slaves attached to an estate or farm or a white merchant. It is possible to say this because much of the preliminary evidence comes from the Livingston family papers.

By the mid-eighteenth century it is estimated that approximately twenty or more slaves resided on the Livingston Manor as personal property of the Livingston family. From entries in the October 1766 account book of Robert Livingston, Jr. (third Lord of the Manor), it is possible to reconstruct clothing allotments to slaves tailored by a Joseph Elliot. For example, between October 1763 and February 1765, Robert, Jr., outfitted his slaves with two popular pieces of clothing—vest and britches. The entries are interesting not only because they detail how slaves were clothed but how often some of the more favored slaves received certain items. The vest was an item purchased most often for between three and five shillings. Leather britches, at ten shillings, were not purchased as often. One slave, Quash, in January 1764 received a vest and britches and in May of the year was given a suit of clothes, purchased at one pound and four shillings. It is assumed that Quash was a coachman. Ole Tobe received a vest in April 1764 which cost four shillings, and another in January of 1765 at five shillings.[42]

Robert Livingston, Jr., also had the task of keeping his slaves in shoes. From an account he kept with Johan P. Rooses [Roosa], eleven slaves received new shoes or had shoes repaired. One of those slaves, Ben, received a pair of shoes in April 1767 at a cost of nine shillings. In June of that same year, Ben received another new pair at the same cost. Another slave, Caesar, in June 1767 had a pair of shoes soled but later that month was given a new pair. In both May and June of that year, one, Loudon, got his shoes soled twice. Tom received a new pair in May, and in June had the new pair or an old pair soled for three shillings.[43]

Aside from the Livingston Papers, the most important source of wearing apparel for slaves in the Hudson Valley was the colonial newspaper advertisements for runaways. These advertisements also contained other descriptive characteristics of the runaways which allow the historian to build a more complete picture of the slave. For example, the *New York Gazette* of 30 December 1729 to 6 January 1730 recorded that a runaway blacksmith, named William Gilliam, "was but indifferently clothed when he went away having but part of a shirt to his back and a yellowed coloured jacket with pewter buttons."[44] In the *Weekly Post-Boy* of 5 March 1750, Robert James Livingston placed an advertisement for one of his female slaves

> named Nell, about 36 of age. Had on when she went away a blue Penniston Petticoat, a short blue and white homespun gown, with a short blue duffils cloak and straw bonnet; she is mark'd with nine spots on each temple, and nine on forehead.[45]

In the *Poughkeepsie Journal* of 6 January 1796 the following advertisement was entered:

> Runaway—from August Barker of Franklin [Dutchess County], a Negro man named Zack, about 20 years of age, 5 feet 7 or 8 inches high, slender built, sprighlty walk, has lost the sight of his left eye . . . speaks good English, plays on the fife and German flute, and had a fife with him; had on a coat, waistcoat and overall of light-colored homemade bearskin, round hat and shoes; carried with him a new green broadcloth coat, stripped [sic] cotton waistcoat, fustian overalls, namkeen do., white cotton stockings, thread do., several shirts and other clothing.[46]

What is evident from these advertisements is that those who became runaways did so, when it was possible, with an adequate amount of clothing, either that of their masters or their own. Also, the advertisements indicate the degree and extent of craftsmanship and other skills possessed by Hudson Valley slaves.

It would appear that slaves held by wealthy owners were maintained rather well. For those owners not so well off, the welfare of their slaves mirrored their socioeconomic status within the institution of slavery. But within any socioeconomic stratum, the welfare of all slaves remained such only as long as they chose to remain obedient to the master class.

The closeness of the two races in a slave society, where white men were dominant and black men were dominated and powerless concerning family welfare and stability, permitted the development of liaisons between white slave owners and their black female slaves. A natural outcome of this was the birth of mulatto children who carried the slave status of the mother. To date, not much has been written on this topic. Most descendants of early white families in the valley prefer to deny or ignore the fact that such relationships existed.[47] However, the large numbers of light skinned blacks and the growing body of information from family histories and local historians suggest that miscegenation was rather widespread.[48] Further support for race mixing comes from a mid-eighteenth century report on manumission, in which, Frances Jansen, a mulatto, appeared in a Dutchess County court in August 1756 to take out manumission papers for his son, Cornelius Jansen.[49] Also, in the family of General Philip Schuyler, there is the story of a blood relative who took as his companion a Black women, who "to the great offence and scandal of the family, bore a child to him, whose colour gave testimony to the relation."[50] The Schuylers named the child Chalk, saw to his education, and when he "was of age allotted him a well stocked and fertile farm, but two miles from the family seat in Albany, deep in the woods."[51] Also on the question of race mixing, a missionary of the Society for Propagation of the Gospel in Foreign Parts (SPG), Rev. Samuel Seabury, recorded in his report to the Society's Secretary in London on 26 June 1767, that among those he baptized was "one mulatto [sic] adult". [52] The 1723 will of Robert Livingston, Jr., read in part "I do give and bequeath to my son Robert and his son and assigns a mulatto boy called Caesar about 17 or 18."[53] Given what has been said on the topic, it seems safe to conclude that there was a significant amount of race mixing in colonial New York.

Masters and Slaves
A Relationship Impossible to Consummate

Relationships between the slave and masters that appeared to be functionally close (i.e. for the purpose of social and economic stability) were really, from the African's perspective, relationships of convenience. Given the unpredictability of the modus vivendi in a slave society, such relationships were easily susceptible to friction and eventual dissipation. So long as one race held another in bondage against its willed consent, there would always be differences between them. An overwhelming desire on the part of the enslaved to be free both in body and in mind persisted. The differences remained constant and obvious between masters and their slaves over the legal relationship of slave parents and their progeny. Such differences were acted out on the Livingston Manor in 1715 and resulted in the death of one slave owner, John Dykeman. Dykeman was murdered by his slave, Ben, for selling Ben's daughter off the manor to a Mrs. Vetch, Livingston's daughter who resided in New York City. Coming in the aftermath of the 1712 slave rebellion in that city, the Dykeman murder was initially thought to be a part of another growing slave rebellion. After a preliminary hearing conducted by Robert Livingston, Sr., and some county magistrates, it was determined that the murder was the sole act of a heartbroken, revengeful father.[54]

The desire to be free was ever present and overwhelming and at times was expressed in acts of resistance to slavery. Sojourner Truth's experiences with her several owners addresses this point quite clearly. First of all, the reality of slavery remained forever vivid for her. Her childhood remembrances of seeing most of her nine brothers and sisters sold off to other white families "created an open wound on her heart and became fuel in years to sustain her desire to be free." In addition, the debilitating conditions of her living quarters in the cellars of the Hardenburgh house and those of her later masters added to the wound and strengthened her desire for freedom. An account of those conditions revealed that:

> Isabella remembered only too clearly the damp, cold cellars of [her owners]. The small windows admitted little light, even on sunny days, and the flagging and broad floors were invariably cold. The only beds were their straw-filled mattresses, and the older Negroes suffered continually from what Sojourner called the misery.[55]

When one of her five children was sold off by the John I. Dumont family of Ulster Park, Sojourner had had enough of slavery. In the same year that slavery was officially outlawed in New York State (1827), she fled from the Dumonts with her youngest son, Peter, and into hiding at the Quaker family of Issac Van Wagener in Dutchess County.[56]

The consequences of the ebb and flow of interpersonal relations within a slave society affected most slave households in the valley. It was especially evident in those households where there were large numbers of slaves. Two such households were those of the van Rensselaers of Albany-Troy and the Cadwallader Colden family of Newburgh and New York City. In the Van Rensselaers household, Jeremias, although satisfied with the work of his brother's slave, Andries, on their estate, remained alert and alarmed about the slave's strong will against total domination and depersonalization. In a letter to his brother Jan, in Holland, Jeramias expressed his concerns:

> you write of me to send over the negro Andries, but the friends have advised me against this, saying that it would be nothing but foolishness to try to have him serve you in a free country, as he would be too proud to do that. I have noticed that in his manner. It is bad enough here to get him to do so, so that at times I have to punish him for it.[57]

In 1717 Cadwallader Colden alarmed over a female slave's "negative" influence over her children and her growing independence of mind, showed no remorse when he made the decision to break up the slave family by sending the mother to be sold in Barbados. In a letter to a friend on that island he confided:

> I send by this vessel, the Mary Sloope, Capt. Edward Harely Commander, a negro woman and child . . . she is a good house negro . . . Were it not for her allusive tongue, her sullenness . . . I would not have parted with her . . . I have several of her children I value and I know if she would stay in this country she would spoil them.[58]

Even among the van Cortlandt slaves, whose owners have been depicted as benevolent, strained relationships developed between master and slave because of the latter's desire to be free. During the American Revolution when several slaves were left at the Croton manor to care for it while Pierre, Sr., was away, his daughter, Cornelia Beekman, living nearby, discovered a slave plot to escape to freedom behind enemy lines in New York City. Led by the female slave Briget (who had been in the van Cortlandt family for some twenty years, since 1758), six females

of Pierre and Cornelia "planned to join up with the next raid-
ing party from beyond the British lines and return to New York
City and freedom . . . [but] Cornelia successfully routed the
leaders and put an end to the plan."[59]

Slaves implicated in such plots, if not summarily punished,
were frequently shipped to the West Indies to be sold. In her
Memoirs of an American Lady, Anne MacVicar Grant remarks how
an Albany schooner in preparation for shipping goods to the
West Indies "was always looked forward to with unspeakable horror, all the stubborn or otherwise unmanageable [slaves] were
embarked, to be sold by way of punishment."[60] In line with this,
a great, great, great grandson of Rensselaer Nicoll wrote that "an
adult slave was rarely sold, unless one became incorrigible in
which event the slave was shipped to Jamaica Island, in the West
Indies and there sold."[61]

As the eighteenth century drew to a close and the valley
resounded with an atmosphere of newly won freedom and independence from England, so too did enslaved Africans become
affected by such an atmosphere. Slaves within van Cortlandt
households were emboldened by America's independence.
Because the slaves were so emboldened, both Pierre, Sr., and his
wife Joanna threatened to sell what they termed those "unruly,
disobedient, wicked servants."[62] Writing to his son in 1789,
Pierre, Sr., expressed his disappointment that "your mother tells
me she cannot have the trouble and anxiety another year with
the blacks. I know she is the slave to slaves and all that is raised
here is only to support them."[63] The two slaves Pierre, Sr., had
in mind were Ishmael and his daughter, Abby. Pierre, Sr. provided for Abby's early education. Both Ishmael and his daughter were characterized as having shown too much independence
and a complete disregard for prescribed boundaries within the
system of slavery. They appeared to have consistently "worked to
reshape that system to fit their goals and desires."[64] Content to
go his way without the approval of the van Cortlandt family,
Ishmael continued to build a so-called cushion for himself
"between the theory of slavery and the society as he lived it" by
nightly visiting the establishment of James Mandivile where he
was the official fiddler at "frolicking times".[65] Ishmael's independence of action forced Pierre, Sr., in 1799 to threaten court

action against Mandivile or "any person that encourages, or suffer him [Ishmael] to play the fiddle at night in their houses."[66]
Ishmael's daughter, Abby, mirroring her father's attitude and
temperament, drew unpleasant feelings from Maria Clinton,
the sister-in-law of Pierre, Jr. Although Abby's duties were those
of the personal servant to the ladies at both Peekskill and Croton
manors of the van Cortlandt family, she was almost uncontrol-
lable in terms of when, whom, and how she was to serve them.
Her unbridled attitude soon precipitated concern from Maria
at Peekskill that "I have every reason to be glad that Abby is not
here. I feel much interest for the child but I see more and hear
more of [Abby] than I think prudent to write."[67] On 3 March
1812, she wrote to Pierre. Jr., about her disappointment with
Abby during her stay at Peekskill. particularly Abby's lack of
docility. She wrote: "Abby . . . was here last week. I don't care for
Abby coming up if she is more contented there. I can do as well
without her [here]."[68]

The independent actions of Abby and her father and the
female slave plot to escape from the Van Cortlandt household
are only two examples along a continuum of many such attitudes, plots, and actual escapes by slaves to achieve total freedom. The Hallett murders, the Negro Plot of 1712, and the slave
conspiracy of 1741, all around the mouth of the Hudson River,
reveal the insatiable desire of slaves to be free. In the Hudson
River Valley, such events never reached the proportions of those
of the Stono Rebellion, the Prosser and Vesey conspiracies, or
the Nat Turner rebellion, but the explosive potential, nevertheless, was there. Where bloodshed did occur, it was normally
a single, isolated act of vengeance committed by a slave against
a white he or she knew. The execution of "Negro Charles" for
the murder of Colonel Wynkopp in 1793 and that of "Negro
Jack", both in the Kingston area (discussed above), are examples
of those single isolated cases.[69]

But there did occur in the valley in the eighteenth century, two events that had potential to reach a scale of resistance
to slavery which was comparable to those on the lower Hudson.
The first took place just before the start of the American
Revolution and was a foiled slave conspiracy to kill the inhabitants and burn the town of Kingston. Almost a year before the

Americans were to declare their independence from England, African slaves in the vicinity of Kingston sought to get the edge by striking a blow for their own freedom. On Saturday, 18 February 1775, led by two determined and calculating Blacks, York and Joe, neighboring slaves had agreed to be divided into parties in order to accomplish their goal of catching the town by surprise. They agreed that one group would converge to fire the homes of the whites; another would beat the drums to muffle the cries from the victims; and a third group would kill the people as they fled the burning buildings. At the time of the planning, it was rumored that, if the uprising proved successful in the opening stages, African slaves in the Kingston area would be joined by six hundred neighboring Indians.

Hours before the plot was to unfold, the two leaders met in Kingston to go over the plans. A contemporary transcript recounted the conversation between the two conspirators:

> York: How Many? [Meaning the number of slaves involved.]
> Joe: A great many.
> York: From where?
> Joe: From Keyserch [?] Hurley, [Marbletown], and Kingston.
> York: How much powder have they?
> Joe: Two pounds.
> York: That is not enough, they should have more to get through with it, and drums enough to prevent hearing the cries. They will begin, two at your house, two at John De Puis, and in proportion more at other houses. It will be put in execution between this [Saturday night] and Wednesday night. When once begun we must go through with it. We are to set fire to the houses, and stand in the doors and windows to receive the people [kill them] as they come out.[70]

Before York and Joe and their co-conspirators could carry out their attempt to gain their freedom, whites moved quickly to squelch the plot. The town's people were alerted after Johannes Schoomaker of Kingston overheard the conversation his slave, Joe, had with York. The two along with about eighteen other slaves were questioned the next day by four magistrates, and subsequently imprisoned because of the strong evidence against them. That evidence was the considerable amount of confiscated "powder and shot" found in their possession.[71]

The other potentially explosive event occurred in Albany in the fall of 1793 and involved one male and two female slaves: Pompey, a slave belonging to the estate of Matthias Visscher; Bet, whose master was Philip van Rensselaer, and Deane, the slave of Volkert A. Douw. All three were apprehended and tried for one of a series of acts of arson that swept Albany in November 1793. They were found guilty of the act but were not hanged until 14 March (Bet and Deane) and 11 April 1794 (Pompey). It is not certain that their act of "arson" against Leonard Gansevodt's property was proven conclusively, as simply an act of personal gain done for a Mr. Beesbrown and another individual distinguished only by his blue coat and living in the "plains".[72] Even after the three had been jailed, fires continued around the city, indicating that perhaps the act of arson (for which they were convicted) was part of a much wider crime than at first detected. Taken together, the aforementioned events suggest that the potential for African resistance in the Hudson River Valley mirrored that of the lower south and chesapeake regions.

The so-called "Black Arson" of Pompey, Bet, and Deane was a rebellious act aimed at venting grievances and frustrated hopes built up over time in a system that denied them their freedom. What was really tragic and unfortunate about this particular case was that all three were hanged five years before the passage of the gradual emancipation bill of 5 July 1799. In addition, they were not even considered for leniency under the "March 1790 law, by which they might have been transported out of the state upon conviction of a capital offense."[73]

Conclusion

New York was a typical slave society but modified by the absence of large plantations and longer growing seasons like its sister colonies of the Chesapeake and lower south. The existence of large capital schemes within the economy of the colony (lumber, grain, iron, foodstuffs, and river commerce) necessitated the use of large numbers of slaves to sustain that economy and the economies of many households in the valley. The very existence of a leisure class, similar to that of the southern colonies, accustomed to a way of life it had known for generations, also necessitated the use of slave labor to maintain that lifestyle. Sumptuous elegance of the Livingston, van Rensselaer, Van Cortlandt, Philipes, and Schuyler holdings as well as those of families among the Huguenots in New Paltz, could not have been maintained without African slave labor.[74]

Within the setting of a slave society, what appeared to be functionally close relationships between masters and slaves were really the result of African accommodation to such a society. And because of the constant fear and violent nature of the institution of slavery, such interpersonal relationships as did exist were always threatened by the desire of the slaves to be free as well as by the use of force by masters to keep the enslaved docile and obedient. But in spite of such longings and severe consequences for transgression of slave boundaries, just enough cracks in Hudson Valley slave society did develop to foster some, seemingly convenient and advantageous relationships between slave and freemen. Moreover, the very existence of a mulatto population demonstrates the presence of interracial sexual relationships.

The African who arrived in the Hudson River Valley as early as the seventeenth century was a resilient and resourceful individual. He was able to integrate old beliefs brought from Africa with those encountered in the New World. He reinterpreted "both to fit a pattern of sanction and value that [functioned] effectively in meeting the psychological needs of life"[75] within the institution of slavery in the Hudson River Valley.

Notes

1. George W. Williams, *History of the Negro Race in America from 1619 to 1880* (New York: G. P. Putnam's Sons, 1883), 2: 134-35.

2. A. J. Williams-Myers, "Hands that Picked No Cotton: An Exploratory Examination of African Slave Labor in the Colonial Economy of the Hudson River Valley to 1800," in this volume.

3. Edwin Vernon Morgan, "Slavery in New York: The Status of the Slave under the English Colonial Government", *"Harvard Historical Review"* 5 (January 1925): 338.

4. Edmond O'Callaghan, *The Colonial Laws of New York From the Year 1664 to the Revolution* (Albany: James B. Lydon, 1894), 1: 597-98; Morgan, 344.

5. O'Callaghan, *Colonial Laws of New York*, 1: 598.

6. *Ibid.*, 761-67; Morgan, 344.

7. O'Callaghan, *Colonial Laws of New York*, 1: 764-64.

8. Morgan, 344.

9. *Ibid.*, 345.

10. O'Callaghan, *Colonial Laws of New York*. 1: 764.

11. *Ibid.*, 1: 765-67, 2: 683; Aaron Hamlet Payne. "The Negro in New York Prior to 1860," *Howard Review* 1 (June 1923): 23.

12. Cf. A. J. Williams-Myers, "Introduction: The African Presence in the Mid-Hudson Valley Before 1800: An Historiographical Sketch," in this volume; A. J. Williams-Myers, "The African American in the Mid-Hudson Valley Before 1800: Some Historical Clues," in *Transformation of an American County*, ed. Joyce Ghee et al. (Poughkeepsie, N. Y.: Dutchess County Historical Society, 1986), 107-16.

13. Thomas J. Davis, *A Rumor of Revolt: "The Great Negro Plot" in Colonial New York* (New York: MacMillian, Co, 1985).

14. *Ibid.*, 6.

15. "Slavery in Ulster Co.," notes from the "Calendar of English MSS, Albany," Senate House Museum, Kingston, New York.

16. "Kingston Court Records, November 27, 1702," Senate House Museum citation, Kingston, N. Y. *Argus*, 3 December 1703.

17. O'Callaghan, *Colonial Laws of New York*, 2: 763.

18. Henry Noble MacCracken, *Old Dutchess Forever. The Story of an American County* (Hastings House; New York, 1956), 122-29.

19. Leo Herschkowitz, "Tom's Case: An Incident, 1741," *New York History* 52, no. 1 (1971): 63-71.

20. Cf. Din R. Gerlach, "Black Arson in Albany," New York, November, 1793," *Journal of Black Studies* 7 (March 1977); Mary Humphreys, *Women of Colonial and Revolutionary Times: Catherine Schuyler* (New York: Charles Scribner's Sons, 1897), 38-39; Joel Munsell, *The Annals of Albany* (Albany, N. Y.: J. Munsell, 1850), 8: 160-61, 163.

21. Payne, 12-13.

22. Hector St. John de Crèvecoeur, *Sketches of Eighteenth Century America*, ed. H. L. Borndin, R. H. Gabriel, and S. T. Williams (New Haven: Yale University Press, 1925), 110.

23. E. M. Ruttenber, *History of the County of Orange, with a History of the City of Newburgh* (Newburgh, N. Y.: E. M. Ruttenber and Son, 1875), 135-36.

24. *Minutes of the Albany Committee of Correspondence, 1775-1778* (Albany: State University of New York, 1923), 2: 585.

25. *Ibid.*, 1: 87.

26. A. J. Williams-Myers, "Pinkster Carnival: Africanisms in the Hudson River Valley," in this volume.

27. Cf. Evarts B. Greene and Virginia D. Harrington, *American Population before the Federal Census of 1790* (1932; reprint, Gloucester, Mass: Peter Smith, 1966) 105; Edmond O'Callaghan, *Documentary History of the State of New York* (Albany, N. Y.: Weed, Parsons and Company, 1850), 1: 693.

28. William Strickland, *Journal of a Tour of the United States of America, 1794-1795*, ed. J. E. Strickland (New York: New York Historical Society, 1971), 163-64.

29. Cf. *Schuyler Mansion: A Historical Structure Report* (Division for Historical Preservation, Bureau of Historical Sites, New York State Parks and Recreation, 1977); *Locust Lawn: A State Historical Landmark* (New Paltz, N. Y.: Huguenot Historical Society, 1985).

30. General Correspondence, 1689/90, *Livingston Family Papers,* Franklin Delano Roosevelt Library, Hyde Park, N.Y. (microfilm, reel 4).

31. Debts due by the Palatines Living in the 4 Villages in the Manor of Livingston, *Livingston Family Papers,* Franklin Delano Roosevelt Library, Hyde Park, N. Y. (microfilm, reel 4).

32. Crèvecoeur, 83.

33. *Ibid.,* 46.

34. James Fenimore Cooper, *Satanstoe or the Littlepage Manuscripts* (New York: W. A. Townsend and Company, 1890), 8-81.

35. Dunkin H. Gill, "Biography of a Slave, 1732-1852, Caesar," New York Historical Society, New York.

36. Jacquetta M. Haley, "Slavery in the Land of Liberty: The Van Cortlandt Response," in *The Van Cortlandt Family in the New Nation* (Tarrytown, N. Y.: Sleepy Hollow Restoration, 1984), 39.

37. *Ibid.,* 40.

38. *Ibid.*

39. Humphreys, 37-38.

40. Anne MacVicar Grant, *Memoirs of An American Lady: With Sketches of Manners and Scenery in America, as They Existed Previous to the Revolution* (London: 1808), 59-60.

41. *Ibid.*

42. Account Book of Cost for Things Made/Service Rendered, 1763-1765, in General Correspondence, *Livingston Family Papers,* Franklin Delano Roosevelt Library, Hyde Park, N. Y. (microfilm, reel 7).

43. John P. Rooses Account of Shoes, April 1767, *Livingston Family Papers,* Franklin Delano Roosevelt Library, Hyde Park, N. Y. (microfilm, reel 8).

44. *The Arts and Crafts in New York, 1726-1776: Advertisements and News Items from New York City Newspapers* (New York: New York Historical Society, 1936), 335.

45. *Ibid.,* 341.

46. Quoted in Helen Wilkinson Reynolds, "The Negro in Dutchess County in the Eighteenth Century," *Yearbook: Dutchess County Historical Society* 26 (1941): 47.

47. Kenneth E. Hasbrouck, New Paltz Historian, correspondence with author, July 1986.

48. William Heidgerd, *Black History of New Paltz* (New Paltz, N. Y.: Haviland-Heidgerd Historical Collection, Elting Memorial Library, 1986), 15.

49. Reynolds, 93.

50. Grant, 1: 59.

51. *Ibid.,* 1, 60.

52. Rev. Samuel Seabury to Dr. Burton, 25 June 1767, Letters Received, Calendar of Society for the Propagation of the Gospel in Foreign Parts,

vol. B2 (1759-1782), 171, Rhodes House Library, Oxford University.

53. Will and Testament, 10 February 1723, General Correspondence, *Livingston Family Papers,* Franklin Delano Roosevelt Library, Hyde Park, N. Y. (microfilm, reel 4).

54. Manor of Livingston, Robert Livingston, Justice of the Peace, February 2, 1715, Livingston Family Papers, Franklin Delano Roosevelt Library, Hyde Park, N. Y. (microfilm, reel 3).

55. Al Green, "Abstracts from history written by Mabel Hall of Hurley, herself a descendent of slaves," New Paltz, N. Y., *Record,* 14 March 1971.

56. Ibid.

57. Jeremias van Rensselaer to Jan Baptist van Rennselaer, 20 August 1659, *Correspondence of Jeremias Van Rennselaer, 1651-1674* (Albany, N. Y.: University of the State of New York, 1932), 167.

58. Cadwallader Colden to Mr. Jordan, 26 March 1717, *Letters and Papers of Cadwallader Colden, 1711-1775* (New York: New York Historical Society, 1918), 1: 39.

59. Haley, 46-47.

60. Grant, 1: 45.

61. Gill.

62. Haley, 47.

63. *Ibid.,* 47.

64. *Ibid.,* 45.

65. *Ibid.,* 48.

66. *Ibid.,* 48

67. *Ibid.,* 49.

68. *Ibid.,* 49.

69. "Negro Education," *Farmer's Register,* 6 July 1798.

70. "Negro Plot in Ulster County, 1795," *Rivington's N.Y. Gazette,* 2 March 1775; Weekly Mercury, 6 March 1775. Cf. Ivor Noel Hume, *1775: Another Part of the Field* (New York: Alfred A. Knopft, 1966), 109-10; Peter H. Wood, "Impatient of Oppression," *Southern Exposure* 7 (November/December 1984): 10-16.

71. Hume, 110.

72. Gerlach, 304.

73. *Ibid.,* 310.

74. Cf. *Schuyler Mansion;* Edgar J. McManus, *A History of Negro Slavery in New York* (Syracuse: Syracuse University Press, 1966); Samuel McKee, Jr., *Labor in Colonial New York, 1667-1776* (Port Washington, N. Y.: Ira J. Friedman, 1963).

75. John W. Blassingame, *The Slave Community* (New York: Oxford University Press, 1972), 17.

Chapter 4

THE SOCIETY FOR THE PROPAGATION OF THE GOSPEL IN FOREIGN PARTS AND EARLY AFRICAN CHRISTIAN EDUCATION[1]

Introduction

Other than Pinkster, the week–long celebration following Whitsunday, which will be discussed in chapter five, not much has been done and not much evidence found to shed light on the possible retention and practice of African religions in the Hudson River Valley. This is probably because the African slave was perceived as "savage," a being without a definable "civilized" culture; one immediate goal was to disarm the slave by removing any vestiges of "savagery" through a process of acculturation—inculcating Western socioreligious values. The process of acculturation also was to be a means of lessening the fear of the whites of the unknown (African). It was, perhaps, as a result of this inculcation of Western values in an attempt to "tame" the African, that many of the socioreligious values the African brought to America were relegated to the annual celebration of Pinkster. Also, because African slaves lived in the homes of their owners or in adjacent buildings, there was little opportunity for the practice of African socioreligious values among New York slaves. Therefore, the historian is limited to an examination of the impact of the Judeo–Christian religious tradition on Africans in New York as propagated by the Anglican Church of England and, rather reluctantly, reinforced by the slave owners.

The job of acculturating the slaves in New York was assumed by the missionary arm of the Anglican Church, the Society for the Propagation of the Gospel in Foreign Parts (SPG). Avoiding advocacy of abolition, the Society maintained a very conservative position on slavery, careful not to alienate slave owners and content with the argument "that Christianizing the slaves would not injure the slave masters [but] in fact would teach the slaves to serve their masters more loyally."[2] Missionaries themselves, if they could afford the cost, were even allowed to hold slaves, around which developed the sarcastic epithet coined for the Society's trustees—"the honorable body of slaveholders."[3]

The SPG and Its Beginnings in the Hudson Valley: An Assessment

For most of the eighteenth century the SPG's formula for the acculturation of slaves was embodied in its program of religious education. One of the very first points clarified in that program, and was also a means of reassuring the slave owners, was that of baptism. In line with a 1674 amendment to the Duke's Laws on Christians Kept in Bond–Slavery, the Society "committed itself to the steady and unswerving conviction that baptism was not manumission or emancipation" but only a recognition of Africans as human beings within the legal boundaries of slavery.[4] It was, therefore, within those legal boundaries that the Society for the Propagation of the Gospel preferred to confine its functions. Forever concerned with the attitude of slave owners concerning religious services they rendered to their slaves and mindful of colonial decrees, the SPG elected not to proselytize in the revolutionary fervor of Jesus Christ but only to do so to the extent that their efforts contributed toward a smoother maintenance of a society of white masters and Black slaves.

The British proscription of African activities (social, travel, economic, religious) was unlike that of the Dutch Reformed Church which, because of a lack of well defined legal restrictions on Africans, rendered religious services to the colonists (freemen and slaves) unencumbered by legal boundaries. As a result, Christianized Blacks under the Dutch, in theory, were acknowledged as equals before God. They were welcomed into the Dutch Reformed Church, married there, and even buried from the church. By 1636 African and white youths together were receiving religious instruction in the church.[5] Prior to the capture of New Netherland by the British in 1664, a Dutch reformed minister wrote of his work among Blacks: he had "taken much trouble in private and public catechizing [Blacks]. This had born little fruit among the elder people who have no faculty of comprehension; but there is some hope for the youth who have improved reasonably well."[6]

Once it began its work in the valley, the SPG assumed a similar position with Black youth but never gave up totally on the adults. Beginning in 1704 at the lower end of the river in New York City, the SPG established its first catechizing school for slaves under the Rev. Elias Neau.[7] Between 1710 and the end of the 1770s, similar efforts at catechizing slaves were begun further up the river at various SPG mission stations located throughout the Hudson Valley. These mission stations became, in essence, "laboratories of education for whites, blacks and Indians" in which missionaries experimented with teaching methods until a suitable one became functional for a particular "Center."[8] Although the emphasis was on evangelizing all three racial groups (Blacks, whites, Indians) through religious instruction (catechism) and administering the Holy Sacraments (baptism, communion, marriage, and burial) to those who professed Christianity, each mission responded to the needs of the people with an enthusiasm peculiar to a particular station within the mission.

Why the disparity in missionary enthusiasm? First, stations, as such, identified respective missions; two or more stations comprised a mission parish in the valley. An example of one of these parishes was that in the lower valley composed of New Rochelle, East Chester, West Chester, and Rye (including the substation of Salem). In the Mid–Hudson Valley, the parish to the east of the Hudson River was comprised of Poughkeepsie, Fishkill, Beekman, and the Nine Partners Patent. In the upper valley, the parish was composed of Albany, Schenectady, and Fort Hunter in the Mohawk Valley among the Indians of the same name.[9] Secondly, much of this disparity centered around the fact that missions were administered by one missionary priest and, at times, with the assistance of a schoolmaster (a catechist), but, in the absence of such an individual the priest catechized. The priest and the catechist were hampered by the distances and difficult terrain between mission stations, and bore the added pain of trying to maintain self and, at times, a family on the meager SPG annual salary (fifty British pounds for the priest and ten pounds for the catechist). These factors contributed to the disparity of missionary enthusiasm from parish to parish expressed in the commitment exhibited by missionaries to their work with Blacks, whites, and Indians, and especially evident in the tone of some of the reports sent back to the Secretary of the society in London. The reports are replete with pleas for increases in salary, reassignments to other mission parishes such as New York City or St. John in New Foundland because of the ill feelings of parishioners, or return to England for holidays or personal reasons. Administrative responsibilities (baptisms, marriages, burials, communicants, and descriptions of religious instructions) are outlined in more detail in some reports than others. Those without descriptive details appeared rushed, and exhibited a lack of enthusiasm and a great deal of disillusion.

With respect to the African presence in the valley, the missionary letters (the form the reports took) are not rich in terms usually associated with the missionaries' perception of a people's cultural background (as in those written from Africa). The letters were written mainly in an dispassionate, *objective* fashion devoid of much detail about Black social life or day–to–day existence during the eighteenth century. This, undoubtedly, mirrored the SPG's position of distancing itself from the ideology of slavery and any doctrinal conflict (initially there was little) in deference to slave owners. Some of the letters, though, did come close to pushing beyond the SPG's stance (especially those from Albany), and it is from these that the historian gets a real sense of an African slave presence in the evangelical activities of the missionaries.

Yet despite this real sense of an African slave presence, and coupled with the fact that Africans were never quoted or wrote (seldom, if ever) anything themselves, the historian is left with the task of recreating an historical situation as it may have existed. This is done by reading into the letters so as to interpret what the African slaves experienced in the process of acculturation to European socioreligious values, and to capture the essence and intent of what was written about the African. What is immediately evident from the letters are the number of Black catechumens, baptisms, and communicants, and glimpses of the education of African slaves through religious instruction.

Missionary Efforts and African and White Reactions: Religious Instruction and Conversion To 1730

Religious instruction and religious conversion among whites in the valley proceeded at a slow pace during the first quarter of the eighteenth century. Religious education for white children was even more difficult because missionary schoolmasters were easily attracted away to other employment because of the low SPG annual salary. Rev. John Bartow intimated as much in his 9 February 1716 letter to the Society's Secretary: "the labourer in husbandry earns 3 pence per diem."[10] The SPG's annual salary, which was drawn from the Queen Anne's Bounty, was no match for wages that could be earned elsewhere.[11] Religious conversion was also difficult at first because many of the people were "generally poor . . . and indeed very ignorant [of religion]," which resulted in their "contempt of baptism [and Holy Communion]," especially among those confessed to be Quakers."[12] In later years, Quakerism was a formidable challenge to Anglicanism in the valley, so much so that the Rev. Ephraim Avery at Rye wrote that his efforts at baptizing Blacks were made difficult "owing chiefly to the great number of people who call themselves Quakers but in truth are nothing."[13]

As a result of these obstacles, religious instruction and conversion among African slaves during the first quarter of the eighteenth century moved at even a slower pace, but it did vary from mission to mission. In the lower valley, religious instruction of African slaves was not as intensive as that of whites because of the small numbers brought into the area. The number successfully converted to Christianity through baptism remained small during the period. For example, a report from Rye, New York, of 20 November 1710 lists a community of 772 "including children, servants and slaves," but does not indicate any Africans among those baptized or who were communicants.[14] Two years earlier in 1708 the Rev. George Muirson wrote the SPG Secretary that "there are only a few Negroes in this parish, save what are in Colonel Heathcote's family, where I think there are more than in all the parish besides. However, so many as we have I shall not be wanting in my endeavors for their good."[15]

A little west of Rye in the community of West Chester, the first evidence of Black interest or curiosity in Christianity had been demonstrated by the Africans. The Rev. John Bartow, writing back to London in July 1710 acknowledged that "our church at West Chester increases, that at East Chester continues constant. We have sometimes Negroes and Indians come to our assembly and behave themselves orderly, but the slight and contempt of Baptism by Quakers and many others I am persuaded keeps them [slaves] from it."[16] In November 1710 he wrote of his success with slaves: "I have lately baptized a free Negroe man and three children and a Negroe woman servant."[17] From New Rochelle (also La Rochelle), the Rev. David Boudet (who was ordained in London after his French Protestant community was absorbed by the SPG), recorded a fair beginning with African slaves during the first quarter of the eighteenth century.[18] On 14 November 1717 he wrote excitedly of having admitted two Blacks as communicants in the church. "I have of late admitted to the communion two Negroes to the satisfaction of the church who heard them often before giving promise of their Christian instruction and having good report among our people."[19]

This small number of Black converts at the outset of SPG activities in the valley was a result of at least three obstacles. There was the initial problem with baptism which was thought to set slaves free; this was later clarified in 1704 in legislation that was supported by the Society "to confirm the right of [slave owners] over their slaves after baptism in the same manner that had it before [the act of baptism]."[20] The second obstacle was fear of slave rebellions such as the one in New York in 1712. The third obstacle was the refusal of slave owners to release their slaves from work to attend catechism classes. The Rev. Thomas Standard of West Chester saw the slave owners' fear of slave rebellion as "an invincible Barr to the Christian instruction [of slaves]." According to Rev. Standard, slave owners were quite sure that if a slave rebellion developed, it would be led by those Blacks imbued with religious fervor (as were at least two of the culprits in the 1712 revolt).[21] The refusal of owners to release their slaves for religious instruction was an obstruction to Black conversion equal to the fear of rebellion. In confirming this, the Rev Standard wrote that "the state of the Negroes being servitude and bondage all the week, they are held to hard labour but only Sundays."[22] In support of this, the Rev. Jenney wrote in 1725 from Rye about the difficulty of getting the "few Negroes and Indian slaves" to be catechized. "The Catechist," he wrote, "has often proposed to teach them the catechism, but we cannot prevail upon their masters to spare them from their labour."[23] As the first quarter of the century drew to a close, catechizing among slaves was still somewhat discouraged at the lower end of the valley, so much so that Rev. Jenney's successor, the Rev. John Wetmore, wrote to his superiors in London about it. He wrote that the catechist had "taken pains with the negroes, so many as their masters would allow to come. But of late they have left coming all together. Those that belong to the Quaker masters they will allow them no instruction."[24] Many owners were also discouraged from sending their slaves to religious instructions because the slaves used the occasion "to absent [themselves] from their masters' service [for] many days."[25]

In the upper valley at the mission parish of Albany, Schnectady and Fort Hunter, the SPG's beginnings were more promising. Because of Albany's large Black population, that mission's efforts at catechizing slaves were to be the most successful in the valley. The Rev. Thomas Barclay was originally sent to the mission to concentrate on converting the Mohawk Indians but later turned that task over to Rev. Andrews. Barclay was responsible for much of the early success with Blacks, especially those in and around Albany. Given the fact that most of a slave's day was taken up with work for his or her owners, Rev. Barclay conducted his religious instructions of Blacks in the evening hours but only after he had acquired the express approval of their owners. Through his diligence in building bridges with Albany's prominent slave–holding families, such as that of Colonel Kilian van Rensselaer, Colonel Peter Schuyler, and the family of Mr. Robert Livingston, Jr., Barclay was able to cate-chize slaves in his own home after Sunday services and on Wednesday and Friday evenings.[26] In addition to religious instruction to prepare slaves for baptism, Rev. Barclay also instructed them in the Dutch language because of their lack of facility with the newly introduced English language. In June 1714 he wrote to his superiors in London:

> I am glad to acquaint the . . . Society that I find in these poor slaves a great forwardness to embrace the faith of Christ and a readiness to receive instruction. . . . The first thing I inculcate upon them is that by being baptized they are not free. I am obliged with the greatest caution to manage this work, and I have publicly declared that I will admit none of them into the church by baptism till I have obtained their masters' consent . . . for some masters are to[o] ignorant and averse that by no entreaties can their consent be had.[27]

That the Rev. Barclay was able to acquire the consent of the slave owners says something about his strategy in Albany vis–à–vis that of this fellow missionaries in the lower valley. His bridge–building among those who held slaves greatly aided his efforts, and the idea of a so–called *tamed* African slave on a hos-tile frontier probably convinced owners of the good services ren-dered by the SPG. Colonel Kilian van Rensselaer and his wife were persuaded by this notion and often sent their slaves to Barclay for religious instruction. They publicly acknowledged "that their Negroes were better for being instructed" by the Rev. Thomas Barclay, which was an essential good of the Society.[28]

In his letter of June 1714 to the Society in London, the Rev. Barclay also listed names of those among his Black cate-chumens who had lately been baptized as well as the names of their owners. This is one of the few times that names are given in missionary letters sent back to London concerned with the hundreds of slaves listed as catechumens, as having been bap-tized, and having become communicants of the Anglican Church. Writing rather elatedly from Saint Peters Church in Albany, Barclay stated the names of the baptized are: Elizabeth, the slave of Barnet Bratt citizen of Albany; Jacob, the slave of Col. Killian van Rensselaer, lord of Rensselaerswick; Brit, slave of Robert Livingston, Junior, Esq., mayor of Albany; Scipio, the slave of Peter Matthews, Commandant of the garrison; and Christiane, the slave of Gerrit Van'est, citizen of Albany.[29]

Three years later in April 1717 the Rev. Thomas Barclay was still writing back to London of the great success he felt he was having at Albany. In a letter to the Society of April 9 he wrote:

Let it be said before the Society, that I have above 40 Black Catachumens, and about 80 white children: 17 Blacks I have baptized and shall quickly form a congregation alone of slaves.[30]

By June of that year, the number of Rev. Barclay's Black baptisms had grown to a total of twenty-three.[31] There were apparently no Black communicants at Saint Peters Church at that time.

The SPG Missionary and Black Converts: A Question of Confidence?

Although it has been said the church in colonial America undertook the conversion of Africans "more effectively in New York than anywhere else [along the eastern seaboard]," it must be mentioned that, at times, missionary doubt about the educability of Africans and the worth of their conversion dampened their spiritual fervor. When the Rev. Bartow began his duties at West Chester, he was plagued by such doubt. After having baptized a number of Blacks in 1710, he wrote home to the SPG offices: "but its very rare that those people [Africans] can be bought [sic] to have any true sense of the Christian Religion."[32] The Rev. Samuel Seabury, Jr., expressed a similar timidity when he stated that he had "baptized eight white infants and one negro, and five negro adults, who I hope were worthy subjects of that sacrament."[33] A successor to Bartow at West Chester, the Rev. Thomas Standard also wrote of his trepidation with Blacks. But they were those of an individual who, because the SPG had elected to distance itself from the ideology of slavery and thus neglect the human element in the slave, was at a loss to understand the trauma to which Africans were subjected as a result of their incorporation into a slave society. This is evident in his concluding remarks in his 5 November 1729 report to the Society's Secretary in London.

> But I had almost forgot one thing . . . and it is this that few of them [Blacks] are capable of being instructed. I have now two Negroes since marriage one of which is a girl about nine years old whom I have had above a twelve month, and have during that time, several times, attempted to teach her to read, but cannot yet make her to know her alphabet. Nor have all the endeavors hitherto used with her, which have not been inconsiderable, been sufficient to make her to number ten, tho' she was born in this country. Nor can a fellow that is at least 20 whom I have lately [bought], tho he hath been seven years in this country count up [to] that number.[34]

Mindful of his primary missionary duty of the instruction and conversion of the African slaves, the Rev. Standard went on to say "but not withstanding what hath been said I hope so far to initiate them in the Christian Religion as to fit them for Baptism."[35]

One missionary was so unsure of his accomplishments with his own slave, one whom he had taught to read and who in turn went about "marrying [other] slaves with the office in the Common Prayer Book," that he alarmingly wrote in his report that such activity "shows . . . they are ambitious of being as free, but I fear their freedom would be unsafe and dangerous as well as very chargeable to the inhabitants."[36] Another, oblivious to the fact that slaves were constantly under duress from a dehumanizing institution, justifiably concluded that because they exhibited no evidence of having moral practices, as a consequence, they had no right to membership in the church nor to the sacrament of Holy Baptism.

> It has always been my practice to use all proper motives I can think of, to bring my own negro slaves to a regular practice of the moral duties, in which most of their colour are very loose, but without which conceive that they have any title [sic] to church membership, nor consequently to baptism.[37]

A most pressing and frustrating issue for missionaries and one which taxed their confidence greatly was the problem of reconciling administering of the holy sacraments to slaves who, because of African customs (polygamy, for one) and legal prohibitions (against recognition of slave marriages), continued to resort to their so–called "heathen ways." The missionary at West Chester in 1725 saw this as an irreconcilable issue.

> I cannot be very zealous to baptize slaves because I know they will not or cannot live up to the Christian covenant in one notorious instant at least, viz. matrimony, for they marry after their heathen way and divorce and take others as often as they please, and Christian baptism cannot [be consistent] with adultery, and should we marry them I fear they would do the same.[38]

Echoing the missionary at West Chester but at the same time qualifying him, the Rev. Robert Jenney observed that slave marriages were made even more difficult to maintain because of the selling off of one spouse or because the spouses had two different owners "which make it almost impossible that they can be joined together till death parts them."

> If Christian persons live together as man and wife without marriage, they live in fornication, and if they are married they must not be parted. . . . Hence it will follow that if both parties are in the same family the master lies under an obligation either to keep both or sell both, let his necessities be even so pressing, which often obliges men to sell one when the other cannot be spared. And if they are in different families (as is most usual) then the removal of one of the family to a different part of the country at some considerable distance is a parting of man and wife. This is the case with my negro woman, and I find it a very difficult thing, almost impossible, to keep them faithful at any considerable distance from one another.[39]

Africans and a Growing Christian Awakening in the Hudson Valley

As the decades passed and appropriate legislation was enacted to define the legal and social boundaries of slaves, much of the missionaries' anxiety about marriage and baptism soon dissipated. By the middle of the eighteenth century, most were reassured that reconciliation of the sacraments with "heathen ways" appeared an impossibility but that their efforts within the legal boundaries of slavery on behalf of Blacks were redemptive. Resolved to this, missionaries settled into their tasks with a heightened evangelical fervor.

Some of the most accomplished work among African slaves in the valley after the end of the first quarter of the eighteenth century continued at the Albany mission. In the 1730s the Rev. John Beasley became known around Albany town as not only a schoolmaster of white children, but also for his personal endeavors at catechizing slaves after hours in his home. John Beasley's work among the slaves was brought to the attention of the SPG in London by the Rev. John Miln, who was the Society's missionary in Albany between 1728 and 1736. The Rev. Miln, in a report to London, implored the Society to give Mr. Beasley encouragement in his work with Africans by officially appointing him their catechist, especially since his work among the Albany slaves dating from 1725, lightened his (Miln's) own ministerial duties.

> There is one John Beasley a school master who contributes not a little to promoting my endeavors toward the propagating [of] Christianity in this place for he not only brings 50 children to prayers twice a week but hath also instructed near twenty negroes in the catechism, whom together with the children I examine in the church on Sunday afternoons; several of them I hope may be fit to be admitted to Baptism before Easter on Whitsunday. This man does as much service to the church as the catechist of New York and deserves at least some encouragement.[40]

In the following year Rev. Miln further alerted the Society to the unstinting efforts of John Beasley:

> I have baptized at Albany 24 children and 10 adult negroes. . . . The 10 negroes whom I baptized were instructed by Mr. Beasley who brought me certificates that their masters were willing they should be Baptized and likewise of their good behavior. I am glad to hear that the Society have taken into consideration the service of that good man who is very serviceable to the church here.[41]

John Beasley corresponded at least twice with the Society in hopes of getting its approval as the official catechist to African slaves in Albany at an annual salary of ten English pounds. In his first letter he attempted to show the Society that, because the large Black population at Albany was "ignorant of God and his holy religion," and because the people were very desirous of religious instruction, he sought to be "instrumental in doing some good amongst them."[42] He also pointed out that when the Rev. John Miln arrived at Albany in 1727, he gave Miln encouragement in his work with Africans. In 1733, word got back to Beasley that the Society was of the opinion that Albany's Black population was not "numerous" enough, and, therefore, they had not agreed to appoint him catechist. Beasley hurriedly wrote back to London:

> Is the Humble Society acquainted of the vast number of ignorant negroes that are amongst us and during the summer months yearly more [are] brought hither to be sold. I humbly conceive they would think it very necessary as well as a charitable work to establish a catechist in Albany; there is more than 300 inhabitants in this city, and by a modest computation there can't be less than 400 negroes. . . . Their [number] must unavoidably increase, since there is yearly such vast numbers of them imported in this province.[43]

To help the SPG decide on his appointment, Beasley wrote once again to London pointing out the value of services to the Rev. Miln in his successful baptizing of several Blacks whom he had instructed.

> Since my last there has been eight negroes baptized in the year 1733 (viz. 6 adults, 2 children) and upon Easter Sunday last 5 adults which makes in all 21 since I have employed my time in instructing them.[44]

The mayor of Albany (Ed. Holland), the official Recorder (Dirck TenBroeck), and four Justices (one of which was Cornelius Cuyler) added their support by certifying "that the number of Negroes in this place amounts to four hundred. We moreover assure you that we think him a person well qualified for catechizing and instructing them, and that he has several years past taken much pain and made some progress in that work."[45] Unfortunately, the Society decided not to fund a catechist at Albany, preferring to have that role performed by its mission minister. The Society did send Rev. Beasley ten pounds gratuity for his efforts. It was, nevertheless, John Beasley's unselfish efforts that contributed towards the growing number of Black converts in Albany.

Beasley's efforts at Albany were continued between 1749 and 1762 under the Rev. John Ogilvie and between 1768 and 1773 under the Rev. Harry Munro, with both cognizant of the importance of gaining the cooperation of the slave owners. Such cooperation had greatly improved since the early beginnings of the SPG in the valley and was constantly confirmed by the owners' certificates of good behavior in support of their slaves' conversions. Between February 1759 and February 1760, Rev. Ogilvie baptized 104 white children and fifteen Blacks.[46] When Munro arrived in Albany he found the Africans eager for religious instruction and their masters "committed . . . to join him in the observation of the parish work for [their slaves]."[47] Writing of his initial success with eighteen Black baptisms, he wrote:

> These and some more blacks I constantly catechize every
> Sunday, after evening prayer, and can with great pleasure
> inform the Society that there is a visible change and reforma
> tion among these poor negroes. I have had no complaints of
> immorality since they were baptized; nor has any proved a
> scandal to [this] Holy profession; and the daily petitions I
> receive from their masters, requesting me to baptize more, is, I
> humbly think, a plain argument in their favor. I have lately
> admitted a negro man to Holy Communion, after due instruc
> tion, and enquiring particularly into his morals.[48]

By 1772 it was recorded that Rev. Munro "had instructed and baptized more than fifty negroes, and that six of them had been admitted to Holy Communion."[49]

For African slaves, the opportunity to receive religious instruction went beyond simply salvation; it was their introduction to an early form of education. Beginning in 1704, separate, primarily part-time, "catechetical schools," where Blacks were involved in catechismic recitation, spread throughout the valley. By the 1730s, such schools were "in operation at Rye,

Westchester County, and Albany; by the 1760s or 1770s also in
Yonkers (Philipsburg) and Schenectady." The one at Albany
operated the longest, approximately fifty–nine years.[50]

The recitation involved in the catechism facilitated the
Africans' ability with the English language and thus enhanced
communication among them and with their owners. As successive generations of native–born African Americans went through
catechism, they developed an almost innate ability to master the
basic songs, prayers, and rituals as part of their religious preparation for the holy sacrament of baptism and, eventually, that of
communion. The method used for Blacks was similar to that
used for whites, except for the different days on which each
group was taught although, as the century progressed, Black
and white were instructed together. Commenting on the days
when the groups were taught, one missionary wrote, "I shall
continue to read prayers and preach twice every Sunday, and
after prayers every Friday afternoon catechize the children . . .
the black children and adults are catechized every Sunday
evening."[51] Another commented on his catechizing methods by
stating that "when I had baptized negroes I use to discourse
[with them] concerning the evidence and excellence of the
Christian religion, the nature of Baptism and the qualification
for it and the obligations lying upon Christians."[52] As for the
educability of African slaves, one missionary as early as 1726
wrote of those he had baptized that "4 of the adults knew the
Lord's Prayer, the Creed, and the Ten Commandments, and
besides were able to give a good verbal account of the Christian
faith."[53] From Philipsburg, at the lower manor (Yonkers), it was
reported that "these poor negroes are very fond of my instructions, and seem to be extremely thankful for my care and attention to their spiritual concerns. Many of them can answer every
question in the catechism properly and distinctly."[54]

Obviously, African slaves were committed to excelling in
this important avenue of religious freedom, where, in addition
to their demonstration of prowess and/or acumen in slave labor,
they could seemingly shed the burden of servitude and be as one
with whites in God's house. A minority of Black children by the
1730s, "attended missionary schools with white children where
they were taught reading, writing and arithmetic, and the prin-

ciples of religion, particularly the church catechism."[55] In 1738, Charles Taylor, the schoolmaster at Rye, New York, in the lower valley, reported that, along with thirty–five white scholars, he had two Black children.[56] In 1739, Charles Taylor's successor at Rye, Flint Dwight, wrote that the number of Black students remained the same and that, after evening service, he taught both Black and white children "with lessons from the Creed, Lord's Prayer, and Ten Commandments, and such other instruction as he was capable of giving and they of receiving."[57] By 1762, the Rye mission school (the most prominent at the time in terms of a mixed student body) under Timothy Wetmore, reported a total of three Black children in attendance.[58] Undoubtedly, the few Black students in formal education during the day were free and male. The education of black female slaves was done informally in the homes of their owner, and handled by their mothers. It was also in the homes that Black females became acquainted with the principles of Christianity. According to one source, in 1717 "the Anglican rector in New Rochelle reported that a number of [female] slaves in this town had learned the principles of Christianity by listening to their masters' family devotions." As a result "he encouraged them by assigning each seats in his church."[59]

Christian Instruction and Conversion to the American Revolution: A Concluding Statement

Although this essay points to a monumental, spiritually dedicated effort by the SPG in the religious education of African slaves in the Hudson Valley, it must be reiterated that it was done within the legal boundaries of New York slavery. Missionary fervor was directed towards an educational process which maintained the master–slave society rather than towards its dissolution. Missionaries remained objectively distant in their involvement with slaves and were more acquiescent than seditiously liturgic of the institution of slavery. If there were to be acts of sedition against the institution, it would come from those who, despite the contribution of hard labor, profited the least— the slaves. In rebellions and escapes, slaves struck out against the system of slavery in spite of missionary efforts to tame them through religious conversion. If anything, religious education contributed towards those very acts. Also, although religious education succeeded in the acculturation of the slaves, it failed to eliminate totally elements of African traditional religious practices. These were syncretized with Christian beliefs and encapsulated in the annual Pinkster festival.

The American Revolution eventually brought the SPG work to an end. Unable to identify with the American cause, missionaries were "jailed or driven out, their churches and schools closed or sacked, their work discredited."[60] With independence the Anglican Church ceased missionary activity in New York, leaving further efforts towards Black conversion and education to the newly established American Episcopal church and other benevolent organizations. But the seeds of Black Christian and educational awakening had been sown in that crucial but revolutionary eighteenth century.

Notes

1. Support for the work on this chapter was provided by two summer research grants from the New York African American Institute in Albany, New York for 1986 and 1987. Data were collected at Rhodes House Library, Oxford University.
2. Frank J. Klingberg, *Anglican Humanitarianism in Colonial New York* (1940; reprint, Freeport, N. Y.: Books for Libraries Press, 1971), 170; Carleton Mabee, *Black Education in New York From Colonial to Modern Times* (Syracuse: Syracuse University Press, 1979), 3. Cf. David Humphrey, *An Historical Account of the Incorporated Society for the Propagation of the Gospel in Foreign Parts* (London: 1730), 232–33.
3. Klingberg, 170.
4. *Ibid.*, 170, 187.
5. Mabee, 1.
6. Hugh Hastings, *Ecclesiastical Records, State of New York,* quoted in Mabee, 1–2.
7. Mabee, 3.
8. Klingberg, 158.
9. *Ibid.*, 121–86; *Letters Received, Calendar of the Society for the Propagation of the Gospel in Foreign Parts,* Rhodes House Library, Oxford University.
10. Mr. Bartow to Secretary Worthy, 9 February 1716, Letters Received, vol. 12, (1716–1717), 273–76.
11. Mr. Beasley to SPG Secretary, 1 May 1732, Letters Received, vol. A24 (1732-1733), 164.
12. Rev. John Bartow to SPG Secretary, 5 July 1710, Letters Received, vol. A5 (1709-1710), 532.
13. Ephraim Avery to SPG Secretary, 29 September 1767, Letters Received,

vol. A6 (1710-1712), 233; cf. Mabee, 14.

14. Rev. Christopher Bridge to SPG Secretary, 20 November 1710, Letters Received, vol. A6, (1710–1712), 4; cf. H. P. Thompson, *Into All Lands The History of the Society for the Propagation of the Gospel in Foreign Parts 1701–1950* (London: SPGCK, 1951), 185.

15. Rev. George Murison to SPG Secretary, January 1708, Letters Received, vol. A4, (1707–1709), 460; cf. Thompson, 185.

16. Rev. John Bartow to SPG Secretary, 5 July 1710.

17. Rev. John Bartow to SPG Secretary, 30 November 1710, Letters Received, vol. A5 (1709-1710), 532.

18. Mr. Boudet to SPG Secretary, 14 November 1717, Letters Received, vol. A12, (1716–1770), 349; cf. Thompson, 72.

19. *Ibid.*

20. Mabee, 11–12; Thompson, 74.

21. Rev. Thomas Standard to SPG Secretary, 5 November 1729, Letters Received, vol. A22, (1729–1730), 363.

22. *Ibid.*

23. Rev. Robert Jenney to SPG Secretary, 14 November 1725, Letters Received, vol. A12, (1716–1717), 157.

24. Rev. James Wetmore to SPG Secretary, 20 February 1727/1728, Letters Received, vol. A20 (1727-1724), 218-19; Klingberg, 167.

25. Rev. James Wetmore to SPG Secretary, 3 December 1726, Letters Received, vol. B1, (1702–1799), 274.

26. Rev. Thomas Barclay to SPG Secretary, 28 June 1717, Letters Received, vol. A12 (1716-1717), 290.

27. Rev. Thomas Barcaly to SPG Secretary, 20 June 1714, Letters Received, vol. A12 (1716-1717), 290.

28. *Ibid.*

29. *Ibid.;* cf. Klingberg, 135.

30. Extract of a Letter from Mr. Barclay to a Friend in London, 9 April 1717, Letters Received, vol. A12, (1716–1717), 284.

31. Rev. Thomas Barclay to SPG Secretary, 28 June 1717.

32. Rev. John Bartow to SPG Secretary, 30 November 1710; cf. Thompson, 73.

33. Rev. Samuel Seabury, Jr., to SPG Secretary, 26 March 1767, Letters Received, vol. B2, (1759-1782), 157.

34. Rev. Thomas Standard to SPG Secretary, 5 November 1729, 363.

35. *Ibid.*

36. Klingberg, 154–55.

37. *Ibid,* 155–56; Rev. Robert Jenney to SPG Secretary, 19 November 1725, Letters Received, vol. B1 (1702-1799), 78.

38. Klingberg, 154.

39. Rev. Robert Jenney to SPG Secretary, 19 November 1725; Klingberg, 157.

40. Rev. Mr. Miln to SPG Secretary, 2 November 1731, Letters Received, vol. A23, (1730–1731), 86.

41. *Ibid.*

42. Mr. Beasley to SPG Secretary, 1 May 1732.
43. Mr. Beasley to SPG Secretary, 5 June 1734, Letters Received, vol. A25 (1734-1735), 17.
44. *Ibid.*
45. Mayor of Albany to SPG Secretary, 15 June 1734, Letters Received, vol. A25 (1734-1735), 19.
46. Klingberg, 176–77.
47. *Ibid.*, 177.
48. Rev. Harry Munro to SPG Secretary, 20 July 1771, Letters Received, vol. B3 (1766-1782), 272; cf. Klingberg, 177.
49. Klingberg, 177.
50. Mabee, 4.
51. Rev. Harry Munro to SPG Secretary, 3 January 1769, Letters Received, vol. B3 (1766-1752), 268.
52. Rev. James Wetmore to SPG Secretary, 3 December 1726.
53. Klingberg, 156–57.
54. *Ibid.*, 134.
55. Mabee, 8. Carleton Mabee's "A List of the First Black Schools in Each Place in New York, from Colonial Times to 1945" (*Afro-Amiercans in New York Life and History 2* [July 1978]: 11-12) includes the following.

	Place	County	Type of school
1714	Albany	Albany	Church
1728	Rye	Westchester	"
1766	Philipsburg (Yonkers)	Westchester	"
1773	Schenectady	Schenectady	"

56. Notitia Scholastica of Charles Taylor, Schoolmaster, Rye, New York, 1 July 1738, Letters Received, vol. B7 (1738-1739), 150.
57. Flint Dwight to SPG Secretary, 12 November 1735, Letters Received, vol. A26 (1734-1735), 75; cf. Klingberg, 167.
58. Notitia Scholastica of Timothy Wetmore, Schoolmaster, Rye, New York, 5 October 1762, Letters Received, vol. B3 (1759-1764), 217.
59. Mabee, *Black Education in New York*, 11–12.
60. Klingberg, 181–86; Letters Received, all series.

Chapter 5

PINKSTER CARNIVAL:
AFRICANISMS IN THE HUDSON RIVER VALLEY

Introduction

In his 1939 study of the Black family in the United States, E. Franklin Frazier wrote: "Probably never in history has a people been so completely stripped of its social heritage as Negroes who were brought to America."[1] Twenty years earlier Robert E. Parks, who was one of Frazier's professors in sociology at the University of Chicago, demonstrated his erudition on the so–called "Negro Question":

> My own impression is that the amount of African tradition which the negro brought to the United States was very small. In fact, there is every reason to believe, it seems to me, that the Negro, when he landed in the United States, left behind him almost everything but his dark complexion and his tropical temperament. It is very difficult to find . . . anything that can be traced directly to Africa.[2]

These bold statements for both teacher and student are, nevertheless, a measure of the superficiality and the extent of the a priorism of sociohistorical research into the Black perspective that prevailed during the early decades of this century. Much of this was soon to be challenged by a rash of books on

Blacks that were published in the decades following Frazier's 1939 statement. These books sought to dispel the belief that there had been no African customs among African Americans. Some examples include: Melville J. Herskovits, *The Myth of the Negro Past* (1969); Lorenzo Turner, *Africanisms in the Gullah Dialect* (1949); John Blassingame, *The Slave Community* (1972); Gerald Mullin, *Flight and Rebellion: Slave Resistance in Eighteenth Century Virginia* (1972); George P. Rawick, *From Sundown to Sunup* (1972); and Peter H. Wood, *Black Majority: Negroes in South Carolina from 1690 through the Stono Rebellion* (1974).

In an attempt to further demonstrate the retention of Africanisms among African Americans within the institution of slavery, this essay will examine a socioreligious tradition of enslaved Africans on the upper and lower Hudson River prior to the New York Emancipation Act of 1827. Through the use of a little-known publication of 1803, titled "Pinkster Ode," as well as other sources not too readily available, the essay will not only demonstrate the existence of Africanisms among early New York Blacks on the Hudson, but will also reconstruct New York's contribution to the carnival tradition that is now evident in New Orleans, the Caribbean, and Rio de Janeiro, Brazil.[3]

But before proceeding, perhaps a little should be said about the number of Africans in the region under study. Although the number of enslaved and free Africans never reached that of their counterparts in the regions of the Chesapeake and lower south, they were, nevertheless, significant. Based on the census figures for 1790, the following counties or areas contained slave and free African populations. Albany had a total population of 75,921, of which 3,929 were slaves and 170 free. (Albany City had a 3,498 total, of which 572 were slaves and twenty-six free.) Ulster had 29,397, of which 2,906 were slaves and 157 free. Dutchess had 45,266, of which 1,856 were slaves, 440 free. Columbia had 27,732, of which 1,623 were slaves and 55 free. Orange had 18,478, of which 966 were slaves and 201 were free. New York City and County had 33,131, of which 2,369 were slaves and 1,101 were free. Queens had 16,014, of which 2,309 were slaves and 808 were free. Brooklyn had 1,603, of which 405 were slaves and fourteen were free. In two adjacent counties in New Jersey, the total population in

1745 for Bergen was 3,006 of which 616 were slaves; for Essex, the total was 6,988, of which 445 were slaves. (Both the eastern New Jersey counties of Monmouth and Middlesex had larger slave populations than either Essex or Bergen in 1745: Monmouth had 899 and Middlesex had 879).[4]

Definition and Origins of Pinkster

Pinkster, as defined, has been associated both with Pentecost and Whitsuntide, a holy day among both Christians and Jews. It is believed that Pinkster is a Dutch corruption of Pentecost and was a religious festival associated with medieval Europe. According to *Webster's Seventh New Collegiate Dictionary*, Whitsuntide is the week beginning with Whitsunday, especially the first three days of the week. It is a Christian feast on the seventh Sunday after Easter commemorating the descent of the Holy Spirit on the Apostles.[5] Pinkster is also associated with the change of season, i.e. the blooming of flowers and the rebirth of life in spring. One flower in particular with which it was associated was the beautiful azalea which bloomed throughout the Hudson River Valley, and along the banks of the Hudson and was called "pinkster blummachee."

Pinkster origins were, undoubtedly, two–fold. On the one hand, Pinkster is believed to have Dutch origins; today in Holland an ancient "Pinkstertool" is celebrated by dancing and singing around a maypole that is topped by a "Pinksterkroon," a crown of flowers.[6] When the Dutch settled in New Netherlands (New York), they continued to celebrate Pinkster. On the other hand, Pinkster is believed to have been an "African religious day" which was brought to the New World by African slaves.[7] This "African religious day" was perhaps associated with a number of Old World rituals. For example, the installation of an African ruler was normally accompanied by drumming, dancing, and various games performed by the King's subjects; the "first fruits ceremony" consisted of agricultural offerings of thanksgiving to the village chiefs just before harvest; a coming out ceremony was held for those youngsters newly received into adulthood after having observed a period of seclusion; the end of a long period of mourning after a funeral which was capped by a "great feast with much singing, dancing and drinking."[8]

"African religion is . . . joyous, [festive, and] celebrated in an atmosphere of music, singing and dancing."[9] Thus, the belief that Pinkster was brought to the New World suggests that "in the process of acculturation the slaves made European forms serve African functions."[10] Over time, therefore, elements of these African rituals were incorporated into the Pinkster festival. And it was probably in this fashion that, in New Netherlands, the festival developed, at least initially, into a syncretism of the two. Until just before the middle of the eighteenth century, Pinkster became all but in name an African festival. In *Satanstoe,* James Fenimore Cooper asserted,

> The features that distinguish a Pinkster frolic from the usual
> scenes at fairs, and other merry–makings, however, were of
> African origin. . . . The traditions and usages of their
> [Africans] original country were so far preserved as to produce
> a marked difference between this festival and one of European
> origin.[11]

From the beginning, African slaves and early generations of African Americans adopted Pinkster and combined it with the worship of their African god, "Totau," whom they acknowledged with dance and drum during the week–long celebration. In Albany, New York, the god, "Totau," was personified by an African–born slave named King Charles who reigned over the celebrations from atop "Pinkster Hill" (the site of the present state capitol) and who was alleged to have descended from royalty in Angola. On the lower Hudson, the Pinkster carnival, celebrated without a King Charles, took place in York (present–day Manhattan, but New Amsterdam under the Dutch) on the "commons," where City Hall now stands, and, at times, at the old Brooklyn "Fly Market."[12] Also, at this end of the river, Pinkster was described as being "never . . . the perfect Saturnalia that was for a long period exhibited in its observance at Albany."[13]

Pinkster Carnival on the Upper and Lower Hudson River

Historically Pinkster was celebrated in cities adjacent to the Hudson River as well as in Brooklyn and on Long Island. During months, weeks, and even days and hours before the

advent of Pinkster, many Africans, slave and free, busied themselves at tasks that could earn them enough money to be used
throughout the week–long celebration. Therefore, it was not
uncommon to see many free and enslaved Africans roaming
about the cities and towns peddling delights such as sassafras
and swigled tow.[14] Cooper painted a vivid description of such
merchandising in *Satanstoe:*

> Just as I got into Hanover Square, I saw a gray–headed Negro,
> who was for turning a penny before he engaged in the amuse-
> ment of the day [Pinkster], carrying two pails that were
> scoured to the neatness of Dutch fastidiousness, and which
> were suspended from the yoke he had across his neck and
> shoulders. He cried "white wine!" in a clear sonorous voice;
> and I was at his side in a moment. White wine was, and is still
> my delight of a morning; and I bought a delicious drought of
> the purest and best of a communipaw vintage, eating a cake at
> the same time.[15]

For Pinkster, a carnival village was always constructed adjacent
to the parade and dance grounds and was normally completed
by sundown the Saturday before Whitsunday. This village was an
assortment of colorfully decorated booths and stalls from which
carnival–goers could purchase an array of savory African and
African American dishes as well as various drinks such as cider
and applejack. There were also tents erected to house sideshows
of caged animals, rope dancing, bareback riding and many
other attractions. In Albany, the Monday after Whitsunday was
characterized by the absence of "Black royalty" from the carnival village—it was considered "ungenteel for the colored nobil-
ity" to make their appearance on the commencing day.[16]
Monday was usually the day when whites and Indians along with
the majority of Blacks who were not a part of King Charles's
entourage, descended upon the village strolling among the
booths and stalls savoring the edible delights and being amused
by the activities of the sideshows.

Albany's Pinkster celebration was officially sanctioned or
commenced on Tuesday with the appearance of King Charles.
Accompanied by royal retainers, the King made his grandilo-
quent entry onto Pinkster grounds amidst his assembled subjects
and visitors. A late eighteenth century description of the King

depicted him as impressively "tall, thin, and extremely agile" despite his seventy-odd years. He was traditionally attired in a cast–off costume of a "British brigadier of olden times," the coat of which was scarlet and ornamented with tracings of golden lace. His yellow buckskin clothes were much too small for his tall and thin frame. But his black buckled shoes and the tricornered cocked hat upon his head painted a picture of one who, without a doubt, was the most prominent figure on the Pinkster grounds.[17] According to an early nineteenth century description, if one looked carefully about the parade grounds, King Charles could not be missed because

> You'll know him by his graceful mien;
> You'll know him on the dancing ground,
> For where he is folks gather round;
> You'll know him by his royal nose,
> You'll know him by his Pinkster clothes,
> You'll know him by his pleasant face,
> And by his hat of yellow lace;
> You'll know him by his princely air,
> And his politeness to the fair;
> And when you know him, then you'll see
> A slave whose soul was always free.
> Look till the visual nerves do pain,
> You'll never see his like again.[18]

As people poured onto the grounds, King Charles, as the Master Drummer with the musicians, made the necessary preparations to begin the Pinkster celebrations. Couples, groups, and troupes gathered to commence the dance, and, with the cue from King Charles, the week–long Pinkster "jubilee" was underway.

Since very little is known about Pinkster, the little-known 1803 literary piece, "Pinkster Ode," provides valuable evidence. Written in Albany by Absolom Aimwell, Esq., the "ode" was perhaps "the earliest description of a folk festival in the United States."[19] From it, one can construct a clearer picture of other Africans who were involved in the various dances, the instruments used, as well as the visitors assembled at Pinkster with King Charles.

The "Ode" tells us that King Charles was an incomparable terrestrial to the Africans in the Albany region. Neither the grandeur of King George of England nor the military genius of Napoleon were any match for the magnificence of Charles.

> On wing'd Pegasus, Laureat Pye
> May raise King George above the sky;
> And Gallic poets strain their art,
> To swell the fame of Bonaparte;
> These bards of gas can never raise
> A song that's fit for Charle's praise.
> Tho' for a sceptre he was born,
> Tho' from his father's kingdom torn,
> And doom'd to be a slave; still he
> Retains his native majesty. . .
> From Hudson's stream to Niger's wave.[20]

Because the celebration of Pinkster only encompassed a week, the Africans sought to maximize their short–lived freedom. Once again the "Ode" reveals the extent of pleasure and gratitude the Africans showed for the privilege of being allowed a respite from their work regimen in order to sing and dance the praises of their African deity, "Totau."

> Rise then, each son of Pinkster, rise,
> Snatch fleeting pleasure as it flies.
> See Nature spreads her carpet gay,
> For you to dance your care away. . .
> All beneath the shady tree
> There they hold the jubilee.
> Charles, the King, will then advance
> Leading on the Guinea dance. . .
> But–hush–now Charles the King harangues,
> A hundred fiddles cease their twangs.
> 'Harken, ye sons of Ham, to me;
> 'This day our Bosses make us free;
> 'Now all the common on the hill,
> 'Is ours, to do what e'er we will.
> 'And let us by our conduct show,
> 'We thank them as we ought to do. . .
> 'Let us, each woman, man and boy,
> 'Strive who can freedom most enjoy. . .
> 'Tho' torn from friends beyond the waves
> 'Tho' fate has doom'd us to be slaves,

'Yet on this day, let's taste and see
'How sweet a thing is liberty.'[21]

In his own right, King Charles was a Master Drummer, and, as such, he occasionally participated in the rhythmic beating of drums during the festivities. In his later years, the more furious activities were reserved for younger men. Two names come down to us as having been the Master Drummer at one time during the eighteenth century: Adam Blake, who was the body servant of the old patroon van Rensselaer, and Jackey Quackenboss. The role of the Master Drummer was to set the pitch and pace of the dance through rhythmic beatings of the drum accompanied by various stringed and wind instruments. The main drum has been described, at times, as a large wooden box with dressed sheepskin drawn tightly over one end. It was accompanied by several smaller drums, ellpots also covered with sheepskin. From an eyewitness account, we get a picture of the Master Drummer's pace–setting touch and the response of onlookers as well as the dancers.

> Astride this rude utensil [the large drum] sat Jackey
> Quackenboss, then in his prime of life and well known energy,
> beating lustily with his naked hands upon its loudly sounding
> head, successively repeating the ever wild, though euphonic
> cry of Hi–a–bomba, bomba, bomba in full harmony with the
> thumping sounds. These vocal sounds were readily taken up
> and as oft repeated by the female portion of spectators . . .
> accompanied by the beating of time with their ungloved
> hands. . . . [and from the "Ode"] Briskly twirled the lads and
> lasses over the well trampled greenwards; loud and more
> quickly swelled the sounds of music . . . as the excited move-
> ments increased in energy and action; rapid and furious
> became their motions . . . and there, enclosed within their
> midst, was [their King] his stately form beheld, moving along
> with all the simple grace and elastic action of this youthful
> days, now sometimes displaying some of his amusing antics to
> the delight and wonderment of the surrounding crowd.[22]

As the day wore on, couples, groups and troupes moved in and off the dance area performing an array of dances. Three of the most noted ones were: "the double–shuffle heel–and–toe break-down," the "jug," and the highly emotive, "sexually provocative" and, as once described, "the most indecent dance that can well

be imagined," "Totau" of the African deity.[23] The pitch of the
music grew higher and the pace of the dance increased.
Musicians became so engrossed in their renditions of African
rhythms and songs that they appeared intoxicated with the
sonorous tunes. The "Pinkster Ode" describes the wind and
stringed instruments which accompanied the drums and offers
a further glimpse of the assembled crowd.

Now they strike the lyre again,
With louder and louder strain.
The fiddles touch their sweetest strings,
While the ebon lassie sings.
And the pipe and tabor plays,
Brisk and merry rounde lays.
Again the fife and hollow drum
Calls you—come together come. . .
Afric's daughters full of glee,
Join the jolly jubilee.
Up the green and round the ring,
They will throng about their King;
Dancing true in gentle metre,
Moving every limb and feature.
Or under shades they talk and laugh,
And the cheering nectar quaff.
Handsome Phillis sings and shows
Fine white teeth in ivory rows;
And suffers him she fain would please
To give her now and then a squeeze.
While the young Africs every where
Merry as the pipers are.[24]

Although it is from the "Pinkster Ode" that one of the most
vivid descriptions of the carnival is rendered and the activities
are those which took place in Albany, New York, it must be
remembered that additional celebrations took place in towns
with significant Black populations throughout the upper, middle, and lower Hudson River Valley. On the western end of Long
Island, Africans celebrated Pinkster but often preferred to make
their way into York for the festivities. Africans from both
Brooklyn and New Jersey were also in attendance at Pinkster. In
York, people gathered on the "commons." At this end of the
Hudson River, Pinkster was characterized as "the great

Saturnalia of the New York blacks," where they not only danced
simply for enjoyment but competed individually and as regional
groups (Brooklynites, Long Islanders, Jerseyites, Yorkites) in the
nimble art of such dances as the "jig" and "breakdown." One
dance in particular, which seems to give every indication of an
Africanism, was the "shakedown." De Voe had captured the
essences of this dance.

> But some of them did more in "turning around and shying off"
> from the designated spot then keeping to the regular
> "shake–down," which caused them all to be confined to a
> "board" (or shingle, as they called it), and not allowed off it;
> on this they must show their skill; and being several together in
> parties, each had his particular "shingle" brought with him as
> part of his stock in trade. This board was usually about five to
> six feet long, of large width, with its particular spring in it, and
> to keep it in its place while dancing on it, it was held down by
> one on each end. [Some] of their music or time was usually
> given by one of their party, which was done by beating their
> hands on the sides of legs and the noise of the heel.[25]

In *Satanstoe,* Cooper depicted an interesting encounter during
a York celebration of Pinkster between Africans born in America
and those "native" Africans who had been brought to the country as slaves. He indicates that the Old World Africans were held
in very high esteem by American–born Africans who looked
upon them as their "African teachers."

> A party of native Africans kept us for half an hour. The scene
> seemed to have revived their early associations, and they were
> carried away with their own representation of semi–savage
> sports. The American Blacks gazed at this group with intense
> interest also, regarding them as so many ambassadors from the
> land of their ancestors, to enlighten them in usages and super-
> stitious lore, that were more peculiarly suited to their race. The
> last even endeavored to imitate the acts of the first, and though
> the attempt was often ludicrous, it never failed on the score of
> intention and gravity. Nothing was done in the way of carica-
> ture, but much in the way of respect and affection.[26]

During Pinkster, people from as far as thirty or forty miles were
attracted to the week's festivities. In the cities, whites were as

eager to join the celebrations as Blacks. White school children were especially overjoyed for more reasons than simply missing classes: the dancing, booths and stalls with edibles, and the sideshows were uppermost in their minds. The gathering also allowed many people to catch up on the latest news or gossip. Once again the "Pinkster Ode" has encapsulated in its words the realism of such a scene.

Now, there will be, the eye to lure,
All the world in miniature.
Men of every grade you'll see,
From lowest born to high degree.
Indians from the west will come,
And people from the rising sun.
There you'll see brave Mountaineers—
The independent Vermonteers.
You'll hear them ask for warlike news,
Of Bonaparte and Jarsey blues.
Then point out all the ways and means,
To drive the French from New Orleans;
Where jealous Spain, our trade to stop,
Has damn'd the Mississippi up . . .
Every colour revels there [on Pinkster ground],
From ebon black to lillie fair.
Ah! how much happiness they see,
In one short day of Liberty!
And now they move around the ring,
To see again the jovial King.
Charles rejoices at the sight,
And dances, bowing most polite.[27]

The activities of the official opening were repeated day after day until the following Saturday when Pinkster drew to a close with the annual parade through the streets of Albany, with participants decked out in colorful dress and King Charles at the lead. The parade signaled the official end of Pinkster until spring of the following year. At that time all would converge once again onto Pinkster field to enjoy a time when liberty was theirs.[28]

Pinkster, A Threat to White Society?: Some Concluding Remarks

It has been alleged that the Albany Common Council passed in 1811 a City Ordinance banning the celebration because of the so-called "boisterous rioting and drunkenness."[29] The Ordinance read:

> No person shall erect any tent, booth or stall within the limits of this city, for the purpose of vending any spirituous liquors, beer, mead or cider, or any kind of meat, fish, cakes, or fruit nor to collect in numbers for the purpose of gambling or dancing . . . or to march or parade, with or without any kind of music during the days commonly called pinxter, under penalty of ten dollars or confinement in jail.[30]

As written, the real motives behind the passage of the ordinance can be deduced. To partake of "spirituous liquors" was, undoubtedly, a given on such an occasion as Pinkster, and to become somewhat tipsy or excited as a result of such indulgence was possible. But to say that it was total rioting and drunkness is to beg the question. In *Satanstoe,* Cooper is explicit about the lack of drunkenness among those Africans gathered for Pinkster on the "commons" in York: "while drinking was far from being neglected, still not a man was drunk. A drunken Negro, indeed is by no means a common thing."[31] Most Africans were still slaves in 1811 (slavery was ended in New York on 4 July 1827). As the ordinance was passed one year before the young Republic's involvement in the War of 1812, whites, as they had been during the French and Indian War, were very suspicious of Africans favoring the cause of the enemy. Another possible motive for the ordinance was the Gabriel Prosser conspiracy of 1800 in Virginia. That conspiracy came on the heels of the Haitian Revolution, which left whites throughout the Americas quite alarmed, wondering where the next Toussaint L'Ouverture would strike. Also, 1811 was the same year in which the state of Louisiana experienced a serious slave revolt which almost caught her white population unprepared. The ordinance dealt a serious blow to the carnival in Albany; gradually, over the years, the idea of Pinkster slipped from memory. King Charles continued to personify the African deity, "Totau," until his death in

1824.[32] Lower on the river, Pinkster activities continued too, but, in time, the idea of Pinkster lost its significance among successive generations of African Americans.

Pinkster may have originated in Europe with the Dutch, but, shortly after it reached the New World, it was taken over by African slaves who incorporated into it their African traditions. As a result, for almost two hundred years, some forms of Africanisms were able to survive within the institution of slavery in New York encapsulated in the Pinkster carnival. These were passed on from generation to generation, from Old World African to New World African, so that by the nineteenth century Pinkster carnival had become an African celebration.

Notes

1. E. Franklin Frazier, *The Negro Family in the United States* (Chicago: University of Chicago Press, 1939), 211.
2. R. E. Park, "The Conflict and Fusion of Cultures with Special Reference to the Negro," *Journal of Negro History* 4 (1919): 116.
3. Absolom Aimwell, *A Pinkster Ode for the Year 1803* (Albany, N. Y.: n.p., 1803); see also "Pinkster Ode, Albany," 1803 copied by Geraldine R. Pleat and Agnes N. Underwood in *New York Folklore* Quarterly, n.d. xeroxed copy on deposit Albany Institute of Art and History, Albany, N. Y.
4. Evarts B. Greene and Virginia D. Harrington, *American Population before the Federal Census of 1790* (1932; reprint, Gloucester, Mass: Peter Smith, 1966), 105, 111.
5. Cf. Gabriel Furman, *Antiquities of Long Island* (New York: J. W. Bouton, 1875), 266–67; Eileen Southern, *The Music of Black Americans: A History* (New York: W. W. Norton, 1971), 50–51; Henry R. Stiles, *A History of the City of Brooklyn* (Brooklyn, N. Y.: n.p., 1869), 2: 39.
6. Allison Bennett, "Pinksterfest's Foreign Origins," and John Wolcott, "Albany had a Folk Festival," Albany Institute of History and Art, Albany, N. Y.
7. "Pinkster Notes", Albany Institute of History and Art, Albany, N. Y.
8. Cf. John Blassingame, *The Slave Community* (New York: Oxford University Press, 1972), 17-18; A. J. Williams-Myers, "The Nsenga of Central Africa: Political and Economic Aspects of Clan History from the Eighteenth Century to the Late Nineteenth Century, " (Ph.D. diss., UCLA, 1978); Daryll Forde and P. M. Kaberry, *West African Kingdoms in the Nineteeth Century* (London: Oxford University Press, 1967), 110-11.
9. Roger Bastide, *The African Religions of Brazil* (Baltimore, Md.: Johns Hopkins University Press, 1978), 261.
10. Blassingame, 17.

11. James Fenimore Cooper, *Satanstoe* (New York: W. A. Townsend and Company, 1890), 74-75.
12. John F. Watson, *Annals and Occurrences of New York City and State in the Olden Time* (Philadelphia, Pa.: Henry F. Anners, 1846), 204.
13. Furman, 70.
14. Cf. Alice Morce Earle, *In Old New York* (1896; reprint, Port Washington, N. Y.: Ira J. Friedman, 1962), 199; Furman, 266.
15. Cooper, 70.
16. Earle, 197; Southern, 51.
17. Southern, 51–52; James Eight, *Reminiscences of the City of Albany* (Albany, N. Y.: By subscription, 1836), 6.
18. Pleat and Underwood, 34.
19. *Ibid.*, 31.
20. *Ibid.*, 32–33.
21. *Ibid.*, 33–35.
22. Joel Munsell quoted in Southern, 51–53; Pleat and Underwood.
23. Furman, 267. "Other authorities state that the dance was called 'Toto [Totau] Dance,' and partook so largely of savage license that at last the white visitors shunned being present during its performance" (Earle, 198).
24. Pleat and Underwood, 36.
25. Thomas F. De Voe, *The Market Book: Containing a Historical Account of the Public Markets in the Cities of New York, Boston, Philadelphia and Brooklyn* (New York: Thomas F. De Voe, 1862), 1: 344.
26. Cooper, 80.
27. Pleat and Underwood, 37, 42.
28. Perhaps it was unjust of Alice Morce Earle to suggest that "these Pinkster holidays became such bacchanalian revels in other ways" (198).
29. Furman, 268.
30. Bennett; Wolcott.
31. Cooper, 74.
32. Pleat and Underwood, 31.

Chapter Six

THE AMERICAN REVOLUTION, THE STRUGGLE FOR CONTROL OF THE HUDSON RIVER VALLEY, AND THE ROAD TO VICTORY: THE AFRICAN AMERICAN FACTOR

Introduction

When Thomas Jefferson penned the Declaration of Independence in July 1776, he, and his co-conspirators, had only white colonists in mind. What he did not anticipate was that thousands of Africans held in bondage (and those that were free) would view the Declaration and the ensuing conflagration between two groups of whites as a means to their own freedom. Because the modus vivendi between masters and slaves in New York remained precarious, the African had no qualms about choosing either of the combatants to assist him in becoming his own liberator. In the words of Benjamin Quarles, "Insofar as [the African] had freedom of choice, he was likely to join the side that made him the quickest and best offer in terms of those 'inalienable rights' of which Mr. Jefferson had spoken."[1] For the African, the Declaration of 1776 was his call to arms to battle for independence and freedom. Caught up in the rhetoric of the Declaration, the African's undeclared war on the peculiar institution became an open campaign against the evil of slavery.

For him, "whoever invoked the image of liberty, be he American or British, could count on a ready response from the [B]lacks."[2]

There were many incentives for Africans—free and enslaved—to seek the challenge of war, the foremost being personal freedom. Free Africans saw the offer of a land and cash bounty as a way to begin a new life filled with much promise as well as a way to be adventuresome and "express support for the revolutionary ideals of freedom."[3] Runaway slaves viewed enlistment as a means of security, employment, and eventual freedom. The fate of the slaves was at the mercy of the whims of their owners, who, if they so desired, could send the slaves in place of themselves or could accept cash or a land bounty. The slaves were promised that they would be free after serving three years or after the war. For the enslaved, free, and runaway Africans, the Revolution also afforded them the opportunity to demonstrate their prowess as combatants and as men—something denied to them in a slave society which defined them as infantile, and untrustworthy sambos.

The efforts to dispel, to demystify, and to destroy these notions of the majority community toward Africans mobilized the slave community of the Hudson River Valley from the time of the Dutch. Continual African resistance to the peculiar institution was demonstrable proof, in its own subtle way, that those white society held in bondage did not fit the pejorative descriptions which were merely figments of white imagination. Although slavery for the African was a trek into "the valley of the shadow of death," where he was abandoned to confront the "slings and arrows of outrageous fortune," it was, nevertheless, a temporary sojourn for Ethiopia's children. During their accommodation to slavery, the Africans awaited the day Gabriel would blow his horn at the dawn of a new day of freedom.[4]

African participation in the American Revolution was nothing new. Impatient of oppression, Africans were ever alert to ways of hastening the day Gabriel's horn would resound across the land heralding freedom. Two decades before the Revolution, African warriors, under the Dutch and English, comprised part of the fighting force in the European colonial conflicts. Because of their need to pacify the "owners of the land" (the Native Americans) in the Hudson Valley, the Dutch, under their Governor Peter Stuyvesant, sought "clever and strong" Africans. In his request to officials on the Caribbean island of Curaçao, Stuyvesant indicated that he needed such men to "pursue the Indians," because it was "evident that in order to possess this country in peace and revenge affronts and murders we shall be forced into a lawful offensive war against them [the Indians]."[5] Under the British, Africans—free and enslaved—were very conspicuous among colonial enlistees in the French and Indian War fought in New York. Among the 1762 enlistees in the company of Captain Van Dyck were Peter Lucus and Peter Primus both laborers from Schenectady, New York.[6] John Murray, a cordwainer, served in the Ulster, Orange, and Dutchess 1762 detachment under Captain George Brewerton.[7] Cato Thomas, a laborer from Rye, New York, was in the 1760 Westchester County company of Captain William Gilchrist.[8] Peter Lucus, Sr., and Peter Lucus, Jr., both farmers; William Sisco, a laborer; and Francis Matysa, cordwainer, served in the 1759 Orange County regiment of Colonel Abraham Hering.[9] These fighting men were proud African warriors in support of the British war effort, as well as in quest of their own manhood and freedom. In a letter to his Philadelphia cousin from Lake George, a white soldier wrote of a fierce fire-fight with enemy forces under the French and Native Americans: "the Blacks fought more valiantly than the whites."[10] What this lone, white combatant shared with his cousin was a fact of history that lay buried, forgotten, and unsung. African warriors and their deeds of valor were forgotten and unsung after the American Revolution.[11]

The African Factor in the American Revolution

The heroism of these unsung African warriors became evident at the inception of the revolutionary conflict at the battles of Lexington and Concord and even at the Boston Massacre of 1770.[12] As with previous wars, it was the Africans distributed throughout the forces of the Continental lines, state levies, and militias, who were to turn the tide of war in favor of the Americans. The American army suffered defeat at Brandywine, Schuykill, and Germantown after having been driven out of New York City by British forces, and lingered "dispiritedly" in winter quarters at Valley Forge, apparently on the verge of defeat in the winter of 1777-1778.[13] "In the midst of his starving, half-naked, freezing rabble, Washington saw hopes of an American success fast ebbing away . . . plagued by [mutinies and] by the continual departure of recruits whose time had expired (three-months enlistment for state militia men), [he had] tartly commented in 1776 that 'short enlistments—a mistaken dependence upon militia—have been the origin of all our misfortunes.'"[14] Short enlistments were an important variable prolonging revolutionary conflict. Of the 395,858 men recruited into the Revolutionary armed forces, those in the field at any one time never exceeded 35,000. Because the British forces in America never exceeded 42,000, if half of the 395,858 had "been available regularly, the Americans should easily have overwhelmed the British."[15] But this was not the case by 1777 and would not be the case until General George Washington, in that memorable winter of 1777-1778, concluded that the presence of Africans— free and enslaved—was necessary for the eventual defeat of British forces.[16]

Blacks and the War Effort

An important strategic objective of the American forces was to hold the Hudson Valley against British attempts to cut a wedge between the New England states and others further south. The job of insuring valley security fell to the forces of the Northern Army (first under General Philip Schuyler and later under Horatio Gates) and to those of the Valley Command (under Major-General William Heath and others). Integrated among the forces were Africans from the valley, many from regiments in New England and New Jersey, and from various southern regimental units. The Africans' presence among white combatants predated the official acknowledgment of their use in the revolutionary struggle.[17] When Ethan Allen and his Green Mountain Boys accompanied by Benedict Arnold, made their dash to the northern slopes of the valley in the region of Lake Champlain in order to capture Fort Ticonderoga and Crown Point in 1775 (subsequently turned over to the command of the Northern Army under General Schuyler), African American warriors were among the regimental units.[18] Barzillai Lew of the Twenty-Seventh Massachusetts regiment and Lamuel Haynes of a Connecticut unit both saw duty at Fort Ticonderoga.[19] In addition to Lew and Haynes, many other African Americans were dispersed among the assault troops that captured the two British fortifications: Cash Affrica, Caesar Parkhurst, Caesar Spensor, Prince Done, and Samuel Pomp. The men were enlistees in four of Connecticut's fighting units: the First, Sixth, Ninth, and Tenth regiments. Later that year when Arnold dashed through the woods of Maine to rendezvous with the New York regiments of General Clinton and General Montgomery to join in their disastrous invasion of Canada, Jack Roosa, Cato Dederick, Jack Gaul, Cato Van Aken, and Prince Danforth of various Ulster County regiments and from mid-Hudson towns such as Kingston, Marbletown, and New Windsor, participated in the failed attempt on Quebec City.[20]

As the valley developed into a prime theater of war, adequate space and provisions had to be made available to support the fighting forces. The Peekskill, New York command post for the valley forces had the strategic task of protecting the passes at the foothills of the Highlands against British intrusion. Near there Continental Village sprang up not only to quarter the troops but also to supply them with materiel.[21] When regiments were not engaged in combat in the valley, they were in winter quarters. In 1780-1781, Connecticut regiments wintered in Connecticut Village above the Tory estate of Beverly Robinson, "opposite West Point, about one mile and a half from the river" and in what is today Putnam County.[22] Further south and southwest at Philipsburgh and White Plains, continental forces bivouacked and wintered. To help shore up the American's position in this war theater, African Americans assumed an array of roles in addition to combatants. They were drivers, orderlies, waiters, cooks, bakers (especially at Tarrytown, Continental Village, and at Fishkill where there were numerous ovens for baking bread), skilled craftsmen, and common laborers.[23] Many were also engaged at New Windsor on the "works," a point on the Hudson River where the huge iron chain, manufactured at the Sterling Iron Works in Orange County, was assembled in sections and floated down to West Point. There, sometime after 1777, its five hundred yards was assembled and stretched across the Hudson to Constitutional Island in order to prevent British ships from ascending the river.[24]

As combatants, orderlies, drivers, or cooks, Africans in the Revolutionary struggle were America's unsung heroes. Their deeds of valor are not usually praised and, therefore, do not live on after them: they lay buried in the annals of history. African Americans from New York and other states who were engaged in the revolutionary campaigns in the valley were steadfast and valiant in their contributions to the war efforts. Blacks of the First and Second regiments of Rhode Island repeatedly demonstrated their military prowess. They performed extraordinary feats of valor defending Rhode Island and Red Bank, New Jersey. African Americans of the Rhode Island First Regiment under the command of Colonel Christopher Greene held the British guerrilla group, the "Cowboys," at bay in the Neutral Zone, a region of the lower Hudson Valley which stretched across the extent of southern Westchester County into parts of western New Jersey.[25] Immortalized in James Fenimore Cooper's *The Spy*, the Neutral Zone was a desolate, sparsely populated buffer zone between the forces of the English to the south and the Americans to the north. It was a zone in which those few brave families who elected to remain had to contend with theft, murder, and destruction by renegades, such as the "Cowboys" and "Skinners," who cloaked their plundering under an alleged allegiance to one of the combatants.[26] In it, the major combatants foraged for goods to sustain both men and beasts of burden: "the Americans foraging from a point on the Long Island Sound extending west from Rye, Mamaroneck, East Chester, and Chester to a point as close as possible to King's Bridge."[27]

Major-General Heath ordered Colonel Greene and his Black regiment into the Neutral Zone to hold Pines Bridge on the Croton River against the marauding "Cowboys," who frequently made incursions from their base at Morrisiania (South Bronx) under the command of Colonel James Delancey. In an early morning raid on 14 May 1781, Delancey and his "Cowboys" caught Greene and his command by surprise and overran the Pines Bridge post at the Davenport House, killing Colonel Greene, another officer, and many of the Black troops. The Black troops "defended their beloved Col. Greene so well that it was only over their dead bodies that the enemy reached and murdered him."[28] These are some of America's unsung heroes from the Hudson River Valley.

General Benedict Arnold's dishonest attempt to sell the plans for West Point and the capture and execution of his co-conspirator Major John Andre are recorded in history.[29] Yet, the heroic deed of the Black revolutionary fighter, James Peterson, of Cortlandt in Westchester, remains unsung. At Croton Point on the Hudson, it was, "ironically, the sharp-shooting of Peterson that [forced Andre to seek escape] over-land through Westchester rather than to a waiting ship in the river and down the Hudson [but instead] led ultimately [to his] capture" and hanging in October 1780.[30]

Another unsung deed of a Black hero involved Pompey Lamb. General "Mad" Anthony Wayne's successful capture of Stony Point on the east bank of the Hudson then held by British forces was as a result of Pompey's ability to move unobtrusively between his owner's home and the fort to sell fresh fruits and vegetables, eventually acquiring the secret password from the British guards. Using the password "the fort is ours," Pompey was among those who overpowered the sentries and allowed Wayne's 1,350 continentals (many African American warriors) to successfully capture Stony Point on 16 July 1779.[31]

Among those who died at Valley Forge during the cold winter spent there were heroic sons of slaves like Philip Field, Second New York Regiment, Dutchess County.[32] Private Field had enlisted in the Second New York with a number of African Americans from the Hudson Valley region. Those enlistees included Cornelius Woodmore of Sedman's Cove, Henry Smith of Fishkill, and William White of Kingston, New York. In addition, it is believed that the Revolutionary pensioner Lewis Bradley, of Pawling in Dutchess County, was also a member of the Second New York.[33]

There were other young African American warriors who gave of themselves so that white America might be free of colo-nial oppression and enslaved, Black America might be free of the yoke of the peculiar institution. These included Henry Crandle, who also suffered through that severe winter of 1777-1778. He was a private in a company of the Third New York

Regiment, under the command of Captain Aorson. Private Crandle had been sent to serve in the army by his owner John Crandle of Fishkill.[34] John Ripley of Albany County served in the Third Massachusetts Regiment of Colonel Greaton and was at the battles and surrender of General Burgoyne at Saratoga in October 1777. After the war, he took up residence in Kinderhook, New York, Columbia County.[35] On the muster rolls of a revolutionary regiment from Orangetown, Rockland County, New York, is the name of an African American known only as "Negro Tom," who, as early as 18 March 1776, is listed as a drummer in the regimental company of Captain Egbert.

Although the African Americans' deeds of valor lay unsung, unheralded, and forgotten, they were fighters in most of the Hudson Valley engagements of the Revolutionary War. In addition to the early exploits of battle in the Lake Champlain region and the capture of Stony Point, African Americans fought and died at the Battle of White Plains in 1776, at the several skirmishes at Horseneck/Greenwich within the Neutral Zone, the Burgoyne/Gates campaign of Bennington, Stillwater, and Bemis Heights, as well as at the formal surrender of British forces and their Hessian allies at Saratoga in October 1777. These young warriors were involved in the cannonade by shoreline batteries along the Hudson River at the British frigates HMS *Phoenix* and HMS *Rose* as they attempted to ascend the river in July and August 1776.[36] Many of these young brave African Americans gave of themselves as defenders of the river and the American cause during the cannon fire directed at a British flotilla under the command of General Henry Clinton which had successfully penetrated the river as far north as Kingston, New York, in 1777. The ultimate goal of the flotilla was to join General Burgoyne's army in Saratoga. Foiled in this attempt, Clinton had to content himself with the burning of Kingston, the capture of three African slaves of Colonel Abraham Hasbrouck (Henry, Nancy, Flora), and the destruction and burning of vessels and buildings to the east of the river around Poughkeepsie as the flotilla, under bombardment from shoreline batteries, retreated down the river.[37] African American soldiers were conspicuous at the 1777 defeat of General St. Ledger's forces by General Herkemer in the Mohawk Valley. St. Ledger had moved down the valley in an attempt to join with General Burgoyne and Sir Henry Clinton on the Hudson at

Albany, New York in a three-pronged move to cut the American forces and, thereby, isolate New England.[38] African American involvement was also evident in other campaigns in the Mohawk valley: with American forces under General Sullivan in campaigns in the western part of the valley against the Onadaga Indians and their allies as well as against the forces of Sir John Johnson of Canajoharie.[39] In the little-known July 1779 Battle of Minisink in the southwestern part of Orange County, fought between the combined forces of British agent Colonel Joseph Brant, the famous Mohawk chief, and those of Colonel John Harthorn of Warwick, New York, African Americans were combatants on both sides.[40]

The African American Warrior: For "Whomever Invoked the Image of Liberty"

Thousands of Blacks in Virginia who heeded the declaration of Lord Dunmore to escape to British lines as well as those in the Hudson River Valley who responded to Sir Henry Clinton's 1779 declaration from his Westchester headquarters took up arms for "whomever invoked the image of liberty" and could guarantee them their freedom.[41] In the Hudson Valley in addition to unnamed African Americans who manned the British "Negro fort" on the point east of King's Bridge in the vicinity of New York City (in what is now Riverdale), there were many other Blacks in the service of the British who, because they were familiar with the back country and knew the rivers and stream beds well, aided fellow Blacks and whites in their efforts to reach British lines.[42] Pompey and James Week, both slaves, were apprehended attempting to reach British lines and were sent to the "works at New Windsor."[43] Jonathan, a mulatto, had conspired to convey "draft dodgers" in the vicinity of Poughkeepsie and Beekman Precinct in Dutchess County to Long Island.[44] A "Negro" was found to have assisted loyalists and others in a safe passage through the Neutral Zone. He was charged with conducting them "through the woods in Westchester County cross Croton River, at a point three miles above the bridge, into British held territory."[45] A 1777 letter to Pierre van Cortlandt in Poughkeepsie reported that "a mulatto wench has lately passed through this place from New York; she brought intelligence to the inhabitants from their friends in New York, and in all probability she [has] gone to Burgoyne's army."[46] Perhaps even the foiled attempt of the van Cortlandt female slaves led by Bridget to reach the British lines was a response to Sir Clinton's proclamation because it invoked the "image of liberty."[47]

The African known as Colonel Cuff, who at times commanded the British "Negro fort," had responded to that "image of liberty" invoked by the British.[48] When not at his command post, Colonel Cuff, like his New Jersey counterpart Colonel Tye, often combined his regimental efforts with those of Delancey's "Cowboys" in their rampages in the Neutral Zone.[49] Cuff and his men were part of Sir Henry Clinton's advanced guard the Ethiopian Regiment operating in the Neutral Zone. The twenty or so African Americans among Rodgers's Rangers posted at King's Bridge were part of that advanced guard as well.[50]

Patriots, Allies, and the African American Warrior: On the Road to Victory

African American heroism enabled the English to prolong the war and enabled the Americans to achieve victory. Whether slave, free, or runaway, the African American was equal to the challenge of war. He put to rest the sambo myth. As a crack infantryman in the personal bodyguard of General Washington or as a fifer and teamster in the Fifth New York, he was every inch that "stout Black man" sent off to war in place of his owner.[51] Baron Ludwig Von Closen's description of Blacks in the American fighting forces is far from pejorative. While at White Plains with his French contingent, he remarked that "a quarter of them [American fighters] were Negroes, merry, confident, and sturdy."[52]

Indubitably, when conventional historians write the true history of the African American's role in the Revolution, they will have to confront the assessment not only of Von Closoen but also that of Rochambeau's aide, Jean-Baptiste-Antoine de Verger. As the French and American allies prepared to cross the Hudson River from Verplanck Point at King's Ferry for the long march south to confront the forces of Cornwallis at Yorktown, Verger observed in July 1781:

The whole effect was rather good. Their arms were in good condition; some regiments had white cotton uniforms. Their clothing consisted of a coat, jacket, vest, and trousers of white cloth, buttoned from the bottom to the calves, like gaiters. Several battalions wore little black caps, with white plumes. Only General Washington's mounted guard and Sheldon's legion [included among both were African Americans] wore large caps with bearskin fastenings as crests. *Three-quarters of the Rhode Island regiments consists of Negroes, and that regiment is the most neatly dressed, the best under arms, and the most precise in its maneuvers.*[53]

On 22 January 1828, Congressman Martindal of New York recalled the African American soldiers as they had marched through the counties of Clinton, Franklin, Saint Lawrence, and Jefferson on their way to Lake Ontario. "Slaves or Negroes who had been slaves, were enlisted as soldiers in the War of the Revolution; and I myself saw a battalion of them, as fine martial-looking men as ever saw, attached to the Northern army . . . on its march from Plattsburg to Sackett's Harbor."[54] Of the 2 September 1781 passage of the allied armies through Philadelphia, James Forten remarked: "And I remember . . . for I saw them, when the regiments from Rhode Island, Connecticut, and Massachusetts marched through Philadelphia, that one or two companies of colored men were attached to each."[55]

The African American's quest, therefore, for his own freedom was intertwined with that of whites who confronted one another in what was essentially a family feud. The family member who won would do so only as he effectively appealed to the Blacks. It didn't matter which of the major combatants won; freedom from the peculiar institution for African slaves was assured. The quest for personal freedom from the constraints of a racist, oppressive society remained an arduous journey for Blacks in the Hudson River Valley.

Notes

1. Benjamin Quarles, *The Negro in the American Revolution* (Chapel Hill: University of North Carolina Press, 1961), viii.
2. *Ibid.*, vii.

3.   Lisa A. Bull, "The Negro," in *Westfield Bicentennial Committees and Historical Journal of Western Massachusetts,* ed. Frederick F. Harling and Martin Kaufman (Westfield, Mass.: Bicentennial Committee, 1976), 69; cf. Quarles.

4.   Cf. Clement Alexander Price, *Freedom Not Too Far Distant A Documentary History of Afro-Americans in New Jersey* (Newark: New Jersey Historical Society, 1980).

5.   Quoted in Roi Ottley and William J. Weatherby, eds., *The Negro in New York: An Informal Social History* (Dobbs Ferry, N. Y.: Oceana Publications, Inc. 1967), 12.

6.   *Collections of the New York Historical Society for the Year 1891* (New York: New York Historical Society, 1892), 476.

7.   *Ibid.,* 446.

8.   *Ibid.,* 316.

9.   "Men Enlisted Out of Colonel Abraham Hering's Regiment in Orange County, Mustered the 24th Day of April 1759, and Appendix D," *Orange County Historical Society 3* (1973-1974), 34-35; *Collections of the New York Historical Society for the Year 1891,* 332.

10. E. B. O'Callaghan, ed., *Calendar of Historical Manuscripts in the Office of the Secretary of State* (Albany, N. Y.: Weed, Parsons and Company, 1866), 6: 1005.

11. Cf. Debra Scacciaferro, "Blacks in the Revolution," in *Times Herald Record,* 3 July 1988, "Sunday Magazine" quotes Williams-Myers on his research into the African factor in the American Revolution in the Hudson River Valley.

12. Quarles, 4, 9.

13. Robert W. Cookley and Stetson Conn, *The War of the American Revolution* (Washington, D. C.: Center of Military History, United States Army, 1975), 101, 111; Lorenzo J. Greene, "Some Observations on the Black Regiment of Rhode Island in the American Revolution," *Journal of Negro History* 37 (April 1952): 144-45.

14. Francis V. Greene, *The American Revolution* (New York: 1911), 292.

15. Willard W. Wallace, *Appeal to Arms* (New York: Harper & Row, 1951), 271.

16. Walter H. Mazyck, *George Washington and the Negro* (Washington, D. C.: Associated Publishers, 1932), 44. In addition to manpower needs, Washington "bowed before the fear of the Negro in the enemy's ranks" (Quarles, 52). Wishing to create two regiments of African combatants, commanded by whites, (which never materialized) the New York State Legislature offered a land grant bounty, on 20 March 1781, "To any person who delivered his able-bodied slave(s) to a warrant officer. The slave was to serve for one to three years, or until 'regularly' discharged" (*Laws of the State of New York* [Poughkeepsie, N. Y.: 1782], 179, quoted in Mazyck.

17. Mazyck, 38; Quarles, 10-13. Cf. David F. Phillips, "Negroes in the American Revolution," *Journal of American History* 5 (1911), 143-46; *New Hampshire Provincial and State Papers* (Durham: University of New

Hampshire, 1886), 434-39; David White, *Connecticut Black Soldiers 1775-1783* (Chester, Conn.: Pequot Press, 1973); Morris J. MacGregor and Bernard C. Nalty, eds., *Blacks in the United States Armed Forces: Basic Documents* (Wilmington, Del.: Scholarly Resources, 1977), 1: 11; Robert Ewell Greene, *Black Defenders of America 1775-1973* (Chicago: Johnson Publishing Company, 1974); Robert Ewell Greene, *Black Courage 1775-1783, Documentation of Black Participation in the American Revolution* (Washington, D. C.: National Society of the Daughters of the American Revolution, 1984); William C. Nell, *The Colored Patriots of the American Revolution* (New York: Arno Press, 1968). For New York, see chapter six.

18. Cf. Henry P. Johnson, ed., *The Record of Connecticut Men in the Military and Naval Service during the War of the Revolution 1775-1783,* (Hartford, Conn.: State Library, 1889), 29-30. James A. Roberts, *New York in the Revolution as Colony and State,* 2d ed. (Albany, N. Y.: Press of Bandow Printing Company, 1898), 8; *Heath's Memoirs of the American War* (1798; reprint, Freeport, N. Y.: Books for Libraries, 1970), 40, 405-6.

19. R. E. Greene, *Black Courage,* 9, 31, 42, 48; Quarles, 11; White, 17; Johnson, 39-44, 75, 99.

20. Ewards Park, "Could Canada Have Even Been Our Fourteenth Colony? or Arnold's Dash to Quebec," *Smithsonian* 18 ((December 1987): 41-49; Ruth P. Heidgerd, ed., *Ulster County in the Revolution: A Guide to Those Who Served* (New Paltz, N. Y.: Huguenot Historical Society, 1977) 4, 20, 57, 99, 204, 251; Alan and Barbara Ainone, "The History of the 2nd New York, 1775-1783," United States Military Academy Library, West Point, N. Y.; Cookley and Conn, 92-94.

21. Otto Hufeland, *Westchester County during the American Revolution 1775-1783* (Harrison, N. Y.: Harbor Hill Books, 1974), 209-10; Samuel Tallmadge et al., *Orderly Books of the Fourth New York Regiment, 1778-1780 and The Second New York Regiment, 1780-1783,* (Albany: University of the State of New York, 1932), 31; *Heath's Memoirs,* 95.

22. Johnson, 303; *Heath's Memoirs,* 95; George F. Scheer, *Private Yankee Doodle* (Boston: Little, Brown and Company, 1962) 164 note 4.

23. Conte Jean-François-Louis de Clarmon-Crevecoeur, "Journal of the War in America During the Years 1780, 1781, 1782, 1783," in *The American Campaigns of Rochambeau's Army 1780, 1781, 1782, 1783,* ed. Howard C. Rice, Jr., and Anne S. K. Brown (Princeton, N. J., and Providence, R. I.: Princeton University Press and Brown University Press, 1972), 1: 34 note 39, 35. Jared Spards, ed., *Correspondence of the American Revolution: Being Letters of Eminent Men to George Washington from the Time of his Taking Command of the Army to the End of his Presidency* (Boston: Little, Brown , 1853), 1: 417; *The Hudson Valley and the American Revolution* (Albany, N. Y.: New York Historic Trust, 1968), 17; Quarles.

24. *Hudson Valley and the American Revolution,* 6; Scheer, 278; Spards, 2: 59. In the winter "when military operations were suspended," the chain was hauled out of the Hudson by windlass for repairs.

25. L. J. Greene; Philip S. Foner, *Blacks in the American Revolution* (Westport, Conn.: Greenwood Press, 1975), 57; William Nell, *Services of Colored*

Americans in the War of 1776 and 1812 (Boston: Prentiss & Sawyer, 1851), 10; Sidney Kaplan, *The Black Presence in the Era of the American Revolution 1770-1800* (Washington, D. C.: Smithsonian Institution Press, 1973), 42, 55-56; George H. Moore, "Historical Notes on the Employment of Negroes in the American Army of the Revolution," in *The Negro Soldier: A Select Compilation* (New York: Negro Universities Press, 1970), 19; Laura A Wilkes, "Missing Pages in American History Revealing the Services of Negroes in the Early Wars in the United States of America, 1641-1815," in *The Negro Soldier: A Select Compilation* (New York: Negro Universities Press, 1970), 34-35; Quarles, 73, 77,79, 80-82. Cf. R. E. Greene, *Black Courage;* Sidney S. Rider, "The Black Regiment of the Revolution," *Rhode Island Historical Tracts* 10 (1880): 1-50.

26. James Fenimore Cooper, *The Spy* (Philadelphia, Pa.: MacRae-Smith, 1821); Louis de Clermon-Crevecoeur, 30 note 28; Robert Bolton, *The History of the Several Towns, Manors, and Patents of the County of Westchester from its First Settlement to the Present Time* (New York: Charles F. Roper, 1881), 2: 678.

27. Howard C. Rice, Jr., and Anne S. K. Brown, eds., *The American Campaigns of Rochambeau's Army 1780, 1781, 1782, 1783* (Princeton, N. J., and Providence, R. I.: Princeton University Press and Brown University Press, 1972), 1: 249.

28. Allison Albee, "The Defenses at Pines Bridge," *Westchester Historian,* 1958-1961 editions, see especially vol. 37, (January, February, March 1961), 15-20. Kaplan, 56; Wilkes, 35; *Heath's Memoirs,* 303; Rider, 3-4; Hufeland, 279-82; L. J. Greene, 169-70; Bolton, 678-80, 686.

29. *Heath's Memoir's,* 267, 268, 269.

30. "A Hudson River History Narrative," *Westchester African-American Historical Society Newsletter,* 8 August 1987: 2-3. As a militiaman Peterson apparently manned the cannon "that blew a hole in the British ship *Vulture* as it waited [on the Hudson] for the British spy, [Major] John Andre, to return from Haverstraw on the west shore, where he had met with General Benedict Arnold, who had given him the plans to West Point."

31. Herbert Aptheker, *Essays in the History of the American Negro* (New York: International Publishers, 1969), 108-9; Benson J. Lossing, *The Pictorial Field-Book of the Revolution* (Rutland, Vt.: Charles E. Tuttle Company, 1972), 2: 744-46, 744 note 3. Cf. Henry P. Johnston, *The Storming of Stony Point* (New York: James T. White & Co., 1969). Pompey Lamb does not appear as a significant actor in the capture of the Point, nor is there any mention of other African combatants from among various regimental units, such as those of Connecticut, Massachusetts, Maryland, and New York, who participated in the capture of the fort as described in the text by Johnston.

32 . Aptheker, 100; Ainone, 6; Berthold Fernow and E. B. O'Callaghan, eds., *Documents Relating to the Colonial History of the State of New York* (Albany, N. Y.: Weed, Parsons and Company, 1887), 15 (State Archives, vol. 1.): 188. Cf. Howard H. Peckham, *The Toll of Independence*

Engagements: and Battle Casualties of the American Revolution (Chicago: University of Chicago Press, 1974).

33. Death Certificate, Lewis Bradley of Pawling, New York, 13 May 1837, Dutchess County Surrogate Office, Poughkeepsie, New York.

34. Cf. T. W. Egly, Jr., *History of the First New York Regiment 1775-1783* (Hampton, N. H.: Peter E. Randall, 1981), 205-9.

35 . MacGregor and Nalty, 181; R. E. Greene, *Black Courage*, 32, 42, 60, 81.

36. Cf. Richard J. Koke, "The Struggle for the Hudson: The British Naval Expedition under Captain Hyde Parker and Captain James Wallace, July 12-August 18, 1776," in *Narratives of the Revolution in New York* (New York: New York Historical Society, 1975), 36-79; Spards, 1: 277.

37. George Pratt, "An Account of the British Expedition above the Highlands of the Hudson River and of Events Connected with the Burning of Kingston in 1777," in *Ulster County Historical Society Collections*, (1860; reprint, Kingston, N. Y.: Ulster County Historical Society, 1977), 111, 115.

38. Cf. Roberts, 9; *The Champlain Valley In the American Revolution* (Albany, N. Y.: New York State Revolution Bicentennial Commission and Champlain Valley Committee for the Observance of the Bicentennial of the American Revolution, State Education Department, 1976), 12.

39. Cf. Frederick Cook, *Journals of the Military Expedition of Major General John Sullivan 1779* (Ann Arbor, Mich.: University Microfilms, 1967), especially "Journal of Lieutenant John L. Hardenbergh, 2nd New York Regiment," 115-36.

40. Vernon Leslie, *The Battle of Minisink: A Revolutionary War Engagement in the Upper Delaware Valley* (Middletown, N. Y.: T. Emmett Henderson, 1976). Cf. R. Emmet Deyo," Colonel Lewis DuBois and the 5th N. Y.. Continental Regiment in the Revolution," *Historical Papers* (Historical Society of Newburgh Bay and the Highlands) 13 (1906): 191-98.

41. Quarles, vii, 19-32, 113-14; Hufeland, 296-97. Clinton's proclamation read in part: "I do most strictly forbid any Person to sell or claim right over any Negro, the property of a rebel, who may take refuge with any part of this army. And I do promise to every Negro who shall desert the rebel standard, full security to follow within these lines, any occupation which he shall think proper" (Hufeland, 277).

42. Cf. Bolton, 2: 528; Hufeland, 189; *Heath's Memoirs*, 119-21; Lossing, 2: 625. The Negro Fort was situated on the Post Road east of King's Bridge and slightly southwest of the Valentine's Hill, in what is today Riverdale. It was on the "point," and undoubtedly was the "tripline" for the British giving evidence of an advance south by the American forces. Given its name, it was manned by Black troops fighting for the British, who were probably composed of elements from either the British Company of Pioneers raised in Philadelphia in 1772 or the Negro Horse unit raised in New York in 1782. See Philip R. N. Katcher, *Encyclopedia of British, Provincial, and German Units 1755-1783* (Harrisburg, Pa.: Stackpole Books, 1973), 83, 92. Private Joseph Plumb Martin recorded that the Negro Fort was "garrisoned by a gang of fugi-

tive Negroes, commanded by a black by the name of Cuff—Colonel
Cuff (Scheer, 205).

43.   *Minutes of the Committee and the First Commission for Detecting and Defeating
Conspiracies in the State of New York, December 11, 1776-September 23, 1778
and Minutes of the Council of Appointment, State of New York, April 2, 1778-
May 3, 1779* 2 vols. (New York: New York Historical Society Collections,
1925), 1: 70.

44.   *Ibid.,* 1: 57-58.

45.   *Ibid.,* 1: 271-72.

46.   *Ibid.,* 2: 443.

47.   Jacquetta M. Haley, "Slavery in the Land of Liberty: The Van Cortlandt
Response," in *The Van Cortlandt Family in the New Nation* (Tarrytown, N.
Y.: Sleepy Hollow Restorations, 1984), 46-47.

48.   Scheer, 205. While on patrol one night in the lower Hudson Valley in
1780, Private Martin encountered a runaway slave who asked: "Is this
Colonel Cuffee's blockhouse?" Unfortunately for the runaway it wasn't,
and he was apprehended and returned to the American lines.

49.   Cf. Price, 68.

50.   *Minutes of the Committee and the First Commission for Detecting and Defeating
Conspiracies,* 1: 121. For additional evidence of Blacks among British
fighting units, see *Minute Book of Proceedings of a Board of General Officers
of the British Army at New York 1781* (New York: New York Historical
Society, 1916) and Kenneth Scott, comp. *Rivington's New York Newspaper:
Excerpts from a Loyalist Press, 1773-1783,* (New York: New York Historical
Society, 1973).

51.   Cf. Evelyn M. Acomb, ed. and trans., *American Revolution: 1776-1783,
The Revolutionary Journal of Baron Ludwig Von Closen 1780-1783* (Chapel
Hill: University of North Carolina Press, 1958), xxxv; Scacciaferro, 6.
One known Black member of Washington's Bodyguard was Tobias
Gilmore in the Massachusetts regiment of Colonel George Williams.
See Moore, 32; John C. Miller, *Triumph of Freedom 1775-1783* (Boston:
Little, Brown, 1948), 510.

52.   Acomb, 89. It is estimated that 5,000 African Americans served as regu-
lar soldiers in the Continental forces during the Revolution (Acomb 89
note 17/89). Cf. Aptheker, 30-32; Quarles.

53.   Clermon-Cervecoeur, 33 note 36.

54.   Quoted in Cook, 150.

55.   Nell, *Services of Colored Americans,* 16. Scheer, 222.

Chapter Seven

POST-REVOLUTIONARY AND ANTEBELLUM
PERIODS: THE STRUGGLE FOR A BIRTHRIGHT

Introduction

The Revolution ended British oppression in America for whites, but most Blacks, in spite of their contributions to the revolutionary struggle, had to wait forty to seventy years before the oppressive yoke of white America was lifted. For some of those who participated in the revolutionary conflagration, freedom was their reward, and, if they persevered, they received a land bounty as well.[1] Many of those who fought with the British were evacuated from the ports of New York and Staten Island for the West Indies and Nova Scotia in Canada. The Hessians even kept their promise to evacuate their Black auxiliaries; a Brunswick contingent under Baron Von Riedesel of the Burgoyne Conventional Army evacuated its corps of Black drummers to Germany.[2] An African known only as Tone (see chap. 1), who was freed from bondage by his owner, John Warring, for his service in the revolutionary cause, developed a prosperous business in boat rentals to fishermen and operated a tavern on a pond named after him in Dutchess County.[3] But Tone and others like him were few. The majority had to wait until the passage of the Gradual Emancipation Act, which freed all newborns of slave mothers on 4 July 1799. To placate the owners, the law required that the newborns remain the servants of the "master or mistress of the mother—the male children until they reached the age of 27, and the females until the age of 25, provided the master or mistress cause the children to be taught to read the holy scriptures previous to their becoming 21 years of age."[4]

The dynamics of emancipation in New York in itself is a fit subject for a book, especially if one considers the Gradual Emancipation Act as a convenient way for owners to dispose of their human property without much loss.[5] With the passage of subsequent legislation, particularly the bill in response to Governor Daniel D. Thompkins's directive to the State Legislature in 1817, slavery in New York was officially abolished on 4 July 1827.[6] The time was exactly forty-four years after the end of the Revolution and forty years after the Constitutional Convention in Philadelphia: a convention which agreed to let the trade in slaves from Africa run its course for another twenty years, gave support to the peculiar institution in the South through provisions in the document, and made Blacks in America three-fifths of a person.[7]

Being considered three-fifths of a person did not deter Black New Yorkers from celebrating the arrival of a not too distant freedom. Nowhere was it celebrated in such splendor as in the City of Albany on 5 July 1827. A great procession, lead by what the *Albany Argus and City Gazette* described as "African bands and Marshals," and followed by "state officers, the Judiciary, Senate, members of Congress, members of Cincinnati, revolutionary worthies and citizens," edged its way up State Street and along several other principal streets to the Second Baptist Church on Hamilton Street. In the pulpit to give the oration was the Reverend Nathaniel Paul, pastor of "the African congregation in this city."[8] With the crowd spilling over into Hamilton Street, Reverend Paul was overwhelmed by the spectacle before him. Bright colorful banners could be seen around the church, and they bore the names of "distinguished men whose efforts [had] been directed towards the extinction of slavery, and the amelioration of the conditions of those who [had] been the subjects of it." The names on the banners included those of Thompkins (Governor), Jay (first president of the New York Manumission Association), Clarkson, Eddy, Murray, Jr., and Wilberforce, as well as the inscriptions, "Albany African Association," "Legislature of 1817," and "New York Manumission Society."[9] It was fitting that such a celebration took place in Albany: a city and county in which the peculiar institution had been second behind New York City in the number of slaves held and the city in which the state legislature abolished what it had for years so fervently protected.

The Post-Revolutionary Period: New Challenges and New Strategies

Personal freedom did not bring economic and political freedom or social acceptance. The first half of the nineteenth century brought a new challenge for African Americans in the Hudson River Valley and the adjoining region of the lower Mohawk. Freed of their slave shackles, African Americans had to contend with growing socioeconomic and political ostracism, intensified by the entrance into the valley of waves of European immigrants. What had been touted as a beneficent, open slave society in its heyday, metamorphosed into a society where one's socioeconomic status was determined by race, when large numbers of poor white immigrants began to compete for jobs traditionally held by Blacks. As racism became more and more a factor, Blacks found themselves in an intolerable predicament. With many families still attached to their former owners and others barely eking out an existence from the land, many more were driven to become day laborers moving from farm to farm or work project to work project. William Strickland's observation about free Blacks in the vicinity of Albany and Saratoga reveals the socioeconomic blight that had descended upon many of them.

> They lead the life of Indians, cultivating a little mays [maize], but living chiefly in the woods . . . [and] are unable to bring up their families;they spend in the summer what they earn, and in the winter are in want and must be supported by their neighbors. . . . Their families in general are numerous, and their children though naked and neglected, they will not suffer to go from home to work. In the vale of Saratoga and other parts of the country I have met with families of Negroes bearing much the same character.[10]

In spite of these conditions, the nineteenth century brought challenges of a new kind to the region linking the African American community to the larger world of abolitionism, enfranchisement, education, European immigration, and economic security. The fight for total liberation had just begun. The arduous journey had not ended with slavery's demise. White society had simply redefined the rules of the game and at the expense of African Americans. This time the battles would not be fought in the trenches but in the very halls of government where legislation was used to deny Blacks their humanity and where, during the post-revolutionary period, legislative action was undertaken to create a society of "Brahmins and Pariahs" whose life-chances would be determined by race.[11]

Not all Blacks in the Hudson Valley and its environs suffered the deprivations Strickland observed. Although many remained attached to their former owners' estates or homes, others began little independent Black or mixed communities on the peripheries of major urban areas, or they migrated to the cities and towns to be near a larger array of job possibilities as well as larger bodies of Black residents. Nuclear and extended families were possible. The first five Federal Censuses (1790, 1800, 1810, 1820, 1830) recorded many Black heads of households, and, for some, residential stability was a fact.[12] For the first fifty years of the nineteenth century, Black residential patterns were evident in most areas, but African Americans were not concentrated in one general area in any large city. Pockets of African American communities were dispersed throughout the general population, although in some rural areas marginal farming land was targeted for Black and poor white families.

In some urban areas, like Albany and Poughkeepsie, Black residential patterns were dispersed. For example, in two predominantly white communities in Albany prior to 1840, the area east of Eagle Street and south of State Street and Arbor Hill contained pockets of African Americans. But by 1850 there was a clear shift away from these areas to a more concentrated, well defined African American residential pattern.[13] Equally, in Poughkeepsie during the first half of the century, African Americans were located in three defined residential clusters: "on the fringes of the central business district bounded by

Washington and Market Streets where some working class whites and recently arrived German immigrants also resided; second, on 'long Row' by the Almshouse; third, in the area of Catherine, Cottage, and Pine Streets."[14] By 1880 though, segregated residential patterns were definitely recognizable in Poughkeepsie.[15]

Dispersed Black residential patterns were related to the employment of many African American bread winners who needed to be near their white employers. If they did not live adjacent to the employer in a rented building or one provided for workers, then accommodations were arranged for them in the home of the employer. For example, in Saratoga Springs forty-three percent of households "consisted of blacks who lived in white households, including three of the village hotels, acting as live-in servants much as they had done in the days of slavery."[16] By 1880 and into the first decades of the twentieth century, preferential residential patterns, similar to those of Poughkeepsie, had become a way of life for African Americans in Saratoga Springs.[17]

Prior to the 1880s, on the peripheries of some towns in the region well defined concentrations of African Americans could be found. They were in the Slote (Sparkill) region on the western bank of the Hudson River where the Sparkill Creek empties into that river below Nyack,[18] in the Skunk Hallow community on the Palisades where New York meets New Jersey,[19] and among other various mixed mountain people in the Hudson Valley, the Ramapo (Jackson Whites) west of Nyack and those from Eagle's Nest near Hurley.[20] Also, there were two communities that sprang up in the late eighteenth-early nineteenth century period on marginal land close to concentrations of prospective white employers. One was known as "The Hills" and was located in the lower Hudson Valley "on the rugged land north of Saint Mary's (Silver Lake) where Harrison, White Plains and North Castle [Westchester County] are joined."[21] The other community was located north in Dutchess County near the present-day village of Poughquay and was founded by Charles Freeman, the community's biggest landowner whose acres stretched to West Pawling.[22] Both communities were referred to as "Nigger Hill" by white outsiders. Community residents preferred to use the name "Guinea Town" because of its historical connection with the Guinea Coast in West Africa from which many of their ancestors were taken as captives. Charles Freeman and others, including women, appeared as heads of households for censuses taken between 1800 and 1830, evidence of the existence of nuclear and extended families at the time.[23]

A counterpart of Charles Freeman in Rockland County was the prominent Black head of household, John Moore, of Orangetown (Piermont). He was the town's first industrialist. By 1800, John Moore was already operating his own sawmill and gristmill and, by 1815, also owned a carding mill which employed fifteen people. Moore was also responsible for the production of grinding wheels made of stone taken from Piermont's "mine hole." [24]

Although individuals like John Moore, Charles Freeman, and others were able to maintain families and remain economically viable in early-nineteenth-century Hudson Valley society, they, nevertheless, had to contend with a white society that was determined to fashion an "aristocracy of the skin." Faced with this, African Americans in the Hudson Valley and adjacent Mohawk region did not sit by calmly, content with "jubilee day," while their small gains were under attack. Imbued with the spirit of the Revolution and, to an extent, spurred on by the populism of Jeffersonian and Jacksonian democracy, African Americans in communities around the region met the new challenges steadfastly and with determination. They began to fight to insure that guarantees of the franchise written into the New York Constitution of 1777 would apply equally to white and Black. In 1821 African Americans became disturbed by the inequities written into the Constitution by the Constitutional Convention held in Albany. In order for a Black male to vote in an election, he had to have been resident in the state of New York for three years and to have controlled property valued at $250. A white male did not need to meet such qualifications. In the wake of this egregious injury, Blacks began a determined campaign of petitions to the legislature and held periodic Black national conventions to deliberate and formulate strategy. By the early 1870s, white society had no alternative but to enfranchise completely the Black male electorate. [25]

Challenges and Strategies: The Rise of a New Corps of Black Leadership

Until the day of full enfranchisement of the African American male, the Black community of the entire state of New York had to deal with an ultra-conservative, racist Democratic party. New York Democrats viewed potential Black voters as tools of the Federalists/Whig/aristocratic political faction, and individuals were singled out as possible obstacles to Democratic political supremacy in the state. The Democratic Party was well aware that Black males, if enfranchised, had the potential to determine the outcome of an election. In fact, in 1800 the vote of a single "Negro ward" won the election for the Federalists. Again in 1813, the "votes of 300 free Negroes in New York City decided the election and [again] swept the Federalists into power and determined the character of the State Legislature." In 1830 and 1840, it was the Black vote that carried the contest against the Tammany machine in the fifth and eighth wards in New York City.[26] In order to prevent this from happening again, the Democratically-controlled constitutional conventions submitted referenda for equal suffrage to the predominantly white New York electorate [which it repeatedly voted down] in 1826, 1846, 1860, 1869.[27] Despite these defeats, the African American community did not relent. The residency and property-holding requirements prevented most Blacks from exercising this constitutional right. (There were only seven qualified Black voters in Albany and four in Buffalo in 1835, but increased to twenty and twenty-one, respectively in 1840, to a total Black electorate of one thousand registered voters.)[28]

Using the convention strategy, combined with numerous petitions and resolutions, the African American leadership not only brought the franchise question into clear focus before the people, it also tied that fight to a host of other antebellum themes: abolition and colonization, education and economic development, and the overall general health of the Black community in the state and the country. The involvement of Black New Yorkers in the larger issue of abolition throughout the United States was really an extension of their fight against slavery and its legacy in New York. African Americans felt shackled to that legacy as long as their brethren in the South remained in a state of enslavement. Abolition, therefore, combined with the issues of colonization, education, economics, and politics presented the African American leadership in the state with a spectrum of challenges whose successful resolve was crucial to their freedom.

Prior to the 1840s the convention strategy, in which many whites were participants, was initially identified with William Lloyd Garrison's strategies: nonviolence and moral suasion. Black suffrage at that time was not a priority.[29] Eventually, a new Black leadership arose to challenge that approach. Interestingly, the Hudson Valley and its adjacent Mohawk region (from the St. Lawrence to the western slopes of New England and from the Lake Champlain-Hudson northern tier to the southern tier of the lower Hudson Valley) produced many of those new African American leaders who immersed themselves in the fight through the use of conventions. The first National Negro Conventions of the 1830s were attended by men from the Hudson region; there were none from the Mohawk region. Men such as George Richardson and David Ruggles of Poughkeepsie, Charles Smith and William P. Johnson of Newburgh, William Rich of Troy, John G. Stewart of Albany (selected second vice president), and Henry Sipkins of the cities of Hudson and Catskill were delegates at the 1833 convention in Philadelphia.[30] Two subsequent national conventions held before the end of the 1830s saw the Hudson Valley delegation widen to include such men as Nathan Blout and Jared Gray of Poughkeepsie, Robert Jackson of Catskill, Charles S. Morton, and John G. Stewart from Albany. All attended the 1834 New York convention; when the convention returned to Philadelphia in 1835, there was only a Troy contingent headed by William Rich (who would remain active to 1864) and newcomers William M. Livezeley and Clarence Seldon.[31]

Before the 1840s these men were considered representative of the "old guard," men who either had been born in the region or had arrived early in the century. As the 1840s began, these earlier leaders were joined and challenged by the "new guard," men, and later women (native born or recent settlers), who represented a new militancy and came from a wider area of the Hudson-Mohawk region. Among these were T. Woodson, James Fountain, and B. S. Anderson of Utica; John Wendell of Schenectady (in whose city the Annual Convention of Colored

Citizens was held in September of 1844 and 1846); Norris Lee from Watertown; and Enoch Moore from Little Falls. From the Hudson Valley came such notables as William H. Johnson, William H. Topp, and Stephen Myers of Albany; Henry Highland Garnet and his associate G. H. Baltimore of the Liberty Street Presbyterian Church of Troy; W. H. Decker of Newburgh in Orange County; Samuel Ringgold Ward, Isaac Deyo, and A. Bolden of Poughkeepsie; and Walter K. Mower of Amenia.[32] This "new guard" would shatter once and for all the stereotypical image of the Hudson-Mohawk African American as docile, timid, and infantile.

These new leaders were stout-hearted. They came from all walks of life: artisans, cooks, common laborers, professionals. Henry Highland Garnet of Troy and Samuel Ringgold Ward of Poughkeepsie reflected the multifaceted nature of Black talent. Garnet, described by Frederick Douglass (with whom he clashed on the appropriate liberation strategy for African Americans) as "the ablist thinker on his legs," began his teaching and ministerial duties in Troy, New York.[33] A graduate of both the African Free Academy in New York and Oneida Institute in the western part of the state, Garnet became a moving force, from the 1840s, at Liberty Street Negro Presbyterian Church of Troy, where he published and distributed his small periodical, *The Clarion*. The paper's objective was "to aid the Negro in all aspects of his emancipation."[34] Until 1847 he associated himself with William G. Allen, also of Troy, and together they produced the periodical, *The National Watchman.* [35]

Henry Highland Garnet represented a new generation of African orators who took center stage in the 1840s espousing a new militancy in the fight for full citizenship. "He was one of a number of young men caught in a generational break with older leaders who espoused caution in the struggle for racial freedom."[36] He understood the use of the convention as a potent weapon in the struggle with white America. Using it to its fullest extent, Garnet set in motion a new Black agenda that broke with Garrison and Douglass, who stressed moral suasion, nonviolence, and gradualism. Instead Garnet emphasized "militancy and greater independence from white abolitionists."[37] Garnet's involvement in the national and state Black conventions to the

1864 Syracuse convention molded the ideological direction conventions took on abolition, suffrage, education, Black-owned newspapers, support of political parties and their candidates, and Black economic development.[38] Troy, where state and national Black conventions were held, was his base throughout the 1840s, but Albany was the fulcrum of the debate on Black liberation. Garnet's leadership brought many African Americans into the abolition movement and, in turn, brought new followers of the Liberty Party, and, later, the Free Soil Party.[39] His most memorable National Convention of Colored Citizens was held in Buffalo in 1843 where Garnet's so-called "Black Power" stand intimated that slaves should take up arms against their oppressors. In his "Address to the Slaves," Garnet, almost advocating violence, remarked: "Brethren, arise arise! Strike for your lives and liberties. Rather die freemen than live to be slaves."[40] It was a memorable, forceful, and courageous statement, and it put Garnet squarely at the center of the abolition struggle, although, at the Troy convention of 1847, Garnet's militancy lost out to Frederick Douglass's "more diplomatic or palliative policy."[41]

Another of those new Black leaders from across the Hudson-Mohawk region was Samuel Ringgold Ward, who, like Garnet, began his illustrious career engaged as a teacher of Black students in a Lancasterian school in Poughkeepsie.[42] The year in which he began his teaching duties, 1839, was the same year Garnet began in Troy. In May of that year, Ward was officially "licensed to preach the gospel by the New York Congregational Association assembled at Poughkeepsie."[43] He was described by Douglass: "in depth of thought, fluency of speech, readiness of wit, logical exactness, and general intelligence, [he] has left no successor [of] the colored men amongst us." In November 1839, he became an orator for both the American and the New York Anti-Slavery societies and a founding member of Poughkeepsie's branch of that society established in 1832.[44] He and Garnet were identified with the convention movement and the political aspirations of the Liberty and Free Soil parties. Samuel Ringgold Ward was present at the founding of the Liberty Party in Albany in 1840 and was reputed to have said, "I then became for the first time a member of a political party; with it I cast my first vote; to it I devoted

my political activity; with it I lived my political life—which ter-
minated when eleven years subsequently I left the country."[45]

Before that departure, Ward and Garnet labored diligently
for the Liberty Party, attending the party's conventions in
Rochester and Buffalo in 1842 and 1843 as the first Black delegates.[46] Ward also fought for Black suffrage and equal education. Both he and Henry Highland Garnet represented the new
militant breed of Black orators, who profoundly affected the
direction of the African American struggle for full citizenship
during the antebellum period. Together with other African
American leaders from across the region they shattered once
and for all the stereotypical images of the Hudson-Mohawk
Black residents.

The African American Response to the Ideology of Southern Slavery as it Impinged on the Hudson River Valley and its Environs: A Concluding Statement

The African American from the region believed the image
of Blacks as docile, timid, and infantile was conjured up by white
society to rationalize its enslavement and oppression of Blacks
and to convince itself of its own race superiority. The African
American always believed the contrary and, therefore, sought
freedom from oppression on his own initiative. His fight for
abolition and his stand against the American Colonization
Society were perceived as one and the same, demanding stout-
hearted, resolute, and aggressive Black leaders to go into the
halls of white political power and confront it. Brave Black leaders eventually persuaded the State Legislature in 1841 to pass a
law against Southern slave holders bringing their slaves into the
state for a period of nine months.[47] The New York African
American community took this as an affront, putting the state
in the position of appearing to support Southern slavery. It was
the stout-hearted and their white allies who developed the intri-
cate network of stations on the Underground Railroad throughout the valley to assist southern fugitive slaves in their flight
north to freedom.

One of these brave souls was the antebellum leader from
Albany, New York, Stephen Myers. Born in 1800 in Rensselaer

County, Stephen Myers was labor-bound to the family of Dr. Eights. A prominent representative from Albany to four of the National Negro Conventions (Troy 1847, Rochester 1835, Philadelphia 1855, Syracuse 1864), Stephen Myers was also a member of the Antislavery Society. Working with an individual in Albany referred to as its "General Superintendent," Stephen held the post of conductor on the Underground Railroad.[48] Stephen Myers's leadership, with the assistance of William H. Topp, a leading Black merchant tailor of Albany, enabled many fugitives from the South to make it safely across the Canadian border to freedom. The Albany station was on the direct route from Washington, D.C., the southern terminus of the Underground Railroad. At Albany, the Underground radiated east into New England, north into Canada, and west towards Utica and beyond. North of Albany at Troy, where many slaves took refuge after their trek along the Hudson River, there were African American conductors, Henry Highland Garnet and Martin I. Townsend. At Troy, fugitives were "supplied with money and forwarded either to Suspension Bridge on the Niagara River, or by way of Vermont and Lake Champlain to Rouse Point" on the Canadian border in Clinton County.[49] In the western part of the Hudson-Mohawk region, the Underground Railroad system was fed by a spur radiating out from Petersboro (home of Garrit Smith) in central New York, running through Oswego to Cape Vincent in Jefferson County at the mouth of the St. Lawrence. From Cape Vincent fugitives were then ferried across to Canada, with many, no doubt, settling in adjacent towns like Watertown and Ogdenburg in Jefferson and Saint Lawrence counties, respectively.[50] Because of Stephen Myers and others like John G. Steward, William H. Topp, and William H. Matthews, many additional fugitives from Albany and Troy were settled in the vicinity of the North Elba home of John Brown (the abolitionist of Harper's Ferry fame) in Essex County on land owned by Garrit Smith.[51]

In addition to his efforts on behalf of the Underground Railroad, Stephen Myers was an indefatigable lobbyist for the New York Anti-Slavery Society. By 1856 he was the publisher of "[three] short-lived abolitionist sheets: *The Elevator* (ca. 1842), *The Telegraph*" (ca. 1852), and the Underground Railroad tract,

Circular to the Friends of Freedom, established some years before the first two.[52] In his letter of 22 March 1856 to the head of the New York Office of the Anti-Slavery Society, Garrit Smith, Myers wrote of his efforts with the state legislature on behalf of the society:

> Sir I have been striving hard this winter with the members of the Senate and Assembly to recommend an amendent [sic] to the constitution of this state so as to strike off the property qualifications and let us vote on the same footing as the whitemail [sic] citizens. So as to have it once more handed down to the people [voters for approval] I have got Senitor [sic] Cuyler some weeks ago to get up a resolution in the Senat [sic] which is now under discusin [sic] and will come up again Monday or Tuesday. I shall have one up in the assembly in a few days [which] I have received from colored men from different sections of the state which I have presented. . . . I have also devoted my time to defeat the collensisation [sic] bill to appropriate five thousand dollars to the collenisation [sic] Society —I have gotten about sixty members pledged to go against it in a final vote, it [is] now under discussion. When it comes up again they will iether [sic] vote it down or strike out the enacting clause which will eventually kill the bill. . . . I have since Mr. Smith was in our city six fugitives from Maryland.[53]

What is clearly evident in the letter is that Myers, as an African American leader, appeared to have been aggressively persuasive in getting members of the legislature, if not to vote in favor of a certain piece of legislation, at least to consider the views he represented.

Much of the activity associated with the Underground Railroad continued in spite of severe penalties for aiding, comforting, and interfering in the apprehension of slave fugitives as set forth in the 1850 Fugitive Slave Law. That law and its equally pernicious counterpart, the Dred Scott Decision of 1857, completely undermined the tenuous existence of all free African Americans around the state, sending many communities fleeing into Canada for refuge because of endlessly having to prove one's status to bounty hunters of fugitive slaves.[54] But many people remained and stood their ground in defiance of the fugitive law, brazenly attempting to foil the recapture of slaves and, through daring rescue attempts and slave purchases, succeeding in securing the freedom of fugitive slaves.

The stout-hearted, aggressively brave African American leaders and their white allies (especially Quakers) in the Hudson-Mohawk region attempted and even succeeded in the rescue of fugitive slaves from the hands of Federal Marshals and in the eventual purchase of freedom for fugitives. Two such known cases took place at Troy and Poughkeepsie. The one at Troy was a daringly successful attempt at the rescue of Charles Nalle, reputedly an escaped slave from Culpepper County, Virginia. On 27 April 1860, after about two years of working as a teamster in the town of Sandlake and for Uri Gilbert in the city of Troy as a coachman, Nalle was apprehended by a Federal Marshal. While Nalle was being prepared for transport out of Troy, a large crowd broke into the jail and whisked him across the Hudson River to West Troy. He was recaptured but shortly afterwards was successfully retaken from his captors and placed in a wagon driven out of town on Shaker Road by Hank York and another Black man known as Parker. Although more than a hundred African Americans participated in the rescue, *The Troy Daily Times* featured a "somewhat antiquated colored woman," posted to alert the rescuers. When the time came to signal the rescue, as "the most conspicuous person opposed to legal course," she was heard to shout "give us liberty or give us death!" and, by "vehement gesticulation urged the rescuers on." This person was probably Harriet Tubman. Eventually Charles Nalle returned to Troy as a freed man after benefactors in the city raised the sum of $1000 as the cost of his freedom.[55] John Bolding, the second case, had escaped from South Carolina to Poughkeepsie where he had married and operated a small tailor shop until identified and arrested in 1860. Bolding was returned to the South but was bought for $1700 by the Dutchess County Anti-Slavery Society and other leading citizens.[56]

In Kinderhook, Columbia County, an alleged escaped slave from Baltimore, Maryland, was identified while in the employ of General Whiting. In May 1830 the fugitive was taken before Judge Vandepoel where a writ of ownership and extradition was issued to permit his owner, Richard Dorsey, to return him to Baltimore.[57] Not even the most insignificant, out-of-the way place could completely shield the slave who hoped for freedom.

Even free Blacks were not safe from the consequences of the law; indiscriminate bounty hunters made fast bucks selling freemen to slave holders in the South. One who got caught in this web was Solomon Northrup of Saratoga Springs. In 1841 he was convinced that the two men who encouraged him to join their troupe as a short-term musician were legitimate. Instead, he was sold into slavery in Louisiana for twelve years until rescued by New York authorities.[58]

In Fishkill Landing (now Beacon, New York), a fugitive slave from Baltimore, James Brown, was successful in avoiding the long arm of the law. Befriended by the Gulian Verplanck family, Brown began working for them in the early 1820s and eventually was purchased by the Verplancks and personally purchased his wife, Julia. An experienced gardener, Brown is credited with the elaborate gardens surrounding the Verplanck house and the bountiful fields fronting the property on the east bank of the Hudson River. He also was one of the first African Americans in Fishkill Landing to qualify for the vote in 1837.[59] The years spent with the Verplancks and in and around Fishkill Landing are reported in Brown's diary kept between the 1820s and the year 1866. It chronicles Brown's ability to make his way and prosper in Hudson Valley society which was difficult for African Americans. This real tale of the rewards of patience, resoluteness, and aggressiveness records the success of one who had the will to forge his image on the land.[60]

Notes

1 . The New York Legislature subsequently freed all slaves who participated in the war, and in 1784 and 1786 freed all slaves of British loyalists. See E. B. O'Callaghan, *Calendar of Historical Manuscripts Relating to the War of the Revolution in the Office of the Secretary of State*, 2 vols. (Albany: Weed, Parsons and Company, 1868), 1: 650; Harry B. Yoshpe, *The Disposition of Loyalist Estates in the Southern District of the State of New York* (New York: James A. Roberts, 1939). Cf. *New York in the Revolution as Colony and State*, (Press of Brandow Printing Company, 1898) 2: 207-9.

2. Benjamin Quarles, *The Negro in the American Revolution* (Chapel Hill, N. C.: University of North Carolina Press, 1961), 158-81; Sidney Kaplan, *The Black Presence in the Era of the American Revolution 1770-1800* (Washington, D. C.: Smithsonian Institution Press, 1973), 67.

3. Philip H. Smith, *General History of Dutchess County from 1609 to 1876* (Pawling, N. Y.: P. H. Smith, 1881), 470.

4.   "Celebration of the Abolition of Slavery," *Albany Argus and City Gazette,* 6 July 1827.

5.   There is ample archival material to support this contention, and it is a topic in itself.

6.   "Celebration of the Abolition of Slavery"; Leo H. Hirch, Jr., "New York and the Negro, from 1783 to 1865," *Journal of Negro History* 16 (January 1931): 395-96.

7.   Cf. Floyd McKissick, *Three-Fifths of a Man* (Garden City: Doubleday and Company, 1969).

8.   "Celebration of Abolition of Slavery." Nathaniel Paul was an avid abolitionist and pastor of the church for many years, while at the same time a supporter of the idea to establish a school in the Black Canadian colony of Wilberforce. In 1831 he went to England to raise funds for the school. With his English wife, Elizabeth, Paul left Albany for Wilberforce but returned and died there in 1839. William Lloyd Garrison described the Reverend Nathaniel Paul as "a gentleman with whom the proudest or best man on earth need not blush to associate" quoted in Charles H. Wesley, "The Negroes of New York in the Emancipation Movement," *Journal of Negro History* 24 (January 1939): 79. Paul Family Printout: Nathaniel, Thomas, Benjamin, Nancy, Albany Hall of Records, Albany, N.Y.

9.   "Celebration of the Abolition of Slavery."

10.   William Strickland, *Journal of a Tour of the United States of America 1794-1795* (New York: New York Historical Society, 1971), 169.

11.   E. S. Abdy, *Journal of a Residence and Tour in the United States of North America from April, 1833, to October, 1834* (London: John Murray, 1835), 1: 44.

12.   Cf. Alice Eichholz and James M. Rose, eds., *Free Black Heads of Households in the New York Federal Census, 1790-1830* (Detroit, Mich.: Gale Research Company, 1981).

13.   Leonard P. Curry, *The Free Black in Urban America, 1800-1850* (Chicago: University of Chicago Press, 1981), 62, 72.

14.   Lawrence H. Mamiya and Lorraine M. Roberts, "Invisible People, Untold Stories: A Historical Overview of the Black Community in Poughkeepsie," *Year Book: Dutchess County Historical Society* 72 (1987): 78.

15.   Cf. Clyde Griffen, "The Changing Neighborhoods of Poughkeepsie 1850-1900," *Year Book: Dutchess County Historical Society* 72 (1987).

16.   Myra B. Young Armstead, "An Historical Profile of Black Saratoga, 1800-1925," in *A Heritage Uncovered: The Black Experience in Upstate New York, 1800-1925* (Elmira, N. Y.: Chemung County Historical Society, 1988), 31. Cf. Myra B. Young Armstead, "Black Families in Saratoga Springs 1870-1930," *Grist Mill* 19 (July 1985): 1-4; Theodore Corbett, "Saratoga County Blacks, 1720-1870," *Grist Mill* 20 (1986): 1-6.

17.   Armstead, "Historical Profile," 31-32.

18.   Cf. *The Village of Piermont: A Brief History* (Piermont, N. Y.: Piermont Bicentennial Committee, 1976), 11; Leonard Cooke, Nyack, N. Y., interview with author, 5 June 1988.

19. Joan H. Geisman, *The Archaeology of Social Disintegration in Skunk Hallow, A Nineteenth Century Rural Black Community* (New York: Academic Press, 1982).
20. Cf. David S. Cohen, *The Ramapo Mountain People* (New Brunswick, N. J.: Rutgers University Press, 1974); Olive M. Clearwater and John J. Hofler, *Hurley in the Days of Slavery* (Hurley, N. Y.: Clearwater and Hofler, 1986), 22.
21. Edythe Quinn Caro, *"Black Civil War Soldiers from The Hills,"* *Westchester Historian* 63 (Winter 1967): 9-16; "'The Hills' in the Mid-Nineteenth Century: The History of a Rural Afro-American Community in Westchester County, New York," *Afro-Americans in New York Life and History* 14 (July 1990): 35-50.
22. Smith, 135; Charles Freeman Land Deeds, Dutchess County Deeds Office, County Office Building, Poughkeepsie, N. Y.; Charles Freeman Death Certificate, January 1834, Dutchess County Surrogate Office, Poughkeepsie, N. Y.
23. Eichholz and Rose.
24. "The Mystery of the Old Mine," *Piermont Newsletter* 8 (October 1974): 2-3; Local Black History, personal collection, Leonard Cooke, Nyack, N. Y.; Louise Seymour Zimm et al., *Southeastern New York* (New York: Lewis Historical Publishing Company, 1946), 2: 728; Eichholz and Rose. John Moore's economic success followed a century and a half after that of Captain John De Vries, his son, and Nicholas Claus Mande Emmanuel, original holders of eight hundred acres (De Vries had 1600) of the Tappan Patent (Local History).
25. With the passage of the Fifteenth Amendment to the U. S. Constitution in 1870, African American males had equal voting rights.
26. Dixon Ryan Fox, "The Negro Vote in Old New York," *Political Science Quarterly* 32 (1917): 253-56; Herman D. Bloch, "The New York Negro's Battle for Political Rights, 1777-1865," *International Review of Social History* 9 (1964): 66-67.
27. Leon F. Litwack, *North of Slavery: The Negro in the Free States, 1790-1860* (Chicago: University of Chicago Press, 1961), 77, 85, 91.
28. Curry, 218. In Fishkill Landing (today Beacon, N. Y.) one of the first Blacks to vote was James Brown in 1837 (James Brown Diary, The New York Historical Society, New York). Cf. Clearwater and Hofler mention George Pete Newkirk as one of the first Blacks to vote in Hurley, New York (22-23).
29. Bloch, 76.
30. Howard Holman Bell, ed., *Minutes of the Proceedings of the National Negro Conventions 1830-1864* (New York: Arno Press, 1969), 36; Wesley, "Negroes of New York in the Emancipation Movement," 73.
31. Bell, *Minutes,* 1-36, 1-32 (reprints of proceedings).
32. Ibid., 1-39. 1-32. 1-57 (reprints of proceedings).
33. Quoted in Charles H. Wesley, "The Participation of the Negroes in the Anti-Slavery Political Parties," *Journal of Negro History* 29 (January 1944): 9.
34. Cf. "Rev. Henry Highland Garnet (1815-1882) Troy's First Negro

Minister and Abolitionist," in Samuel Rezneck, *Profiles Out of the Past of Troy, New York, Since 1789* (Troy, N. Y.: Rezneck, 1970), 118-22; W. M. Brewer, "Henry Highland Garnet," *Journal of Negro History* 13 (January 1928): 36-52; Joel Schor, *Henry Highland Garnet: A Voice of Black Radicalism in the Nineteenth Century* (Westport, Conn.: Greenwood Press, 1977); Litwack, 189-90; Wesley, "Negroes of New York in the Emancipation Movement," 73.

35. Benjamin Quarles, "Letters from Negro Leaders to Gerrit Smith," *Journal of Negro History* 27 (October 1942): 438-39; Wesley, "Negroes of New York in the Emancipation Movement," 89.

36. Schor, *Henry Highland Garnet*, 35.

37. Ibid., 48.

38. Cf. Bell, i-ii; Joel Schor, "The Rivalry Between Frederick Douglass and Henry Highland Garnet," *Journal of Negro History* 64 (Winter 1979): 30-38; Bloch, 76.

39. Schor, *Henry Highland Garnet*, 68, 96; Wesley, "Participation of the Negroes in the Anti-Slavery Political Parties," 32-74.

40. Schor, *Henry Highland Garnet*, 54-56; Howard H. Bell, "Expressions of Negro Militancy in the North, 1840-1860," *Journal of Negro History* 45 (January 1960): 11-20.

41. Brewer, 43. Historian G. W. Williams has written, "Garnett created the idea which Frederick Douglass tempered and presented to the world in a more palliative and acceptable form" (quoted in Schor, *Henry Highland Garnet*, xii).

42. Carleton Mabee, "Separate Black Education in Dutchess County: Black Elementary Schools and a Proposed Black College," *Year Book: Dutchess County Historical Society* 65 (1960): 61.

43. Samuel Ringgold Ward, *Autobiography of a Fugitive Negro: His Anti-Slavery Labours in the United States, Canada, and England* (New York: Arno Press, 1969), 31-50.

44. Wesley, "Participation of the Negroes in the Anti-Slavery Political Parties," 39. *Poughkeepsie Anti-Slavery Society (Auxiliary to the American Anti-Slavery Society) 1832* lists Ward as a founding member (Franklin Delano Roosevelt Library, Hyde Park, N. Y.)

45. Quoted in Wesley, "Participation of the Negroes in the Anti-Slavery Political Parties," 39-40.

46. Ibid., 52; Litwack, 144-45; Schor, *Henry Highland Garnet*, 68-69, 99.

47. Edgar J. McManus, "Anti-Slavery Legislation in New York," *Journal of Negro History* 46 (October 1961): 214-15.

48. Wilbert H. Siebert, *The Underground Railroad from Slavery to Freedom* (New York: Russell & Russell, 1967), 70, 125-26.

49. Ibid., 126-27. Cf. Schor, *Henry Highland Garnet*, 43. Quarles describes Topp as a Garrisonian, second only to Stephen Myers in the work of the Albany Committee on Vigilance (434 note 5). Siebert lists John H. Hooper as a Black conductor from Rensselaer County (415).

50. Siebert, 127; Hirch, 406-7.

51. Siebert, 127. In the Mid-Hudson Valley, which was part of the Albany-

Troy route and points further north, an underground station was
opened at the Orthodox Quakers' Nine Partners Boarding School in
south Millbrook in the 1830s. See Susan J. Crane, "Antebellum
Dutchess County's Struggle Against Slavery," *Year Book: Dutchess County
Historical Society* 65 (1980): 37-38. The home of David Irish on Quaker
Hill in Dutchess County participated in the underground railroad,
receiving "slaves coming from Jacob Willett's station in south
Millbrook."

52. Quarles, 447 note 45.
53. Ibid., 447-48.
54. Cf. Litwack, 237, 249, see also, 49-50; Schor, *Henry Highland Garnet,* 151.
55. Cf. "A 'Jerry Rescue' in Troy," *Troy Daily Times,* 28 April 1860; "Fugitive
    Slave Case at Troy —A Mob Rescue and Rearrest," *Albany Atlas and
    Argus,* 28 April 1860; Samuel May, *The Fugitive Slave Law and Its Victims*
    (1861; reprint, Freeport, N. Y.: Books for Libraries Press, 1970), 134-35;
    Siebert, 85. The famous "Jerry" McHenry rescue took place in Syracuse,
    New York on 1 October 1851.
56. May, 19-20.
57. Edward A. Collier, *A History of Old Kinderhook* (New York: G. P. Putnam's
    Sons, 1914), 148.
58. Armstead, "An Historical Profile," 28, 34; Corbett, 8. Cf. Sue Eakin and
    Joseph Logsdon, eds., *Twelve Years A Slave* (Baton Rouge: Louisiana
    State University Press, 1977).
59. James F. Brown Diary. Cf. Virginia E. Verplanck, *The Verplanck Garden at
    Mount Gulian Fishkill-on-Hudson* (n.d.), 12.
60. See, A. J. Williams-Myers, "An African Voice Among the River Folk of
    the Hudson River Valley: The Diary of an Ex-slave, 1827-1866" (New
    Paltz, N. Y.: by author, 1992).

CHAPTER EIGHT

THE RISE OF AFRICAN AMERICAN ORGANIZATIONS

Religious and social organizations served as spiritual, socioeconomic, and political vehicles in the African American communities in the Hudson region during the fight against slavery and racial proscription. The churches were spiritual abodes and the ministers were religious-political leaders at the forefront of the struggle. The founding of the African Methodist Episcopal Church (AME) by Richard Allen in Philadelphia in 1787 attempted to create a place of worship where Blacks were welcome and at ease with themselves and their God. The rise of separate Black churches came in response to a highly proscriptive, white dominated society. A nineteenth-century traveler, after visits to white churches at the Spa in Saratoga, wrote "few people of colour [were] in the churches, and such of them as were there assembled in a corner separate from the rest of the people."[1] The so-called separatist movement within established, white religions by Blacks was simply a movement to concretize what in fact had already been a reality.

The AME Church and its counterpart, the AME Zion (founded by James Varick, who was born a slave in 1750 in Newburgh),[2] were not only places of worship but with the Baptist and Presbyterian churches also, were social service agencies and vehicles of political leadership in African American communities. Many of the early spokespersons for African American causes were church leaders such as Henry Highland Garnet, Samuel Ringgold Ward, Sojourner Truth, and William P. Butler (former pastor of churches in Hudson and Poughkeepsie). The church was their training ground. Perhaps the AME Zion Church best "illustrated the close linkage between religion and abolitionism among Black people," and many of its branches served, along with other Black demoninations, as stations on the Underground Railroad.[3]

Branches of most denominations were established throughout the region, with their ministers serving the spiritual, sociopolitical, and economic needs of their congregations. AME Zion and AME churches were established in such places as Sparkill (the "Old Swamp" Church, St. Charles AME Zion under Reverend William Thompson in 1865), Newburgh (AME Zion), Poughkeepsie ("Catherine Street " AME Zion, 1840), Kingston (by 1860, three AME churches), Albany (Hamilton-Israel AME, 1828), Kinderhook, Columbia County (Bethel AME, 1851, first pastor, Peter Burgett), and Saratoga (Dyer-Phelps AME Zion, 1863).[4]

Black fraternal and sororal organizations were also centers of Black social life, sponsoring many literary and cultural events. Cities in the Hudson-Mohawk region had Masonic and Odd Fellows Lodges which "generally provided members with financial insurance during difficult times" and "opportunities for Black male fellowship . . . and extending charity to the indigent."[5] One fraternal organization, the Charles Sumner Benevolent Association organized in Albany in 1875, had as its motto, "We care for our sick and bury our dead."[6] Another in that city was the Burdett-Coutts Benevolent Association. One of its most prominent presidents was Adam Blake, the owner of the Kenmore Hotel on North Pearl Street in the late nineteenth century; by his death in 1881 he had amassed an estate estimated at between $100,000 and $500,000.[7]

Sororal organizations duplicated some services the fraternal groups provided. Two of these sororals, the Albany Female Lundy Society founded on 19 June 1833, and the Nyack United Sisters of Friendship, founded in 1874, had mottoes similar to that of the Sumner Benevolent Association. In the United Sisters of Friendship dues for members were twenty-five cents monthly. When a member was disabled through sickness, she received benefits of two dollars per week. At the time of death of a member the benefits totaled thirty dollars, while those for a child who died was five dollars.[8] The Lundy Society had similar benefits and responsibilities and was composed of women who "thought of themselves as very elite" but who nevertheless were conscious of their charge to be a society of "earnest and benevolent colored ladies for mutual benefit and the development of social, intellectual and religious principles."[9] Prospective members were screened, and scrutiny of them continued during their active membership. When and if behavior unbecoming a member was revealed, the rules of the society were enforced. Those rules read, in part, that "if any member commits a scandalous sin or walks on truth, and after having been reproved continues manifestly impertinent, she shall be excluded from office until she gives satisfactory evidence of repentance."[10]

African American religious and social organizations served important functions in the Hudson-Mohawk region in the nineteenth century. In addition to the spiritual, economic, and political functions, those organizations promoted group cohesion, established values, and set appropriate behavioral patterns for Blacks in a predominantly white society.

Notes

1 .   Quoted in Roger Haydon, ed., *Upstate Travels British Views of Nineteenth-Century New York* (Syracuse, N. Y.: Syracuse University Press:, 1982), 117.

2.   Leonard Cooke, interview with author, Nyack, N. Y., 7 June 1988; New Haven, Conn., *Zion Trumpet,* January 1907, 18.

3.   Lawrence H. Mamiya and Lorraine M. Roberts, "Invisible People, Untold Stories: A Historical Overview of the Black Community in Poughkeepsie," *Year Book: Dutchess County Historical Society* 72 (1987): 79.

4 .   Cooke; An Historical Sketch of St. Charles AME Zion Church, Sparkill, New York, 1865-1945, Leonard Cooke Collection, Nyack, N. Y.; Stuart M. Blumin, "Church and Community: A Case Study of Lay Leadership in Nineteenth-Century America," *New York History* 56 (October 1975): 398-99; Edward A. Collier, *A History of Old Kinderhook* (New York: G. P. Putnam's Sons, 1914), 282; Myra B. Young Armstead, "A Historical Profile of Black Saratoga, 1800-1825," in *A Heritage Uncovered: The Black Experience In Upstate New York, 1800-1925* (Elmira, N. Y.: Chemung County Historical Society, 1988), 34.

5.   Armstead, "Historical Profile of Black Saratoga," 35.

6. George R. Howell and Jonathan Tenney, eds., *Bi-Centennial History of Albany: History of the County of Albany, N.Y. from 1609 to 1886* (New York: W. W. Munsell & Co., 1886), 726.

7. Judy Shepard and Pamela Newkirk, "Adam Blake: Black Hero or a White Man?" *Knickerbocker News,* 4 March 1987.

8. "The Origin and Progress Together With the Quarter Century Report of the United Sisters in Friendship," William H. Myers, founder, n.d., pamphlet for members.

9. Howell and Tenney, 726.

10. Harriette Bowie Lewis Van Vranken and Virginia Elaine Lewis Brown, interview with author, Albany, New York, 3 May 1988.

CHAPTER NINE

CONFLICT WITH WHITE IMMIGRANTS AND RACIST ATTITUDES

Introduction

In addition to having to contend with the many forms of racial proscription, African Americans had faced socioeconomic problems resulting from a massive influx of European immigrants. Arriving in America in successive waves, as did the Irish in the 1820s, 1840s, and 1850s, these white immigrants competed with Blacks for employment. Initially shunned by white society because of their accents, language, and customs, many Irish and German families, after one or two generations, found the avenues of social and economic mobility more open to them than they were to the African Americans who had been in the country for generations.

The antebellum period was also a time in which mob violence and racial attacks against Blacks were widespread throughout the Hudson-Mohawk region.[1] It was a time in which racism was used to keep the various elements of the working class opposed to one another, even though their socioeconomic needs were similar. The consequence was constant white mob violence directed indiscriminantly against communities of Blacks. White mob violence was also a major obstacle to Black access to opportunities in the work place. According to Edgar

McManus, much of the lower class white resentment was, perhaps, part of the legacy of slavery: "as the working class grew and the wage rate fell, *negrophobia* became the anodyne of lower class frustration. Free Negroes were brutalized by ruffians and excluded from skilled employment by the hostility of white workers. Indeed, free Negroes in the nineteenth century remained as much a class apart as in the days of slavery."[2]

White immigrants were aided in their lawlessness by a society that was determined to slow Black socioeconomic mobility through a limited franchise, segregated education, job discrimination, and social ostracism. This was clearly evident in the successive constitutional conventions during and after the antebellum period and the racist pontifications of political leaders from the Hudson-Mohawk region. Representatives from the region to the 1821 Constitutional Convention held in Albany stated their position on the *Negro suffrage question*. Colonel Samuel Young of Saratoga County was an open and bitter opponent of Black suffrage. It was his position that the constitution should conform to a society having no social intercourse with Blacks, and, therefore, Blacks should not be given the vote.[3] Justice Ambrose Spencer, who represented Albany County, averred "that just as minors were excluded from the polls because they were not considered sufficiently intelligent, so it was that Negroes, who lacked intelligence should be excluded."[4] P. A. Livingston of Dutchess County asked, "What has been their [Blacks] conduct that should entitle them to your hospitalities and associations? What privilege have you conferred . . . that they have not abused?"[5] Two newspapers in the city of Poughkeepsie, by siding with pro-slavers over abolition, supported the use of mob violence in breaking up antislavery rallies, thus fueling the flame of racism in the region.[6]

The remarks of an English visitor's driver on a trip from Boston to Albany, perhaps, sums up the general feeling of many whites towards African Americans. When asked a question about the Irish in America, the driver remarked that "they [Irish] are an ugly set of people . . . but there are no people I hate so much as the niggers—I always drive over 'em when they get in my way." When he was asked why he hated Blacks, he responded: "I suppose they are much the same as other people. . . . So they are, to be sure:—I don't know why I hate 'em:—but I do hate 'em."[7] Perhaps most whites across the region didn't know either.

The arrival of German, French Canadian and some early Irish immigrants into the region dates to the pre-Revolutionary period.[8] At that time, their numbers were not significant enough to pose a serious threat in a labor market where certain skilled, semi-skilled, and manual labor positions were traditionally held by Blacks. In the era of industrialization with the growth of textile mills, and breweries (two sectors of the economy in which Blacks were virtually excluded), and with the growth and expansion of canals and rail networks in the region between the 1820s and 1860s, the labor market changed dramatically. Jobs traditionally held by Blacks were assumed by white immigrants and, after only one or two generations, their descendants. This was sustained "intergenerational mobility." However, "the vast number of Black people [in the Hudson region] . . . in the late nineteenth century did not experience intergenerational mobility."[9]

Black and White in the Work Place: The Irish Immigrant

An antebellum immigrant group that constantly clashed with Blacks over jobs was the Irish. In the 1820s and as part of the exodus from Ireland because of the famine, many Irish workers were recruited and brought to the region to dig the systems of canals. In the 1840s and 1850s, they also worked on the construction of railroads. To entice the Irish into the region, Erastus Corning's New York Central rail company even arranged for the transportation and arrival of Irish immigrants into Albany, an economic boom town during the period between 1830 and 1855.[10] The economic boom involved the rail and canal systems, the stockyards adjacent to Corning's New York Central rail shop in West Albany, and "the tremendous lumber market along the canal basin, and the iron stone foundries downtown."[11] It was an economic boom from which the Irish would benefit, but there would be no benefits for African Americans.

The Irish became one of the fastest growing ethnic groups in cities along the Hudson and Mohawk rivers. In the city of Albany, the Irish population jumped from between 1,000 and 2,000 in 1830 (out of a population of 24,211) to as many as 5,100 or more in 1850.[12] African Americans, on the other hand, decreased from a combined (slave and free) total of 4,099 or 5.4 percent of the county's population in 1790 to only 1,194 in 1850 (1.3 percent).[13] By 1830, the Irish had exceeded this percentage in the city of Albany alone, levelling at 5 to 10 percent of the total population.[14]

Black and White in the Work Place: Black Displacement and Growing Conflict

Prior to the influx of immigrants, coachmen, barbers, white-washers, washer women, and other generally defined domestic positions were traditionally held by Blacks. In the decade before the Civil War, whites began to move into the so-called "Negro" jobs. By the Reconstruction period, there had been a wholesale displacement of Blacks. In Poughkeepsie in 1850, Blacks were 43 percent of all coachmen or drivers, while the Irish constituted only 14 percent and the Germans 3 percent. In 1880, Blacks composed 18 percent of this occupation, while the Irish and Germans had increased to 31 and 19 percent, respectively.[15] During the same time period, Black barbers dropped from 27 percent to 13 percent, while Germans rose from 18 percent in 1850 to 50 percent in 1880.[16] The occupation of teamster/carter/carman was completely dominated by whites in 1880 with 59 percent versus 5 percent for Blacks.[17] Black women, who had "fewer occupational choices" even in the pre-Civil War era, sought work in a very restricted market in the Reconstruction era. Because their husbands were limited to "the most menial and low paying of jobs," Black women had to work to make ends meet. During that era, 90 percent of the Black women in Poughkeepsie worked as domestics.[18] At one point, during a period of high unemployment in 1855, Black women in Albany were challenged by the Irish as washer women.[19]

Further north in Troy and Cahoes above Albany, the same employment pattern existed. In the Troy iron foundries the Irish dominated in the unskilled and skilled categories, holding "73.6% of the service jobs [and constituting] 54.7% of the molders, 40% of the peddlers, and 55.4% of the heaters and rollers," between 1855 and 1884.[20] In the censuses of 1860 and 1880, only one Black was listed as "employed in the iron foundries."[21] They were systematically excluded from the industry, and either filled service positions (coachmen and maids) living "gathered in shanty enclaves in alley dwellings in the city near the river," or they left Troy.[22] Similarly, in the Harmony textile mills of Cohoes, the French Canadians and the Irish, after the Civil War, were the predominant workers, with very few, if any, African Americans.[23] In the late nineteenth and early twentieth centuries, similar employment patterns persisted, but Blacks competed with immigrant Slavs and Italians for jobs in the brickyards along the Hudson River as well as for jobs on river boats. As with the Irish, much of the animosity surrounding the competition was expressed in mob violence against Blacks.[24]

The employment conditions in Albany, Poughkeepsie, Troy and Cohoes paint a picture of white inclusion and Black exclusion that was common throughout the region. African Americans, who had been in the region many generations before the immigrant explosion, were systematically prevented from achieving sustained intergenerational socioeconomic mobility. White immigrants, in less than a generation (and at times less than a decade, for example, the Irish in the iron foundries in Troy), were able to achieve entry into most employment categories without much difficulty.[25] It was as if "the newcomers from Europe had to be provided for, even if it was to be at the expense of the indigenous colored American."[26] Because of "preferential treatment in employment," the white immigrants gradually sustained intergenerational mobility, while Blacks slipped downward.[27] For example, John Williams of Poughkeepsie rose from the generic classification of laborer in 1850, to a boatman in 1855-1856, and finally to the pilot of the steamship *Sherman* in 1860. After the Civil War, the city directory once again listed Williams as a laborer—displaced by white immigrants.[28]

The competition for jobs and the growing indifference to the plight of African Americans by a society blinded by its own racism inevitably led to white mob violence against Blacks. Blacks were constantly attacked by white mobs who felt threatened by Black competition and who were confident their actions against Blacks would go uninvestigated and unprosecuted by the white justice system. In Albany, whites were able to destroy completely an integrated residence on Lodge Street they characterized as a "noisy place," without any retribution from the mayor and aldermen who stood by and watched.[29] The attack was perpetrated because Blacks lived at the establishment with whites and because, for most working class whites, the segregation patterns, begun as early as the 1820s, were not developing fast enough.[30] By 1880 in some areas of the region, well defined segregated residential patterns were evident with Poughkeepsie taking the lead. Clyde Griffen observed of this 1880 phenomenon that "four widely-separated pockets would be the residence of nearly two-thirds of black male workers, *an extraordinary level of segregation for so small a group.*" (my emphasis)[31]. In addition to mob violence, African Americans across the Hudson Valley region suffered from ill health (with a higher mortality rate than whites)[32] and "were poorly housed in small buildings or tenements badly built and maintained, that were much more likely than residences of whites . . . to be located in alleys and closed courts, or crammed onto the rear portion of narrow lots."[33] White America had abandoned the cause of its fraternal Black twin to the whims of white mob violence and racist neglect.

Notes

1.   Cf. Henry Noble MacCracken, *Blithe Dutchess: The Flowering of an American County from 1812* (New York: Hastings House, 1958). MacCracken cites the repeated violent confrontations between Blacks and other white ethnic groups on the streets of Poughkeepsie, N. Y., including those of the Italians against Blacks.

2.   Edgar McManus, "Anti-Slavery Legislation in New York," *Journal of Negro History* 46 (October 1961): 216. Cf. Harmannus Hoetink, *Slavery and Race Relations in the Americas; Comparative Notes on their Nature and Nexus* (New York: Harper and Row, 1973), 18. In 1862 at the Lorilland Tobacco factory in New York City, Blacks were forced out of their jobs by whites who threatened management with a "walk off" if management did not promise that Blacks would not be hired in the future. See Herman D. Bloch, *The Circle of Discrimination: An Economic and Social Study of the Black Man in New York* (New York: New York University Press, 1969), 34.

3.   Leo H. Hirch, Jr. "New York and the Negro, from 1783 to 1865," *Journal of Negro History* 16 (January 1931): 418.

4.   *Ibid.*, 418-19.

5.   *Ibid.*, 419.

6. Susan J. Crane, "Antebellum Dutchess County's Struggle Against Slavery," *Year Book: Dutchess County Historical Society* 65 (1980): 37-38. Ms. Crane cites the *Poughkeepsie Telegraph* (1836) and the *Poughkeepsie Journal* (1837). Cf. Amy Pearce Ver Nooy, "Anti-Slavery Movement in Dutchess County, 1835-1854," *Year Book: Dutchess County Historical Society* 28 (1943): 57-65; Phyllis F. Field, *The Politics of Race The Struggle for Black Suffrage in the Civil War Era* (Ithaca, N. Y.: Cornell University Press, 1982).

7. Edward S. Abdy, *Journal of a Residence and Tour in the United States of North America, from April, 1833, to October, 1834,* 3 vols. (London: John Murray, 1835), 1: 251. Frederick Douglass commented on the treatment of Black passengers on board Hudson River steamers: "[Blacks] are compelled sometimes to stroll the deck nearly all night, before they can get a place to lie down and that place frequently unfit for a dog's accommodation" (quoted in Hirch, 425-26).

8. Daniel J. Walkowitz, *Work(er) City, Company Town: Iron and Cotton— Worker Protest in Troy and Cahoes, New York, 1855-1884* (Chicago: University of Illinois Press, 1978). Cf. Bloch, 24; William E. Rowley, "The Irish Aristocracy of Albany, 1798-1878," New York History 52 (July 1971): 275-304.

9. Lawrence H. Mamiya and Lorraine M. Roberts, "Invisible People, Untold Stories: A Historical Overview of the Black Community in Poughkeepsie," *Year Book: Dutchess County Historical Society 72 (1987): 85;* Clyde Griffen and Sally Griffen, *Natives and Newcomers: The Ordering of Opportunity in Mid-Nineteenth Century Poughkeepsie* (Cambridge and London: Harvard University Press, 1978), 31. Lawrence H. Mamiya and Patricia A. Kaurouma, "You Never Hear About Their Struggles: Black Oral History in Poughkeepsie, New York, " *Afro-Americans in New York Life and History* 4 (July 1980): 59; Bloch, 33; Leonard P. Curry, *The Free Black in Urban America, 1800-1850* (Chicago: University of Chicago Press, 1981), 33-34.

10. Rowley, 276.

11. *Ibid.,* 289.

12. *Ibid.,* 289-90.

13. *Ibid.,* 279.

14. Thomas J. Davis, "Three Dark Centuries Around Albany: A Survey of Black Life in New York's Capitol City Area Before World War I," *Afro-Americans in New York Life and History* 7 (January 1978): 19.

15. Rowley, 279.

16. Joshua Gordon Hinderfeld, "The Fading Veneer of Equality," *Year Book: Dutchess County Historical Society* 88 (1983): 93.

17. *Ibid.,* 92.

18. *Ibid.,* 92.

19. *Ibid.,* 92; Griffen and Griffen, 235, 237.

20. Rowley, 287. Mamiya and Roberts, 85.

21. Walkowitz, 31.

22. *Ibid.,* 22.

23. *Ibid.*, 111.
24. Walkowitz., 44.
25. Ms. Berta Proctor, interview with author, Kingston, N. Y., 25 March 1983. Block, 40.
26. *Ibid.*, 33.
27. Bloch, 37.
28. Curry, 98.
29. *Ibid.*, 59. Curry notes an increase in residential segregation in Albany between 1820 and 1840, but later indicates that it abates "with a doubling of the number of wards [in the city]."
30. Clyde Griffen, "The Changing Neighborhoods of Poughkeepsie 1850-1900," *Year Book: Dutchess County Historical Society* 72 (1987): 140.
31. Curry, 136-46; Bloch quotes an 1815 description of health and death conditions in New York City (25 note 29).
32. Curry, 79.
33. *Ibid.*, Leonard Cooke, interview with author, Nyack, N. Y., 9 July 1988.

CHAPTER TEN

CIVIL WAR CLOUDS ALONG THE HUDSON: WHITE FURY AND BLACK HEROISM— TO SERVE THE CAUSE OF FREEDOM AND PERHAPS BASK IN A FREEDOM OF ONE'S OWN

Once let the black man get upon his person the brass letters
U.S.; let him get an eagle on his shoulder, and bullets in his
pocket, and there is no power on earth which can deny that he
has earned the right to citizenship in the United States.
                                        — Frederick Douglass

But Negroes, like other people, act upon motives. Why should
they do anything for us if we will do nothing for them. If they
stake their lives for us, they must be prompted by the strongest
motive, even the promise of freedom. And the promise being
made, must be kept.
                                        —Abraham Lincoln

Introduction

The Civil War period in the Hudson Valley and its environs
was trying for African Americans. Mob violence against them was
increased because working class whites felt the war was intended

to free the slaves and thus to create more competition for them in the labor market. The draft riots in New York of July 1863, in which Blacks were brutally murdered and hanged from trees and lampposts, reached into the upper regions of the river valley. In New York City a foreign correspondent suggested that some whites did not hesitate to "shoot a blackman with as little regard as to moral consequences as they would shoot a dog."[1] In Poughkeepsie in 1863, the Catherine Street AME Zion Church was attacked by drunken white soldiers. The attack caused severe damage to the religious edifice. Later in 1863, Black male parishioners stood guard at the church during a mob disturbance to prevent it from being burned down. The white mob was in such a frenzy that the governor had to ask assistance from the Vermont Volunteers to restore order.[2]

South of Poughkeepsie at Newburgh, twice white mobs attacked the congregation of the AME Zion Church during a service (31 December 1860 and 31 December 1862). Identified as "unruly soggers," the mobs bloodied parishioners and destroyed church property until they were "beaten out of the church." Military units eventually had to be called in to disperse and apprehend whites associated with the mob.[3] Similar violence further south in Tarrytown, Westchester County, forced many Blacks to abandon their homes and leave the town in search of refuge in places like Buttermilk Hill until Federal gunboats appeared on the Hudson to restore order.[4] At Troy, Blacks were subjected to similar conditions. Starting at "the Rensselaer Iron foundries and the Albany Nail Works," the rioting spilled over into the community where threats were made against Black property owners. A boat docked at the wharfs had to weigh anchor because of "threats made against colored workers on board."[5]

A Call to Arms and a Cry of Freedom

Although white men expressed their resentment and anger at the draft and war through violence perpetrated against Blacks, it did not deter Black men from the desire to serve in the war.

Between 1861 and 1865 a sizable group of young black men left Saratoga County to join the Union Army. Their momen-

tous decision would eventually carry them to far-flung battle-
fieds at Grand Gulf, Mississippi, Petersburg, Virginia and
Charleston, South Carolina. Their participation in the Civil
War would also help change the course of politics and race
relations forever.[6]

Young African American men from across the Hudson Valley
and its environs replicated this Saratoga enlistment. Some
joined New York's three regiments of "United States Colored
Troops," the 20th, 26th, and 31st.[7] But because of the pervasive
racist attitudes in New York, many young Black men from the
region, wishing to serve, enlisted in predominantly Black regiments outside the state, such as the famous 54th Massachusetts
Infantry. Among the ranks of the 54th were men such as James
R. Jones—a barber from Albany, Joseph Brown—a hostler from
Cazenovia, and Jacob Williams—a farmer from White Plains.[8]
Warren van Shaik, who at the time of his enlistment was a twenty-
two-year-old laborer from Saratoga, also joined the 54th
Massachusetts. Some of his fellow black Saratogians enlisted in
other New England regiments: "Thomas Walters, 17, a servant
from Greenfield, enlisted in the 5th Massachusetts Cavalry.
Three others, including James Shamus, at 39 one of Saratoga's
oldest soldiers, and two brothers, Richard and George Rogers,
all joined the 14th Rhode Island Artillery."[9] Two other known
enlistees from Saratoga, whose regiments are not known, were
James Atkins, thirty-eight, and William Lattimore, twenty-two,
both of Moreau.[10] These young brave souls joined other young
African Americans from northern regiments in administering
the death blow to the institution of slavery between 1863 and
1865 at such battles as Secessionville, Fort Wagner, Port Hudson,
and Bozkins Mills.[11]

Some time after the war, the AME Zion Church in
Newburgh erected a plaque on its facade to commemorate its
brave sons who served in the Civil War. During the ceremonies
to erect the plaque, each name was read over the muffled
sounds of rolling drums and the faint but melodic voices of the
church choir singing the *Battle Hymn of the Republic*: Henry Allen
. . . Charles Banks . . . Needham Beadup . . . Henry T. Bell . . .
Benjamin B. Brown . . . Lloyd Brown . . . Oliver Brown . . . Peter
Brown . . . Samuel Brown . . . Washington Brown . . . Dock Brush

. . . Daniel Coles . . . George Cooler . . . Jackson Copeland . . . James DeGroat . . . Alex Deyo . . . Charles Deyo . . . George Diamod . . . Louis Downes . . . Hiram DuBois . . . James DuBois . . . Charles Earls . . . John D. Freece . . . August Freeman . . . John Gordon . . . Jacob Hart . . . Moses Hasbrouck . . . Wellington Hawkins . . . William Hawkins . . . John Hill . . . Henry Humans . . . Titus Hunter . . . William Jackson . . . Andrew Johnson . . . George W. Johnson . . . Jacob Johnson . . . John Kimback . . . Theodore King . . . Jacob Levie . . . Jacob Levine . . . Morgan Lewis . . . Franics Low . . . John Ludlow . . . John Mason . . . Samuel Mason . . . George McGinnis . . . John Mangin . . . Henry Matthews . . . George Moran . . . Nathan Penn . . . Harvey Quimby . . . James Richardson . . . Peter Richardson . . . Harvey Roberts . . . Charles Robinson . . . Jacob Robinson . . . Isaac Saylor . . . William Saylor . . . Edward Schoomaker . . . Alonzo Simmons . . . Ephriam Simons . . . John Smith . . . George Stewart, Jr. . . . John Stewart . . . Thomas Setup . . . Elias Van Huesen . . . Samuel Van Dyke . . . Peter Wood . . . James Wright.[12]

Cemeteries along the Hudson-Mohawk rivers and in the Champlain Valley contain the remains of those who served the cause with the hope of basking in freedom. For example, in an unforgotten colored graveyard atop Cedar Hill north of Fishkill Village in Dutchess County repose the remains of two Blacks who served: John W. H. Atkins of Company B, 20th Regiment of the U. S. Colored Volunteers, and William Henry Jefferson of the 8th Regiment of the Pennsylvania Colored Volunteers who died on 14 July 1864 at Yellow Bluff, Virginia.[13] Somewhere in Beekman Precinct, in the same county, repose the remains of two Black brothers who served with the 31st New York Colored Regiment in Company I, Charles and George King.[14] In Union Vale, also in Dutchess County, are the Civil War graves of a Freeman family: Augustus, John, and Perry, all having served in the New York 20th Regiment of Colored Volunteers.[15]

Letters from Simeon A. Tierce to his wife, Sarah Jane, of "The Hill" community near Harrison in Westchester County also give evidence of brave, young Black men who served in the war. Having risen to the position of Sergeant while stationed at New Orleans, Tierce wrote his wife several times before his death from fever in 1864:

> [Feb. 15, 1864] . . . God has answered prayer . . . moved the old slave holders out and colored people . . . keeping stores themselves . . . and capable of doing it. . . . The time won't be long I hope before we can see [one] another once more on our own soil. All the colored people down here welcome us here with glad hands. . . . [Feb. 22, 1864] . . . Tell Sissy that her Poppy has got the fever and ague. . . . I shed a great many tears when I was taken, thinking about you. . . . We caught four rebels just here about. . . . [March 1, 1864] . . . I sit evenings alone and think of home all the time. . . . [July 8, 1864] . . . Give my love to Father and Mother Weeks, Father and Mother Tierce and all the rest. . . . [Aware of the seriousness of his sickness, Simeon wrote in the same letter] There is more or less a death . . . every day . . . the doctor says it is not a cold but inflammation of the lungs and that I waited too long before I went to him. I want you to have that place fixed so that if me or you should die, it will always be a good home for Sis as long as she lives. The reason I say so I don't know how soon it may be my turn for some are taken in the morning and die before night. . . . [Simeon died shortly after writing those words to Sarah Jane.][16]

As a witness to war preparations and troop movements in the Mid-Hudson Valley, James F. Brown of Fishkill Landing recorded in his diary, for 26 April 1861, that "a company of voluntears [sic] left Fishkill in [train] cars for Albany to join the troops at Washington."[17] For James F. Brown, as for most African Americans, the war would once and for all destroy the peculiar institution. It was also their hope that it would push the country in the direction of a more open and equitable society, where the freedom of all Americans, regardless of race, was guaranteed.

Notes

1. J. D. Burn, *Three Years Among the Working Classes in the U.S. during the War* (London: Houlston and Stoneman, 1865), 22-23.

2. Cf. Mamiya and Roberts, "Invisible People, Untold Stories A Historical Overview of the Black Community in Poughkeepsie," *Year Book: Dutchess County Historical Society* 72 (1987) 80.

3. "Newburgh Made Contributions to Union Army," *Evening News*, 28 April 1969.

4. Edgar Mayhew Bacon, *Chronicles of Tarrytown and Sleepy Hollow* (New

York: G. P. Putnam's Sons, 1909), 145.

5. Williston H. Lafton, "Northern Labor and the Negro during the Civil War," *Journal of Negro History* 34 (January 1949): 272.

6. Joan Baldwin, "Saratoga County Blacks in the Civil War," *Grist Mill* 21 (1987): 1.

7. Roger E. Ritzmann to Gail Schneider, 7 September 1984, Gail Schneider, Ulster County Black History Research Notes, State Education Department, Albany, N. Y. The letter indicates that muster rolls of the 20th, 26th, and 31st are on deposit in the New York State Archives.

8. Cf. Thomas Wentworth Higginson, *Massachusetts in the Army and Navy during the War of 1861-1865* (Boston: Wright and Potter Printing, 1869), 2: 680, 689; William W. Brown, *The Negro in the American Rebellion* (Boston: A. G. Brown & Co., 1885).

9. Baldwin, 4.

10. *Ibid.*, 2.

11. Higginson, 689.

12. "Newburgh Made Contributions to Union Army." The plaque was an idea of the Lincoln Patriotic League of Orange County and was erected 12 February 1909 on Abraham Lincoln's birthday. It reads: "To the Memory of the Colored Volunteers of Orange County who Responded to the Call of Abraham Lincoln."

13. Cf. J. Wilson Poucher and Helen Wilkinson Reynolds, *Old Gravestones of Dutchess County New York* (Poughkeepsie, N. Y.: Dutchess County Historical Society, 1924), 2: 120.

14. James H. Smith, *History of Dutchess County New York* (Syracuse, N. Y.: D. Mason & Co., 1882), 548.

15. *Ibid.*, 478.

16. Edythe Quinn Caro, "Black Civil War Soldiers from 'The Hills'," *Westchester Historian* 63 (Winter 1976): 12-15.

17. James F. Brown Diary, New York Historical Society, New York.

CHAPTER ELEVEN

TO FORGE ONE'S IMAGE ON THE LAND: THE RECONSTRUCTION ERA TO THE EARLY TWENTIETH CENTURY— THE STRUGGLE CONTINUES

Introduction: The Politics of Reconstruction

Following the Civil War, the adoption of the Reconstruction Amendments to the United States Constitution offered a ray of hope to African Americans around the country. By the 1870s, African Americans from the Hudson-Mohawk region were convinced that the Republican Party represented their best hope for achieving equality. Albany resident, Stephen Myers expressed this position, "If we should vote against the Republican ticket, we [would be committing suicide], so far as the right of franchise is concerned."[1] The adoption of the thirteenth, fourteenth, and fifteenth amendments to the United States Constitution, which freed the slaves, gave them citizenship, and gave them the right to vote, validated Stephen Myers's assertion. The Republican Party's control of the Federal government during those years was a reminder to African Americans that their ultimate salvation appeared to lie with the Republicans. The slowness of the white electorate to change its views in favor of a bias-free franchise and the existence of a race-conscious white establishment which was indifferent to the welfare of Black New Yorkers combined with other formidable obstacles to thwart the hopes of African Americans for full equality.

The Economics of Reconstruction

In addition to political rights, African Americans in the Hudson River Valley and its environs were also concerned with civil rights, i.e., jobs, housing, health, and public accommodations. The efforts of an African American lobbyist, William H. Johnson of Albany were instrumental in getting the New York Legislature to pass the state's first Civil Rights Bill (referred to as "Janitor Johnson's Law") in 1873. Johnson was aided in his efforts by Charles Lewis, also of Albany; and encouraged by the moral support of the Albany Female Lundy Society.[2] Unfortunately, the bill was New York's "States Rights objections to Congressional Reconstruction," and the bill was so weak that even Democrats voted for it.[3] Although it was better than no bill, it must be said that the strong civil rights laws that African Americans needed in New York were sacrificed for state sovereignty.[4]

The Politics of Quality Education in the Reconstruction/Post-Reconstruction Era

Education was another pressing concern of African Americans in New York in the late nineteenth and early twentieth century. William Johnson, along with the Albany "merchant tailor," William H. Topp (whose "store on Broadway . . . [will] not suffer by comparison with the best in any of the Atlantic cities") were instrumental in setting in motion new prospectives for education reform in the state. The two urged the state government to reexamine the need to abolish laws preventing African Americans from free and equal access to the state's public school system. Johnson and Topp had personal interest in the school systems of Albany, Schenectady, and Troy.[5]

The fight for quality education took its precedent from the eighteenth-century efforts of the catechismal schools of the Anglican Society for the Propagation of the Gospel in Foreign

Parts (SPG, see chap. 4), established throughout the valley for African slaves and Native Americans. In the early nineteenth century, the education of African American children was assumed by the New York Manumission Society, which established African Free Schools in major cities and towns along the Hudson River and used Lancasterian instructional methods.[6] At that time, "An Act to Incorporate a School for People of Color, in the City of Albany" was passed on 12 April 1816. In 1828 and 1829, similar schools were opened in Poughkeepsie and the city of Hudson.[7] From the 1830s through the Reconstruction Period, predominantly Black, independent schools assumed the mantle for educating African American children in the region. The school at the First Liberty Street Presbyterian Church in Troy, which was established in 1839, and the Wilberforce School of the First African Baptist Church on Hamilton Street in Albany under the Reverend Nathaniel Paul, later taken over by the Israel African Methodist Church, were both examples of those early black independent schools.[8] Designed to "combine religious instruction with education . . . to produce literacy," and as a way of getting around the indifferent and segregated policies of the white establishment, these early schools were welcomed.[9] They were such a success that "within two years after the establishment of Albany's African Baptist Church, its Sunday School was in operation, and by the mid-1820s enrolled almost 200 scholars."[10] Referred to at times as a "Sabbath School," the First African Baptist Sunday School also served a large number of adult pupils, some as old as ninety years of age. This kind of service to the Black elderly, as well as "its greater emphasis on developing literacy," made the "Sabbath Schools" more desirable than similar schools operated by whites.[11]

But African Americans were never satisfied with segregated educational conditions. If they were truly to liberate themselves and build a secure future for their progeny, there had to be a concerted, continuous assault, similar to the efforts of Johnson and Topp, on the white educational establishment. During the Reconstruction period and for the balance of the nineteenth century, a crucial battlefield was the Mid-Hudson region where the prestigious, but segregated, citadel of higher education,

West Point, was located. In that region, perseveringly brave Black leaders and parents unflinchingly challenged segregated education.

In Poughkeepsie in 1873, Joseph Rhodes, proprietor of the Eagle Dyeing Establishment, and his wife openly defied segregated school laws "by presenting a test case to the Board of Education of the federal civil rights law" which made no distinction of color in guaranteeing rights to education.[12] The strategy of the Rhodeses was to enroll their two daughters (Josephine, fifteen, and Marietta, nine) in the Fourth Grade Primary School rather than send the young ladies to the Colored School No. 1, established in 1844, then situated in the AME Zion Church building on Catherine Street.[13] After some deliberation on the part of the Poughkeepsie School Board and with more Black children attending classes at the predominantly white Fifth Ward School, the Board relented and unofficially decreed an open-school system in the city.[14] But in 1874, the New York State Legislature, reacting to lobbyist pressure from William H. Johnson, passed legislation abolishing segregated educational facilities. Immediate results of that legislation included the first two Black graduates of the Poughkeepsie High School, Joseph Rhodes (1879) and Gaius Bolin, Sr., (1883). Bolin later went on to Williams College where he was its first Black graduate in 1889.[15]

The Struggle over Higher Education: All-Black or an Integrated Approach

Gaining access to higher education was a slow and difficult road for African Americans around the state. In the 1870s, there were only fifty-nine Blacks attending colleges in New York State, in the 1880s that number dropped to fifty-five, not to rise significantly until 1910 when there were 245 in attendance.[16] In Poughkeepsie, both Vassar College and Eastman Business College refused to admit Blacks. The president of Eastman was concerned about the opinions of the school's Southern students, while Vassar's position, even into the twentieth century, was that "the conditions of life here are such [that we] strongly advise Negroes not to enter."[17] At West Point, Blacks were not admitted until 1870. The first African American cadet, J. W.

Smith from South Carolina, was harassed so much because of his African ancestry that he eventually left the academy. As a result, Frederick Douglass remarked that "the spirit of the Ku Klux Klan had reached West Point."[18] The honor of being the first Black graduate of West Point went to Henry Ossian Flipper, who wrote of his experiences at the school in his *Colored Cadet at West Point* (1889).[19]

Despite the desire of most African Americans for integrated education facilities, a group of Black leaders from the Mid-Hudson region, preferring to avoid the harassment, rejection, and discrimination of a predominantly white school, decided to call for the establishment of a predominantly Black college. They chose the name Toussaint L'Overture, after the Haitian revolutionary.[20] Against the wishes of many African American leaders, especially the fiery AME Zion minister, Reverend William P. Butler formerly of churches in Poughkeepsie and Hudson, the advocates of the Black college continued to push for its establishment. The advocates listed the following requirements: fifteen acres and working capital of $300,000; they boasted of the first all-Black board of trustees.[21] The trustees were drawn from various Mid-Hudson counties:

Dutchess County:
Isaac Deyo, Poughkeepsie (cart man and laborer)
Abraham Bolin, Poughkeepsie (gardener and janitor)
Charles Cooley, Poughkeepsie (laborer)
Samuel Jones, Fishkill Landing (laborer)

Orange County:
Rev. Jacob Thomas, Newburgh (minister)
Rev. W. H. Decker, Newburgh (minister)

Columbia County:
Chauncey Van Heusen, Hudson (laborer)

Greene County:
John Goetchess, Catskill (steward)

Ulster County:

Hanson Harley, Kingston (barber)[22]

Although a modified version of the bill proposing the college was pushed through the state legislature, the proposed Toussaint College ran into stiff opposition from the African American community. The New York Annual Conference of the AME Zion Church, meeting in Poughkeepsie in 1871, refused to endorse the college. A year later the state convention of the New York Colored Citizens Convention meeting in Troy took a stand against separate Black educational facilities: "the convention, eager to capitalize on the gains it believed that African Americans were making during Reconstruction, was urging that Blacks, instead of creating more Black institutions, should work to open more white institutions to African Americans."[23] Without the backing of these two powerful Black organizations the college was doomed. In addition, the growing trend in the 1870s and 1880s was to push for more African Americans to be admitted to New York State Colleges.[24] The Toussaint College idea, therefore, remained on paper, an idea whose time had not come.

Economic Peripheralization: Racist Ideology and the Late Nineteenth Century

During the last two decades of the nineteenth century, there was an increase in the African American population in the Hudson Valley region and its adjacent areas. This came as a result of the in-migration of Southern Blacks fleeing low wages, other forms of economic exploitation, and the general pervasive atmosphere of violence against Blacks.[25] Along with their northern brethren, these newly arrived Southern Blacks sought a better life in the more industrialized North. But instead they found themselves socially ostracized, passed over in their quest for industrial jobs, and economically depressed. At best, the majority of Blacks in the region could find only unskilled and menial seasonal work, leaving them in a state of financial insecurity and easy prey to white racist attitudes. With respect to generational socioeconomic mobility, Clyde Griffen's remarks about such mobility in Poughkeepsie for African Americans is appropriate for the entire region. He wrote: "For Black Americans, unlike the children of the [white] immigrants, moving out into more prosperous native white neighborhoods would not be an option by the turn of the century."[26] Newly arrived Blacks simply joined *native* Blacks in a socioeconomic dream deferred. One prominent Black leader from the valley remarked on the despair that engulfed thousands of African Americans as a result of their socioeconomic marginalization and ostracism "by the white caste system."[27]

National and world events in the closing two decades of the nineteenth century contributed to this despair and demonstrated that the African American in the United States of America and African abroad were marginalized. For example, the rise of the new imperialism and the scramble for Africa (1884-1885) indicated the dependent role the Black man would play in the new economic order being fashioned by the white Western world. In addition, the *Plessy vs. Ferguson* decision of 1896, establishing a national policy of separate but equal, fortified the view that African Americans were pariahs in the land of their birth. The Spanish-American War of 1898 reaffirmed the West's need to resolve the dilemma of the *white man's burden.* For African Americans in the Hudson Valley and its environs, the remarks of valley college president C. C. Gaines at the 1890 Lake Mohonk Conference on the Negro Question, mirrored the general view of African Americans held by whites. In a debate whether African slaves had surnames, it was Gaines's position that the ancestors of late nineteenth century African Americans had been but "a few generations removed from absolute savagery."[28] *Their descendants,* so his intent might have gone, *were perhaps no further from that level of development, and, therefore, the white man's burden held true* (my emphasis).

The last decades of the nineteenth century played a crucial role in creating the marginal socioeconomic and political conditions in which Africans in Africa and those in the diaspora found themselves. In *From Slavery to Freedom,* John Hope Franklin remarked, "For the American Negro the last decades of the nineteenth century were more critical than the Reconstruction years of 1868 to 1876."[29] For W. E. B. DuBois, the last decades of the nineteenth century:

may be epitomized in one word—Empire, the domination of
White Europe over Black Africa and Yellow Asia, through political power built on the economic control of labor, income and
ideas. The echo of this industrial imperialism in America was
the expulsion of the Black man from the American democracy,
their subjection to caste control and quasi slavery.[30]

For Rayford Logan in *The Betrayal of the Negro*, "the period 1877-
1901 [for African Americans was] the nadir in [their] quest for
equal rights."[31]

The Early Twentieth Century: A Continuing Struggle and a Cry of "Am I Not a Brother"?

The nineteenth century drew to a close as it had begun.
Ever resilient and persevering African Americans in the Hudson
region held white America accountable for the dismal socioeconomic conditions confronting the Black community. Racism
in New York was a fact and was the means by which white society limited the intergenerational mobility of African Americans,
while openly assisting and encouraging the intergenerational
mobility of newly arrived European immigrants. Yet in spite of
this preferential treatment for whites, many Black families in
search of better working conditions and a more promising
future for their children were drawn to the region in successive
waves of migration: 1870-1880, 1910-1920, and before and after
World War I. Members of these Black families competed with
newly arrived Italian immigrants for jobs in the brickyards along
the Hudson as well as in the resort industry. For African
Americans, the search for viable employment was difficult
because of racist hiring practices in many of the mills, hotels,
hospitals, and private homes.

In the early twentieth century Private Henry Johnson
returned home to Albany with the coveted *Croix de Guerre*, after
serving with the U. S. 369 Infantry (the former 15th New York
Colored Troops) in France during World War I. In Albany, he
found more white hostility against African Americans than on
the battlefields of France.[32] As economic conditions in the
region deteriorated during the Great Depression, the African
American community and other law-abiding citizens were confronted with the rise of yet another mob, the Ku Klux Klan. In

the Mid-Hudson region, the Klan was quite active in Ellenville, Napanoch, and Unionville in Ulster County, Poughkeepsie in Dutchess County, and in Pine Bush and Walkill in Orange County, two towns reputed to be the cradle of upstate Klan activity. But economic conditions aside, the Klan does attract individuals prone to violence, and the racist conditions prevalent in the region make such organizations ideal conduits for mob violence. Undaunted by the rise of the Klan and unrelenting in their drive to be *American*, Blacks across the Hudson-Mohawk region in the early twentieth century were determined to be heard. Their journey then, as today, continues arduous. Having been in the belly of the beast and now in the eye of the storm, African Americans remain steadfast and resolute in their desire to forge their image on the land.

Notes

1. Phyllis F. Field, *Politics of Race in New York: The Struggle for Black Suffrage in the Civil War Era* (Ithaca, N. Y.: Cornell University Press, 1982), 95.
2. Thomas J. Davis, "Three Dark Centuries Around Albany; A Survey of Black Life in New York's Capital City Area Before World War I," *Afro-Americans in New York Life and History* 7 (January 1978): 17. Harriette Bowie Lewis Van Vranken and Virginia Elaine Brown, interview with author, 3 May 1988. Mrs. Van Vranken states that the work behind the "bill" was that of her father, Charles Lewis. The name Lundy is from the abolitionist Benjamin Lundy. Ena L. Farley, "The Denial of Black Equality Under the States Right Dictum: New York, 1865 to 1873," *Afro-Americans in New York Life and History* 1 (January 1977): 19.
3. Farley, 19.
4. *Ibid.*, 21.
5. Davis, 17; Van Vranken and Brown.
6. Cf. Carleton Mabee, *Black Education in New York, from Colonial to Modern Times* (Syracuse, N. Y.: Syracuse University Press, 1979); Leonard P. Curry, *The Free Black in Urban America, 1800-1850* (Chicago: University of Chicago Press, 1981), 153.
7. The founders and trustees of the Albany "School for People of Color" were Thomas Lattimore, Frances Jacobs, Thomas Elcock, Samuel Edge, John Edward, Boltus Hugenon, and John Williams (Ira De A. Reid, "The Negro Population of Albany, New York, A Survey," in Adele Jacked, ed., *Source Material for Black History, Albany, N. Y.,* (Albany, N. Y.: State Library, 1972), 83; Carleton Mabee, "A List of the First Black Schools in Each Place in New York State, From Colonial Times to 1945," *Afro-Americans in New York Life and History* 2 (July 1978): 11-12.
8. Curry, 55, 162; Paul Family Printout: Nathaniel, Thomas, Benjamin,

Nancy, Albany Hall of Records, Albany, N. Y.

9.   Curry, 55, 156, 162.

10.   *Ibid.*, 156.

11.   *Ibid.*, 156. Curry states that Sunday Schools were opened as early as 1816 in Albany by "a Mrs. Upfold" (155).

12.   Cf. Lawrence Mamiya and Lorraine M. Roberts, "Invisible People, Untold Stories: Historical Overview of the Black Community in Poughkeepsie," *Year Book: Dutchess County Historical Society* 72 (1987): 83.

13.   *Ibid.*, 82.

14.   *Ibid.*, 83.

15.   *Ibid.*, 83-84.

16.   Carleton Mabee, "Toussaint College: A Proposed Black College for New York State in the 1870s," *Afro-American in New York Life and History* 1 (January 1977): 33; Carleton Mabee, "Separate Black Education in Dutchess County: Black Elementary Schools and a Proposed Black College, *Year Book: Dutchess County Historical Society* 65 (1980): 61.

17.   Mabee, "Toussaint College," 26.

18.   Mabee, "Toussaint College," 26.

19.   "First Negro Graduate," *Evening News*, 28 April 1969; John Hope Franklin and Alfred A. Moss, Jr., *From Slavery to Freedom*, 6th ed. (New York: Alfred A. Knopf, 1988), 262.

20.   Mabee, "Toussaint College," 27.

21.   *Ibid.*, 27.

22.   *Ibid.*, 28.

23.   *Ibid.*, 30-31.

24.   *Ibid.*, 32.

25.   Cf. Lawrence Mamiya and Patricia Kaurouma, "You Never hear About Their Struggles: Black Oral History in Poughkeepsie, New York," *Afro-Americans in New York Life and History* 4 (July 1980): 58.

26.   Clyde Griffen, "Changing Neighborhoods of Poughkeepsie," *Year Book: Dutchess County Historical Society* 72 (1987): 140.

27.   Cf. Joel Schor, *Henry Highland Garnet: A Voice of Black Radicalism in the Nineteenth Century* (Westport, Conn.: Greenwood Press, 1977), 100.

28.   Cf. Isabel G. Barrows, ed., *First Mohonk Conference on the Negro Question Held at Lake Mohonk, Ulster County, New York, June 4-6, 1890* (1890), 69-70. 107.

29.   Quoted in Bernard Makhuseqwe Magubane, *The Ties That Bind: African-American Consciousness of Africa* (Trenton, N. J.: Africa World Press, 1987), 31.

30.   *Ibid.*

31 .   *Ibid.*, 31. Cf. Rayford Logan, *The Betrayal of the Negro* (New York: Macmillan, 1965), chap. 5.

32.   Davis, "Three Dark Centuries Around Albany," 19-20.

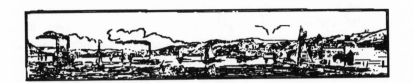

CHAPTER TWELVE

FIELD GUIDE TO IDENTIFIABLE AFRICAN AMERICAN HISTORICAL SITES IN THE HUDSON RIVER VALLEY

1. **Ancram Ironworks, Columbia County**
Established by Philip Livingston in the 1730s and 1740s, the ironworks used complementary, skilled African slave labor along with white workers from nearby Connecticut. With a total African slave labor force of approximately fifteen, the Ancram Ironworks' total output of pig iron by the mid-eighteenth century was 3,318 tons, of which 1,302 were made into bars.

2. **AME Zion Church (Newburgh), Orange County**
Perhaps the church was established in Newburgh in 1820, shortly after the founding of the African Methodist Episcopal Zion Church in New York in 1820 by James Varick, first Bishop of the church, who was born a slave in Orange County near the town of Newburgh.

3. **AME Zion Church (Poughkeepsie), Dutchess County**
Founded in 1837, this AME Zion Church was originally called the Smith Metropolitan. In 1840, its name was changed to the Catherine Street AME Zion Church, and it is the oldest Black church in Poughkeepsie.

4.   **Baxtertown (Fishkill), Dutchess County**

This was an early nineteenth century community west of Fishkill Village, populated by freed African slaves and Wappinger Indians. The two groups were later joined by working-class white families who settled in the community. The community is reputed to have had its own AME Zion Church, which was established in the first half of the nineteenth century.

5.   **Beacon (Fishkill Landing), Dutchess County**

An early ferryboat serviced Fishkill Landing and Newburgh, operated by Martin Wiltse & Son and captained by their slave, Quam. He piloted the ferry during the mid-eighteenth century by means of a rowboat and a piraqua, a two-masted vessel without a jib.

6.   **Bethlehem Estate (Bethlehem), Albany County**

This was the home of the Rensselaer Nicoll family slave, Caesar, who was born 1737 and died in 1852 at the age of 115. He survived six generations of his master's family and five generations of his own descendants. In his younger years, he was the Rensselaer Nicolls' sleighman who handled the large vehicle on the Hudson ice on the family's annual winter trip to New York City. He is buried in the Rensselaer Nicoll graveyard.

7.   **Cedar Hill Cemetery (Fishkill), Dutchess County**

Located north of Fishkill Village, it was an early nineteenth century, predominantly Black cemetery and contains the remains of several Civil War dead. Two of those are John W. H. Atkins of Company B, 20th Regiment of the U. S. Colored Volunteers, and William Henry Jefferson of the 8th Regiment of the Pennsylvania Colored Volunteers who died on 14 July 1864 at Yellow Bluff, Virginia. Perhaps, in some way the cemetery was associated with Baxtertown.

8.   **Coldeham (near Newburgh), Orange County**

This country estate of the colonial Lt. Governor, Cadwallader Colden, was the residence of several of his African slaves. The Lt. Governor was not averse to breaking up slave families, sending an African woman with child at the breast to

Barbados, away from her other children because of her "abusive tongue . . . her sullenness." He sent another slave's (Tomar's) husband, Gabriel, to North Carolina because of his growing influence over her.

9. Connecticut Village (Garrison), Putnam County

In 1780-1781, regimental units of Connecticut's fighting forces wintered here, above the Tory estate of Beverly Robinson. It was described as opposite West Point and a mile and a half in from the Hudson River. Among the Connecticut units were African American troops.

10. Croton Point, Westchester County

It was here during the American Revolution that the course of history was turned by the actions of an African American sentry, John Peterson. His sharpshooting forced Major John Andre to abandon plans to reach a British frigate in the Hudson River for safety. Instead he had to attempt an overland escape through Westchester County. He was eventually caught with plans for the American fortress (West Point), which had been given to him by General Benedict Arnold. Major Andre was hanged in October 1780.

11. Davenport House (Yorktown), Westchester County

At dawn on 14 May 1781 a contingent of the predominantly Black 1st Rhode Island Regiment, under the command of Colonel Christopher Greene, was surprised by elements of the notorious Tory renegades, the Cowboys, commanded by Colonel James Delancy. After a valiant fight, all of the 1st Rhode Island contingent was killed. Contingents of the 1st and 2nd Rhode Island were on guard on the Croton River at Pines Bridge in the Neutral Zone. A plaque to their heroism is located in Yorktown, Westchester County.

12. Eagles Nest (Hurley), Ulster County

This, an early nineteenth century mixed community of freed African slaves, Indians, and working-class whites, was located west of Hurley town in the mountains. Descendants of the early settlers are named Broadhead, Hasbrouck, Cantine, and Elting. The community represents one of many such mountain communities found throughout the Hudson River Valley.

13. Freemanville (Poughquag), Dutchess County

This early nineteenth-century Black community was founded by the free mulatto, Charles Freeman. It started at the base of what was pejoratively referred to as "Nigger Hill," but is now known as Depot Hill. Charles Freeman and his family owned land that stretched to West Pawling. Scattered over the mountain were other African American families such as the Jacksons and the Johnsons. Freemanville was also referred to as Guineatown, in tribute to the African origins and ancestry of many families.

14. Hanging Elm Tree Corner (Albany), Albany County

Located on the northwest corner of Pearl and State streets, this tree was, for most of the eighteenth century, the traditional hanging place. On 14 March 1794 two slave women, Bet and Deane, were hanged here; shortly afterward, on 11 April 1794 Pompey, a male slave, was also hanged. The three had been tried and convicted of setting one of several fires that occurred around Albany in 1793. The punishment for slaves who were convicted of such crimes was death.

15. Israel AME Church (Albany), Albany County

Founded in 1828 by the Reverend William Cornish, the church was originally on State Street but was moved to Hamilton Street in 1842. By 1854 the Israel AME Church housed the all-Black Wilberforce School, which the church operated until 1873 when African American children were finally admitted to Albany's public schools.

16. Kenmore Hotel (Albany), Albany County

The Kenmore was owned by the wealthiest African American in Albany in the late nineteenth century, Adam Blake, Jr., the adopted son of Adam Blake, Sr., a slave of the van Rensselaer family. The elder Blake is reputed to have held the umbrella for General Lafayette on his visit to the city of Albany in 1824. Adam Blake, Jr., also held investments in other properties, and on his death in 1881 his estate was valued at between $100,000 and $500,000.

17. **Kingston Area (Marbletown, Hurley, Kingston), Ulster County**
This area is associated with the Slave Conspiracy of 1775. In February 1775, slaves from the surrounding region of Kingston, under the leadership of York and Joe (a slave of Johannes Schoomaker of Kingston) conspired to burn Kingston and kill its inhabitants. On 18 February 1775 the plot was discovered, and the slaves were later tried by local magistrates.

18. **Kingston Court House, Ulster County**
This is the court house where Sojourner Truth successfully sued for the return of her son sold into Southern slavery in the 1830s.

19. **Kings Ferry (Verplanck Point), Westchester County**
This point on the Hudson River to the east of Stony Point was a strategic crossing for points west and south. In July 1781 a combined revolutionary force of American and French contingents, with state and local fighting units of African Americans attached (1st and 2nd Rhode Island, for example), crossed the Hudson at that point on their way south to Yorktown, Virginia, to confront the British General, Lord Cornwallis.

20. **Lake George, Warren County**
In September 1755 during a fierce battle between American units and those of the French and their Native American allies, a white soldier wrote home to his cousin in Philadelphia, "the Blacks fought more valiantly than the whites."

21. **First Liberty Street Presbyterian Church (Troy), Rensselaer County**
The church was founded in 1840 by the African American abolitionist and Presbyterian minister, Henry Highland Garnet, an escaped slave from Maryland. Henry Highland Garnet was a prime mover in the state and national Black convention movements during the 1840s. The First Street Presbyterian Church

was the focal point for many of the Black conventions, as well as a stop on the Underground Railroad.

22. Montgomery Place (Annadale-on-Hudson), Dutchess County

This is the historic home of General Richard Montgomery, killed at Quebec in 1775, and his wife, Janet Livingston. Between 1835 and 1875 Alexander Gilson, an African American, was the official gardener at Montgomery Place. His mother and sister also worked at Montgomery. In 1875 Alexander moved to Redhook where he opened his own greenhouse business.

23. Historic Cherry Hill (Albany), Albany County

This is the estate of the Elmendorf-Rankin family, where three-year-old Minnie Knapp and her brother were brought in the mid-nineteenth century. Minnie Knapp never married and remained a servant in the Elmendorf-Rankin household until her death. Another African American servant, Mary Jackson, is alleged to have witnessed a murder at the estate.

24. Moore's Mill (Piermont/Orangetown), Rockland County

John Moore was the first African American industrialist in Orangetown who, by 1800, owned a sawmill and gristmill. By 1815 he also owned a carding mill which employed fifteen people. John Moore also produced stone wheels for grinding grain and generating water power: these were all fashioned from stone taken from the old "mine-hole" in Piermont.

25. Nalle, Charles (fugitive slave in Troy), Rensselaer County

At a spot on State Street in Troy, New York, there is a plaque that commemorates the fugitive slave, Charles Nalle, who was freed from the clutches of the law by an excited group of African Americans led by Harriet Tubman on 27 April 1860. The plaque reads: "Here was begun April 27, 1860, The Rescue of Charles Nalle An Escaped Slave Who Had Been Arrested Under The Fugitive Slave Act."

26. **Negro Fort (formerly lower Westchester),**
     Riverdale, N.Y.
     The fort was situated on the Post Road to Boston east of
Kings Bridge and slightly southwest of what was then Valentine
Hill. The fort was on "the point" and undoubtedly was the "trip
line" for the British during the American Revolution to alert
them of a patriot advance south. It was manned by Black troops
("Ethiopian Regiment") fighting for the British. It was under the
command, at times, of an African American known as Colonel
Cuff.

27. **North Elba, Essex County**
     North Elba is the home and burial place of the abolition-
ist, John Brown. It was also the area in which a number of
escaped slaves on the Underground Railroad settled in lieu of
continuing on to Canada. They settled on land given to them by
the abolitionist, Gerrit Smith.

28. **Philipsburg Manor (North Tarrytown),**
     Westchester County
     It was the seventeenth and eighteenth century estate of the
Frederick Philipse family. Prior to the American Revolution the
gristmills and sawmills on the estate were managed by the
Philipses' slaves. One of his slaves, Frank, a cook is said to have
sailed to Madagascar in the late seventeenth century on board
the vessel, *Margaret,* while another was involved in the slave
rebellion of 1712 in New York City.

29. **Pine Hill (Newburgh), Orange County**
     Pine Hill was an estate owned by the French immigrant,
Hector St. John de Crèvecoeur, on which he and his family kept
several slaves for agricultural and household chores. Slaves and
owners shared the same living space, with slaves bedding down
in the kitchen area. In the winter slaves frolicked on the frozen
Hudson with their owner's horse and sleigh.

30. **Pinkster Hill (Albany), Albany County**
     This was traditionally the site on which the annual Pinkster
celebration was held to acknowledge the return of spring.
Originally a Dutch festival, by the middle of the eighteenth cen-

tury it had become an African ritual celebrated as Pinkster Carnival. It was reigned over by an Angolan-born slave honored as King Charles, who also was the embodiment of the African god, *Totau*. Today the State Capitol sits on the site. (In New York City the Pinkster site was located where City Hall is now situated.)

31. Poughkeepsie Rural Cemetery, Dutchess County
Buried in the Gill Family plot is the slave, Dina (Dinah), alleged to have been born in Africa. During the American Revolution she was a slave in the family of Theophilus Anthony. Her freshly baked bread persuaded British soldiers not to burn her owner's home during their 1777 raid up the Hudson River in their effort to link up with General Burgoyne. The home stands today on Route 9 South, at the entrance to IBM Poughkeepsie, and is known as the Treasure Chest Restaurant.

32. Rampo Mountains, Rockland County/Northern Jersey
Descendants of a late eighteenth century community of mixed African, Hessian Germans, and Native Americans reside here. In adjacent towns they are referred to as the "Jackson Whites."

33. Rensselaer, Rensselaer County
The city is the birthplace of Black sculptress Edmonia Lewis (1845-1900?) who made a meteoric rise, producing such works as *Forever Free, Old Indian Arrow Maker, His Daughter,* and *Hagar,* using biblical symbolism to depict the struggles of African Americans. It also is the site of Crealo, the estate of the Rensselaer family, where in 1690 Jeremaias van Rensselaer wrote to his brother, Jan, who was then residing in Holland, about the skill of his slave Andre with horses and of Andre's desire to be a free man.

34. Saratoga Battlefield, Saratoga County
The battlefield is located in and around Schuylerville, New York, where the British General Burgoyne surrendered to General Gates in October 1777. African American soldiers from various state regiments participated in the battles that preceded

the surrender: Bennington (Vermont), Stillwater, and Bemis Heights. Among a contingent of Brunswick German soldiers fighting for the British under the command of Baron Von Riedesel was a corps of Black drummers who were eventually evacuated to Germany. (It is alleged they came from a community of Afro-Germans.) At the end of the war, many African Americans were honorably discharged from their fighting units at Saratoga.

35. Schuyler Mansion (Albany), Albany County

The mansion was build in the mid-eighteenth century, and was the home of General Philip Schuyler. It became a fashionable gathering place for famous American and foreign visitors, who were served by the many household slaves. The slaves resided either in an appropriate space in the mansion's attic or an adjacent building. The families of Diana and Maria, two slaves whose children competed against each other in their assigned chores, have been immortalized in Mary Humphrey's work, *Woman of Colonial and Revolutionary Times: Catherine Schuyler* (1897).

36. Schuylerville, Saratoga County

The town was known formerly as Old Saratoga, where Burgoyne surrendered to General Gates in October 1777. It also was the place where the Schuyler family had its country estate on what was called "the flats." A number of African slaves were attached to the estate operating the gristmills and sawmills and were involved in the production of flax and grain and wood products for the domestic and international markets.

37. Skunk Hollow (Palisades), Northern New Jersey

This African American community was established on marginal lands of the Palisades in the nineteenth century, its population intermarried with Blacks in Rockland County, New York, in and around Piermont. Descendants lived in the Skunk Hollow community into the early decades of the twentieth century.

38.   Stony Point, Rockland County

The Point, located on the west bank of the Hudson River, is a promontory with a commanding view of the region. During the American Revolution, British forces were in control of a strategic fort at the Point. American forces under General Anthony Wayne were able to capture the fort on 16 July 1779, after the African slave, Pompey Lamb, who led an advanced party through British lines, had given the secret password, "the fort is ours," to the guard on duty.

39.   Stormville Slave Cemetery, Dutchess County

The cemetery is located north of Stormville and is one of many such sites (known and unknown) in the valley. Unmarked stones identify individual graves.

40.   Southern Ulster Slave Cemetery, Ulster County

Slaves belonging to white families in the Walkill area were buried in this graveyard, which is located south on Route 208 from New Paltz in a field where Route 300 meets Route 208.

41.   Second African Baptist Church (Albany), Albany County

The church was located on Hamilton Street not far from the present site of the Israel African Methodist Episcopal Church (1828). Founded in 1827 before the demise of slavery, the church was pastored by the Reverend Nathaniel Paul who officiated at the gathering of Black Albanians and officials from local, state, and national government on 5 July 1827 to celebrate the demise of slavery in New York State.

42.   Tappan Patent, Rockland County

Among the original holders of the seventeenth century Tappan Patent from the Dutch government were three Afro-Hollanders: Captain John De Vries and his son who received 1600 acres and Nicholas Claus Mande Emmanuel who received 800 acres. Descendants of the De Vrieses live in the Rockland County-Northern Jersey area today. Some can be found among the so-called "Jackson Whites."

43.   "The Hills" (Harrison), Westchester County

This early nineteenth century, predominantly Black community was established on marginal land perhaps given by Quakers to freed African slaves. African American families resided there for over a hundred years until the 1920s. Many of its young men, such as the Tierces and Weekses, fought in the American Civil War.

44.   Ticonderoga, Essex County

Fort Ticonderoga was captured with another British stronghold, Crown Point, in 1775 by a combined American revolutionary fighting force of Connecticut and Massachusetts units under the command of Ethan Allen and Benedict Arnold. Dispersed among the units were companies of African American soldiers. Barzillai Lew of the 27th Massachusetts was at Ticonderoga and Crown Point as was Lamuel Haynes. Cash Affrica, Caesar Parkhurst, Caesar Spensor, Prince Done, and Samuel Pomp, of Connecticut's 1st, 6th 9th, and 10th regiments, also took part in the capture of Fort Ticonderoga and Crown Point.

45.   "The Works" (New Windsor), Orange County

At this point on the Hudson River south of Newburgh many slaves, escaping to British lines, were assigned to work. Along with other African American and white soldiers assigned there, the slaves assisted in the construction of the iron chain used at West Point. The chain was used to obstruct British naval forces attempting to penetrate the Hudson River. The chain, which was manufactured inland at Sterling Iron Works, was assembled at "The Works," then put on barges and floated down the river to West Point. It was later stretched across the river to Constitution Island.

46.   Treasure Chest (Poughkeepsie), Dutchess County

Today it is a restaurant located on Route 9 South at the entrance to IBM Poughkeepsie. Originally the home of the Theophilus Anthony family, it was saved from burning by the British in 1777 because the soldiers admired the bread of the African female slave, Dina (Dinah). Dina remained at the house

while all others had retreated farther inland from the Hudson
River.

47.   State Capitol (Albany), Albany County

During the antebellum period several prominent African
Americans, some of them former slaves, made presentations
before various Senate and Assembly committees in support of
more protective civil and political rights legislation for New
York's African Americans. Among them were Henry Highland
Garnet, Stephen Myers, James McClune Smith, William H.
Johnson, and William J. Watkins. George A. Johnson of Elmira,
New York, was the doorkeeper of the New York State Senate
(1872-1873). Stephen Myers, a former slave from Rensselaer,
was a lobbyist for the New York Anti-Slavery Society at the State
Capitol.

48.   Underground Railroad Route, Hudson Valley

The Hudson River Valley was one of many routes on the
Underground Railroad along which fugitive slaves traveled to
freedom from Southern slavery. There are many stations
(houses and churches) in cities and towns along the Hudson
route. At Albany, New York, the Underground radiated east into
New England, north into Canada (with many fugitives crossing
at Rouses Point in Clinton County), and west towards Utica and
beyond. In the cities of Albany and Troy, the Israel African
Methodist Episcopal Church and the First Liberty Presbyterian
Church were stops on the Underground. Both Henry Highland
Garnet and Stephen Myers were conductors on the
Underground Railroad.

49.   Van Cortlandt Manor (Croton), Westchester County

The manor was an estate of the van Cortlandt family on
which a number of slaves resided. The female slave Bridget is
remembered for her daring attempt to escape her bondage during the American Revolution. She intended to lead six other
female slaves across British lines to freedom, but the planned
escaped was foiled by Cornelia Beekman, a daughter of the van
Cortlandts.

50.   **Verplanck Estate (Mt. Gulian, Beacon), Dutchess County**

The estate was the home of the prominent eighteenth and nineteenth century Verplanck family. It also was the place where James F. Brown, an escaped slave from Baltimore, Maryland, was employed, between 1827 and 1866 as the Verplanck family gardener. During those years Brown kept a personal diary (ten volumes) in which he meticulously recorded gardening chores, plant experiments, weather conditions, his personal affairs and those of his wife, Julia, and the changing times along the Hudson River between Fishkill Landing (Beacon) and Newburgh.

51.   **Whitehall (Skenesborough), Washington County**

This was the birthplace of the American revolutionary navy comprised of boats used by Lord Philip Skene who exploited the mineral and lumber resources of the southern part of Lake Champlain with slave labor. Prior to the confiscation of Skene's boats and their incorporation into the fledgling patriot navy by Benedict Arnold, many of the boats and scows were manned by Skene's slaves who smelted and forged iron mined from Cheever's hole north of Fort Henry.

52.   **White Plains-Philipsburg Area, Westchester County**

The area was the site of the July 1781 encampments of the combined revolutionary forces of American and French as they prepared to cross the Hudson River at Verplanck Point (Kings Ferry) and other points along the eastern bank of the river such as Fishkill Landing. At White Plains Baron Ludwig Von Closen of the French army described African American soldiers among the American fighting forces as "merry, confident, and sturdy." Also in July 1781, Jean-Baptiste-Antonine de Verger (aide to General Rochambeau), while observing American forces parade before General Washington at White Plains, remarked that "three quarters of the Rhode Island [1st] Regiment consists of negroes, and that regiment is the most neatly dressed, the best under arms, and the most precise in its maneuvers."

INDEX

Mower, Walter K., 123
Mt. Gulian, 175
Mt. Storm, 5
Muirson, George, 70
Mulatto, 5, 44-45, 54, 61, 107, 166
Mullin, Gerald, 86
Munro, 78
Munro, Harry, 78
Murray, 101, 116
Murray, John, 101
Musicians, 90, 93
Myers, Stephen, 123, 125-126, 153, 174

Nalle, Charles, 128, 168
Nash, Gary, 13-14
National Convention of Colored Citizens, 124
National Negro Conventions, 122, 126
Native Americans, 100-101, 155, 170
Neutral Zone, 104, 106-108, 165
New Amsterdam, 6-7, 88
New Challenges, 117, 120
New England Colonies, 21
New England, 21, 102, 107, 122, 126, 149, 174
New Foundland, 68
New Jersey, 31, 86-87, 93, 102, 104, 108, 119, 171
New Netherland, 67
New Netherlands, 17, 20, 87-88
New Orleans, 86, 95, 150
New Paltz, 3, 6, 29, 49, 61, 172
New Rochelle, 67, 70, 80
New Windsor, 103, 107, 173
New World African, 87, 97
New World, 13, 61, 87-88, 97
New York: Anti-Slavery, 124, 126, 174; New York Blacks, 86, 94; New York Board of Trade, 31; New York Colonial Assembly, 45; New York Colored Citizens Convention, 158; New York Colored Regiment, 150; New York Colored Troops, 160;

New York Congregational Association, 124; New York Constitution, 120; New York Democrats, 121; New York Emancipation Act, 86; New York Gazette, 30, 52; New York Legislature, 8, 154, 156; New York Manumission Association, 116; New York Manumission Society, 117, 155; New York Office, 127; New York State Colleges, 156, 158; New York State Legislature, 156; New York State Senate, 174
Niagara River, 126
Nigger Hill, 119, 166
North Carolina, 165
North Castle, 119
North Elba, 126, 169
North Pearl Street, 136
North Tarrytown, 169
Northern Army, 102, 109
Northern Jersey Descendants, 170
Northrup, Solomon, 129
Nova Scotia, 115
Nyack United Sisters of Friendship, 136

Odd Fellows Lodges, 136
Ogdenburg, 126
Ogilvie, John, 78
Old Saratoga, 171
Old Swamp, 136
Old World African, 97
Oneida Institute, 123
Orange County, 24, 30-31, 101, 103, 107, 123, 157, 161, 163-164, 169, 173
Orangetown, 106, 120, 168
Originally, 32, 50, 71, 163, 166, 173
Oswego, 126

Parkhurst, Caesar, 103, 173
Parks, Robert E., 85
Paul, Reverend Nathaniel, 116, 155, 172

חובות הלבבות
שער הבחינה, ועבודת אלוהים

DUTIES OF THE HEART
The Gates of Reflection and Service to God

RABBEINU BACHYA IBN PAKUDA

Translated and Annotated by
Avraham Yaakov Finkel

YESHIVATH BETH MOSHE
SCRANTON, PA.

CONTENTS

הקדמה
מהראש ישיבה
מורינו הרב יעקב שניידמאן שליט״א

עבדות - המלה הזאת מציירת שפלות ופחיתות בעיני בני אדם
ומגמתם תמיד להיות חפשיים לעשות כרצונם ודעתם. אמנם המעיֵ־
ין יראה דדבר זה מן הנמנע ואין לך אדם שראוי לומר עליו שהוא
חפשי באמת אלא כולם משועבדים ובעל כרחם עושים מעשים
שאינם לפי רצונם ודעתם, העני מצד אחד והעשיר מצד אחד. מי
שהוא עני וצריך לעבוד עבור פרנסתו הרי הוא תלוי בדעת אחרים
ממש לעשות מה שתובעים ממנו אף שהוא נגד רצונו. ואפילו עשיר
שאין צורך לו לעבוד בשביל פרנסתו הרי מצוי אצלו חלאים רח״ל
או שאר סיבות המצמצמים אותו ומונעים ממנו לעשות כרצונו. סוף
דבר שענין החפשיות הוא אחד מדמיונות של בני אדם.

ועוד נוסף ע״ז שלהגיע למדה החפשיות המדומה לוחם האדם
מלחמות ועושה ושאר מעשים אשר מעשים פריים השחתת מדותיו ובלבול
דעתו. ונמצא שמטרתו להיות חפשי מוליך אותו שולל ומאבדו
לבסוף.

ע״כ האדם הנבון בראותו כל זה יראה שאין זו הדרך הרצוייה
ויודה שעל כרחו מוכרח הוא להיות עבד ועל כן טוב לו לבחור
עבדות כזו שתועיל לו ולמשפחתו באחריתו וכן אמרו חז״ל כל
המקבל עליו עול מלכות שמים מעבירן הימנו עול דרך ארץ וביאורו
שכפי השיעור שמקבל על עצמו עבדותו יתברך כן לפי זה מסיר ה׳
ממנו שאר עבדות. והרי מבואר מדבריהם דעבדות הוא דבר מוכרח
בעולם אולם אין זה סתירה לבחירה שהרי בידו לבחור לאיזה אדון
יעבוד.

v

ואל יחשוב האדם שעבדות מצד עצמה היא ענין פחותה אלא
הפחיתות בא מחמת פחיתות האדון שהוא עובד אותו. וצא ולמד
מאליעזר עבד אברהם כשבא לבית לבן פתח ואמר עבד אברהם
אנכי והתפאר בזה שהוא עבד לאדם גדול שעי"ז זכה לטוב בזה
ובבא.

והרמב"ן כתב בשם חז"ל שהפסוק אנכי ה' אלקיך הוא מצוה
קראוהו בשם קבלת עול מלכות שמים וזה סמך לדברינו שנקודת
הבחירה הוא הברירה לקבל עליו השי"ת לאדון או ח"ו שיעבוד
לאדון אחר ולכן באה המצוה הראשונה בקבלת עבדותו יתברך.

והנה בשער הבחינה ובשער עבודת אלקים ביאר בעל חובות
הלבבות עומק החיוב לבחר בעבדות השי"ת והדרך לקיים חיובו בזה
במילואו. ויהי רצון שנזכה להיות עבדים למקום ונזכה לעבדו במקום
העבודה בביאת גואל צדק בב"א.

TRANSLATION OF RABBI YAAKOV SCHNAIDMAN'S PROLOGUE

Servitude—the word conjures up a picture of disgrace and degradation in people's minds. Liberty to do as one pleases is their ultimate goal. But a thinking person will realize that this goal is unattainable and that no one is truly free. Everyone has obligations and is forced to do things against his will. This applies both to the rich and the poor. The poor man who works for his livelihood must do what others demand of him and even the rich who need not work for a living often get sick or have other troubles which do not allow them to fulfill their desires. In short, true freedom is a figment of the imagination.

In addition, to attain this freedom, people often fight and get involved in other activities which negatively affect their character. Their quest for freedom causes them to go astray and eventually destroys them.

The intelligent person realizing this, will admit that freedom is not an option, and so chooses such servitude that will benefit himself and his family in the end. Our sages taught "He who accepts on himself the yoke of the heavenly kingdom will be spared the yoke of livelihood." The gist of their words is, that, corresponding to the amount that one accepts on himself the service of The Almighty, Hashem will remove from him other worldly obligations. Though everyone must be a servant, it is up to each person, to decide whom he will serve.

Service is not inherently unbecoming. It is only degrading if the one you serve is of low stature. Remember that Eliezer, the slave of Avraham introduced himself saying "I am the slave of Avraham." He prided himself with the fact that he was a slave to such a noble master through whom he would merit this world and the next.

The Ramban quotes our sages, who referred to the first commandment "I am Hashem your God" as "Acceptance of the kingdom of heaven", for, as we explained, the ultimate choice one must make is whether to accept upon oneself to serve Heaven or to remain bound to serve others.

In the Gates of Reflection, and Service to God, the author of Duties of the Heart explains, in depth, the obligation to choose to serve God and how to fulfill this obligation. May it be His will that we merit to serve Him in His chosen place with the coming of Moshiach speedily in our days.

DUTIES OF THE HEART
GATE TWO

———◦◉◦———

The Gate of Reflection

INTRODUCTION

REFLECTION ON THE CREATION AND ON GOD'S GREAT GOODNESS TOWARD HIS CREATURES

━◉━

We discussed in the First Gate wholehearted acceptance of God's Oneness, and since contemplating the wisdom evident in God's creation is the most direct way to prove His existence and the surest path to knowing Him, it makes sense to link the "Gate of Reflection" to the "Gate of Wholehearted Belief in God's Oneness." This way, the Gates follow each other in logical sequence, and through them you will recognize your obligation to serve God, which is the purpose of your existence. As the wise King Shlomoh said, "*Hashem has acted so that man should stand in awe of Him*" (*Koheles 3:14*).

WHY PEOPLE DON'T APPRECIATE GOD'S GOODNESS

God is good to each and every one of His creations, as it says, "*Hashem is good to all*" *(Tehillim 145:9)*. Nevertheless, most people are blind and do not appreciate this good. There are three reasons for this. Firstly, because people are so engrossed in stockpiling worldly goods and chasing after physical pleasures, they ignore the good the Creator has bestowed on them. They are obsessed by the desire to gratify their lusts and satisfy their wishes. The more they have, the more they want. They also minimize the gifts they receive. They actually reach the point where they believe that the good of others is rightfully theirs,[1] and that everything good that happens to them is really bad.[2] They do not understand that all good things come from God, as it says, "*The wicked man, arrogant as he is, says, 'He does not avenge!' In all his scheming he thinks, 'There is no God, [and I do not owe Him thanks for all the good things that happen to me]'*" *(Tehillim 10:4)*.

The second reason [that people don't value God's benevolence] is because they are born into this world like a mindless, dumb animal, as it says, "*Man is born a wild young donkey*" *(Iyov 11:12)*. As they grow they become accustomed to the abundance of God-given favors [like health, food, shelter and parents]. They take these favors for granted as if they were their inalienable rights and natural, permanent facets of their lives. Even when their minds develop and their intelligence becomes keen, they remain oblivious to all the good God bestowed on them. They are not grateful to God for all He has done, because they do not recognize the good itself nor the One who bestows it.

They can be compared to a baby found in the desert by a kind man. Feeling sorry, he brought the baby home raising, feeding,

---

[1] A merchant thinks that were it not for his competitors all the customers would come to him.

[2] He is never satisfied, even if he earned a thousand dollars, he feels miserable because he expected to earn three thousand. (Marpe Lanefesh).

clothing, and providing for him, until he reached the age that he was capable of appreciating all that was done for him.

Later, the kind man heard about a prisoner, who had been starved and left without clothes for a long time. Overcome with compassion for the pitiful prisoner, the kind man persuaded his captors to release him and forgive all his offenses. He took him home and treated him well, although not nearly as well as he had treated the abandoned baby.

Nevertheless, the former prisoner showed him more gratitude than the child he raised did. Because the prisoner went from a life of misery and pain to a comfortable and tranquil existence while he was a thinking adult, he was fully capable of recognizing the goodness of his rescuer. The child, used to this goodness from childhood, never grasped how much kindness was showered on him, even after he grew up and had gained a mature outlook on life.

Yet no thinking person will doubt that the kindness lavished on the abandoned baby was more far-reaching and important, and that the child had a greater obligation to be forever thankful and full of praise. This idea is expressed in the verse, *"I have pampered Ephraim, taking them by the arm, but they have ignored My healing care"* (*Hoshea 11:3*).

The third reason [people do not value God's benevolence] is because they suffer all kinds of adversities, sicknesses or financial reverses. They do not realize that their hardships may have a happy outcome, or that they are meant as a test, [to reward the one who suffered in the World to Come], or as a reproof [for his sins, to save him from punishment in the World to Come], as it says, *"Happy is the man whom You discipline, Hashem, and whom You teach from Your Torah"* (*Tehillim 94:12*).

They forget that all they own and their very existence are gracious gifts of God, and that He renders just decrees for them, as He sees fit in His wisdom. Therefore they are indignant when God's judgment is brought down on them; and they do not thank Him when He is kind to them. In their foolishness they deny both the good itself and the One who granted it to them. Senselessly, many of them believe that they are smarter than God; that they could run the world better than He, improving on the things He created for their benefit.

They can be compared to a group of blind people brought to a home adapted to their particular needs. Everything had its proper place and it was sensibly arranged with special attention to their disability. Its infirmary was stocked with the most advanced medicines, and an eye specialist was on call to restore their eyesight. But the blind refused to be treated, and did not follow the doctor's orders. They aimlessly roamed around the home, tripping over the equipment that was installed for their benefit, falling on their faces and suffering bruises and broken bones. Their distressful condition went from bad to worse, [as the misery of their blindness was compounded by the pain of their wounds]. In their despair they blamed the director and the builder of the home. They downplayed the [director's] efforts on their behalf and charged the administration with negligence and mismanagement. They suspected that the director, instead of having their welfare in mind, meant to abuse and injure them. In their distorted view they denied that the director was a good and kind person. As the wise Shlomoh said, "*Even when he travels, the fool lacks sense, and he lets everyone know that he is a fool*" (*Ecclesiastes 10:3*).

THE DUTY TO TEACH OTHERS

It is the duty of every learned person to enlighten those who are unaware of God's goodness, teaching them how to appreciate all the favors He bestows on them. People often miss the chance to enjoy the good things [that God grants them] because they are unaware of them, and because they don't understand their value.

But once people are made aware of the many divine favors they receive, they will see the light, and their gratitude and praise to God will know no bounds. They will find pleasure in this world, and a rich reward in the World to Come.

King Shlomoh summed it up, saying, "*The words of the sages are*

like goads, and of the compilers are nails well driven" (*Koheles 12:11*).
He compares the words of the sages to goads because they prod
[people to do the right thing], and he likens their words to well-
driven nails, because through the books they write, their ideas become fixed in the reader's mind and soul, [like a nail driven into a
wall], never to be forgotten.

Please note: The phrase *"the words of"* in the above-mentioned
verse, applies also to the second segment of the verse. Thus it
should be understood as, *"The words of the sages are like goads, and
the words of the compilers are nails well driven."* Their words are
compared to driven nails because books of wisdom remain forever
and are always helpful.

THE SIX CHAPTERS ABOUT REFLECTION

We will discuss six points about reflection:

ONE: The nature of true reflection.

TWO: The requirement to reflect on creation.

THREE: How to reflect on creation.

FOUR: The manifestations of wisdom that can be reflected on in
creation.

FIVE: Reflection on [man], the most obvious sign of wisdom.

SIX: What deters us from reflecting, and the results of contemplation.

CHAPTER ONE

The Nature of True Reflection

———◦◦◦———

Reflection involves contemplating the signs of God's wisdom that are apparent in nature and analyzing these signs to the best of your ability. Although there are many different manifestations of God's wisdom, [for example biology, astronomy, physics or anatomy], all sciences come from one source. Take [the light of] the sun. In and of itself it is essentially one, yet its rays [when passing through colored glass] take on the color of the glass and appear to be either white, red or green. Similarly, when you sprinkle a garden, the droplets adopt the different colors of the flowers they come to rest on.

Reflect on all the marvels of God's creation, from the largest to the smallest, and ponder them deeply. You will see, with God's help, the truth of what I have told you, [that ultimately the source of all God's wisdom is one].

Why there is Great Diversity in Nature

Since the signs of God's wisdom are varied, and each species of creation reveals His wisdom in a different way, meditate on the signs of God's wisdom and think about them until the source of God's wisdom becomes anchored in your soul and fixed in your mind. If the manifestations of God's wisdom were identical in all of creation, no one would have any doubt about His wisdom, and the learned and the ignorant would recognize it equally. God created nature with infinite variety causing his true wisdom to be hidden because if something always acts in one way, it is not acting on his own accord, but is rather forced to act in that particular way, and is powerless to change, like fire which can only burn, or water which can only cool. But one with power to do what he wants, will do different things all the time. God is free to do whatever He wants, whenever He wants, without limitations or constraints. And since He needs nothing and nothing compels Him to do anything, He created things with great variety according to His wisdom, to demonstrate His Oneness and His freedom of action. As it says, "*Whatever Hashem wished, He did, in Heaven and on earth*" (*Tehillim 135:6*).

This is why there are so many different signs of God's wisdom in the world. But only God knows whether this is the true reason why things were created in different shapes and forms causing His wisdom to be veiled. This is just one of many things we do not really understand; only God knows the absolute truth.

CHAPTER TWO

THE REQUIREMENT TO REFLECT ON CREATION

———◈———

Common sense, Scripture, and Rabbinic tradition all require us to reflect on creation and to find proof of God's wisdom in it.

Common sense [requires you to reflect on creation] because through your intelligence you become aware that man is superior to animals being able to think, understand, and grasp the profound wisdom that fills the universe. As it says, *"Who gives us more knowledge than the beasts of the earth, and makes us wiser than the birds of the sky?"* (Iyov 35:11).

The more a person delves into the depths of God's wisdom and reflects on the signs of God's wisdom evident in nature, the more superior he is to the animal. But if he does not [reflect on the signs of God's wisdom], he is not even equal to the animal, as it says, *"An ox knows his owner, a donkey his master's trough; but Israel does not know, My people takes no thought"* (Yeshayah 1:3).

Scripture [demands that you reflect on creation] when it says, *"Lift high your eyes and see: Who created these?"* (Yeshayah 40:26); *"When I behold Your heavens, the work of Your fingers, the moon and the stars You set in place"* (Tehillim 8:4); *"Do you not realize? Have you not heard? Have you not been told from the very first? Have you not contemplated the foundations of the earth?"* (Yeshayah 40:21); *"Listen, you who are deaf; you blind ones, look up and see!"* (Yeshayah 42:18); *"It is better to go to a house of mourning than to a house of feasting, since that is the end of all men, and the living one should take it to heart" (Koheles 7:2). "A wise man has his eyes in his head, whereas a fool walks in darkness" (Koheles 2:14),* and, *"The path of the righteous is like a gleam of sunlight, ever brightening until noon, but the way of the wicked is all darkness, they do not know what will make them stumble" (Mishlei 4:18,19).*

Rabbinic tradition tells us [that it is your duty to reflect on creation] when it says, "About a person who knows how to calculate the cycles of the seasons and the constellations, but does not do so, Scripture says, *"There are harp and lyre and drum and flute and wine at their drinking parties; but they never give a thought to the plan of Hashem, and take no note of the work of His hands" (Yeshayah 5:12).* [The Gemara asks:] "From where do we know that it is a person's duty to calculate the cycles of the seasons and the constellations? Because it says, *'You shall safeguard and perform [the decrees and ordinances], since this is your wisdom and understanding in the eyes of the nations who will hear all these decrees' (Devarim 4:6).* [The Gemara asks:] And what kind of wisdom is recognized by the nations of the world? The science of astronomical cycles and the stellar constellations" (Shabbos 75a). "Calculate the cost of a mitzvah against its reward, and the reward of a sin against its cost" (Avos 2:1). "If the Torah had not been given to Israel, we could have learned modesty from the cat [who covers its excrement], fidelity from a dove [who is faithful to its mate], manners from a rooster [who first courts and then mates], and honesty from the ant [who does not take another ant's food]. (Eruvin 100b)

We have demonstrated that it is our duty to reflect on creation and to find proof of the signs of God's wisdom in it. Keep this in mind.

CHAPTER THREE

HOW TO REFLECT ON CREATION

———≈◦◉◦≈———

Reflect on creation by studying the world's essential elements, and the things that result from the combination of these elements.[3] Next examine the individual parts of these combinations [for example, in the case of a tree, examine its trunk, roots, branches, leaves, and fruits]. Note what function each of these components fulfill, the wisdom that is evident in them, their content, form and shape, and explore the purpose for which these components were created.

Reflect on creation by delving into the spiritual and physical aspects of the world, the rule of cause and effect by which the world is governed, and realize that the ultimate perfection for which the world was created [is to recognize God and serve Him]. Think about [the contrasts in creation:] about humans and animals, about stationary things and mobile things, about minerals that are lifeless and plants that grow, about the elements that rise [i.e. fire and air] and the elements that sink [i.e. water and earth]. Marvel at the way God combined these elements in the right proportions, put them in the places where they are needed, and assigned to each its proper function. God did this to demonstrate that He is the Creator, just as a masterpiece reflects the talent of its artist and a building attests to the genius of its builder.

[3.] The ancients believed that everything in the physical universe is composed of combinations of four elements: fire, air, water and earth.

Remember that the world is a combination of matter and spirit, and the two are so inextricably intertwined that each part sustains the other, like the body and soul of a living creature, [for the body cannot live without the soul, and the soul cannot exist without the body].

THREE CATEGORIES

There are three categories of God's wisdom found in the world.

The first: That which is obvious and self-evident that even fools could not dismiss, much less intelligent people. For example; the way the sun revolves around the earth during the day to illuminate the inhabited area and to benefit everything in it. As it says, "*When the sun rises they (the young lions) come home and crouch in their dens. Man then goes out to his work, to his labor until the evening. How abundant are the things You have made, Hashem, You have made them all with wisdom; the world is full of Your creations*" (Tehillim 104:22-24).

The second: The signs of God's wisdom that are hidden from most people, with only the learned understanding their value. One example is: death, which happens to all living things and is of great benefit to all[4]. Our Sages *(Bereishis Rabbah 9:2)* explained the verse, "*Hashem saw all that He had made, and behold, it was very good*" *(Bereishis 1:31)*, saying that the phrase "*it was very good*" refers to death. And the wise Shlomoh said, "*So I consider more fortunate the dead who have already died than the living who are still alive*" *(Koheles 4:2)*.

The third: Signs of wisdom that are obvious up to a point, but whose main purpose remains obscure at first glance. A person of limited intelligence will never understand them unless he puts his mind to it. These include, the seasonal changes in the weather, and the like. The wise person [will not look for the practical benefits na-

---

[4] Without death man would live forever and never enjoy the bliss of the World to Come as a reward for his good deeds.

ture has to offer. Instead] he chooses to study the spiritual, intangible aspects of this world. He uses this knowledge as a ladder to finding evidence of the Creator's greatness [in everything he sees]. Then, having recognized God's exaltedness, and having understood God's goodness and compassion toward his creatures, he takes it upon himself to serve God wholeheartedly. He acknowledges the kindnesses God has bestowed on him, and how greatly He elevated him [above all other creatures by endowing him with an intellect], although he did nothing to deserve it, and had no commendable character trait that would warrant a reward from God.

He selects the material things he needs for his physical well-being, but only enough to fill his bare necessities. He turns his back on the world's luxuries and enticements that turn the heart away from God. [Instead of indulging in pleasure] he does good deeds that earn him a place in the hereafter, his ultimate destination, the abode he will go to after death. He views the world and material things as the means of gathering supplies for his final journey to the World to Come, and he takes from this world only the things that will stand him in good stead in the World to Come.

But the fool who is blind to the signs of God's wisdom in creation, views the world as his permanent home. He exerts himself, straining every nerve and sparing no effort [to amass worldly goods]. He thinks that material riches will bring him fulfillment. He does not realize that his wealth will go to someone else, possibly during his lifetime, and surely after he dies. And he banishes from his mind any thought of the hereafter.

The wise man and the fool can be compared to the two proverbial brothers who had no possessions other than a plot of uncultivated land they inherited from their father which they divided between themselves. One was wise and hardworking, whereas the other was the opposite.

The wise brother realized that he could not earn a living even if he worked full-time on developing his plot of land, so he hired himself out as a farmhand and worked for others to cover his day to day expenses. In the evenings, after finishing his day's work, he worked diligently on his own field for an hour. When he had saved a day's wages, he worked his own field that day, rather than hiring himself out. He kept up this schedule until his land was fully cultivated. When harvest time came, he gathered his fruit and grain, and storing it, he had enough to live an entire year. Now that he was free to work his land at his own pace, without pressure, he planted more trees. Eventually he produced enough to support himself and to buy more land.

The foolish brother also realized that he could not earn a living by working his own land, so he neglected it altogether. He too, hired himself out as farmhand working for others, but whatever he earned he spent. When he managed to save a day's wages, he took the day off, relaxing and enjoying himself. After work he would spend his evening hours relaxing at the bath house. The thought of working his own land did not enter his mind.

His land was desolate and produced nothing. It was overgrown with weeds, its stone fence was broken, and its trees were swept away by a flood. As Shlomoh described it, "*I passed by the field of a lazy man and by the vineyard of a man lacking sense; it was all overgrown with thorns, its surface was covered with chickweed, and its stone fence lay in ruins*" *(Mishlei 24:30,31)*.

An intelligent person thinking about this parable will understand that it refers to his ultimate destiny and permanent home, and will take pains to prepare for it. [Like the wise brother who tilled his field, he will work hard to gain a share in *Olam Haba*.] When he works for his livelihood, he will do so as if he were working for someone else, doing as much as necessary [to earn a living], but no more. The fool, on the other hand, will do exactly the opposite on both counts: he will work with all his might for worldly matters, and he will be totally oblivious of the hereafter. As the wise Shlomoh said about the fool, "*I observed [the field of the lazy man] and took it to heart; I saw it and learned a lesson*" *(Mishlei 24:32)*.

CHAPTER FOUR

THE MANIFESTATIONS OF WISDOM THAT CAN BE REFLECTED ON IN CREATION

———◦◉◦———

What are the signs of wisdom that are evident in creation about which we can reflect?

There are seven basic categories of wisdom to be found among the world's many species and sub-species.

The first category of signs of God's wisdom is apparent in the positioning of the earth and the [four] elements of the world [earth, water, air and fire, one above the other]. The world is situated in the center with water close by and above it, covered by a layer of air, and then by fire. Note how these are in perfect and changeless balance and proportion, each staying in its designated position. The sea remains in place, its water confined inside it, never overflowing its boundaries no matter how turbulently the waves are raging and the storm is roaring. As it says, *"When I constrained [the sea] with My limits, I set up a bar and bolted doors and said, 'You may come so far and no further. Here your surging waves will stop!'" (Iyov 38:10,11).*

About the positioning of heaven and earth it says, *"Your word will forever stand firm in the heavens; Your faithfulness is for all generations. You established the earth, and it endures. They—[the heavens and the earth]—stand this day to carry out Your decrees, for all are Your servants" (Tehillim 119:89-91).* David also dealt with this subject in the psalm that begins with the words, *"Bless God, O my soul!"* (*Tehillim 104*).

The second category is visible in man, who is a replica of the universe, and for whose sake everything was created. He is the crowning glory, splendor and culmination of creation. David had this in mind when he said, *"Hashem, our Master: how mighty is Your Name throughout the world!"* (*Tehillim 8:2*).

The third category is the wisdom that is apparent in the human anatomy: the structure of the human body, human emotions, and the God-given human intellect which makes man superior to the other living creatures. Man is a small-scale counterpart of the world, and the world is like man in its roots and fundamentals. Iyov implied this when he said, *"You poured me out like milk and curdled me like cheese. You clothed me with skin and flesh and wove me of bones and sinews. You gave me life and were kind to me, and Your providence watched over my spirit"* (*Iyov 10:10-12*).

The fourth category is the wisdom that comes to the fore in other living creatures, from the smallest to the greatest, whether they fly, swim, crawl, or move around on four legs. They have various shapes and sizes, and differ in the way they serve man, and in the pleasure and benefit they provide for him. This was hinted at in God's reproachful answer to Iyov, *"Who provides food for the raven, when its young ones cry out to God and wander about without food?"* (*Iyov 38:41*), and in the references to the other wild animals and sea creatures mentioned in the text that follows.

The fifth category is the wisdom that is manifest in plants and minerals that are available for man's benefit, and in the ways he can make use of them, depending on their nature, composition and properties. The early generations already expressed their views of this in their books, as it says, *"[Shlomoh] spoke of the trees,[5] from the cedar in Lebanon to the hyssop that grows out of the wall"* (*1 Melachim 5:13*).

The sixth category is the wisdom that is evident in the scientists,

---

5. He taught people the scientific and medicinal properties of each species of animal and plant life (Rashi).

artists and the mechanical geniuses that enable man to live life to the fullest, feed his family, and derive other benefits, both of a general[6] and a specific nature[7]. [The fact that it is God Who gives wisdom to scientists and master craftsmen] is alluded to in the verse, *"[Do you know] Who placed wisdom in the innards? Or Who imbued the heart with understanding?" (Iyov 38:36)*, and, *"For Hashem grants wisdom; from His mouth come knowledge and understanding" (Mishlei 2:6)*.

The seventh category is the wisdom that is exhibited in the giving of the Torah and its statutes through which we serve God, and through which the ardent observer comes to have pleasure in this world and can look forward to reward in the World to Come. As it says, *"Listen well to Me and you will eat choice food, and your soul will delight in rich food. Incline your ear and come to Me. Listen, and your soul will be rejuvenated" (Yeshayah 55:2,3)*. The laws of the Torah are also the basis of the legal codes and the rules of conduct that regulate the behavior of the nations of the world. Their ordinances are patterned after the laws of the Torah, and is of benefit to them in this world only.

It has been said that nature is to the Torah like a servant is to his master, because the forces of nature obey the dictates of those who observe the Torah. As it says, *"You will then serve Hashem your God, and He will bless your bread and your water. I will banish sickness from among you" (Shemos 23:25); "He said, 'If you obey Hashem your God and do what is upright in His eyes, carefully heeding all His commandments and keeping all His decrees, then I will not strike you with any of the sicknesses that I brought on Egypt. I am Hashem Who heals you'" (Shemos 15:26)*, and there are many more passages like these.

There are some who are of the opinion that when Shlomoh said, *"With all forms of wisdom did she build her house; she carved out its seven pillars" (Mishlei 9:1)*, he had in mind the seven categories of signs of wisdom we discussed in this chapter.

---

[6] Machines that benefit everyone, like farming equipment.

[7] Machinery that benefits a limited number of people, like tools of the diamond trade.

CHAPTER FIVE

REFLECT ON [MAN], THE MOST OBVIOUS SIGN OF WISDOM

————⊶⊙⊷————

While there is a compelling need for us to reflect on all the seven categories, the most obvious and clearest sign of God's wisdom can be found in that small-scale world, the ultimate purpose of creation: man.

Begin by exploring a human being's embryonic state, his birth, the blending of body and spirit, the formation of his limbs and organs, their purpose, and the reason each was created the way it was. Next, examine the things that help the infant grow, his character traits, his personality tendencies, his intellect, his innate and acquired qualities, his desires, and his mission in life.

When we understand these facets of human life, we will grasp many of the mysteries of the world, because man is a counterpart of the world, [and everything that exists in the world at large is present in man]. A wise man once said that philosophy is man's knowledge of himself. He summed it up in the admonition to "*know thyself*," which means that a person should study the phases of human development in order to recognize God through the signs of wisdom that are evident in man. As Iyov said, "*In my flesh I see God*" *(Iyov 19:26)*.

Since it is so, [that you recognize God's wisdom in the marvels of the human body], let us give a few examples of the phenomena of human development we mentioned, in order to alert a lax person to be aware of these things. This will whet his appetite to study things that I have not mentioned, and, as a result, he will become submissive to God and overflow with gratitude for the kindness and goodness He has bestowed on him. As David said, "*I thank You, for I am awesomely, wondrously made. Your work is wonderful; I know it very well. My frame was not hidden from You when I was shaped in a secret place, knit together in the lowest parts of the earth [the lowest chamber of my mother's womb]. Your eyes saw my unformed limbs; the days on which all [my limbs] would be fashioned were recorded in Your book, not one of [my organs] was unknown to You*" (Tehillim 139:14).

THE EARLIEST STAGES OF HUMAN DEVELOPMENT

Focus on the origin of a human being and you will recognize the divine kindness that brought man into existence out of nothingness. Man passes from the mineral to the vegetable state which in turn becomes food, that subsequently converts into seed and blood.[8] The seed and blood is transformed into animal life, which finally takes on the form of a living, thinking, and mortal human being, who goes through changes and phases, and who, due to changing circumstances, constantly moves, all according to a well thought-out [divine] plan, designed to benefit him.

BODY AND SOUL

Next, look at the human body for evidence of God's goodness, wisdom and complete mastery. Then continue to study the basic com-

---

[8.] The human body originates from semen, which comes from the food that man has consumed. Food is a product of the vegetative state, which, in turn, derives its nourishment from minerals. Thus, man passes all the stages that lead from the mineral to his becoming a living, rational, speaking human being.

ponents that a human being is comprised of, namely, his body and soul. A man's body is made up of opposing elements and discordant natures. God in His might joined them, merged them in His wisdom, and combined them into a body that appears to be one, but actually is a composite of many parts.

He then attached to this body a spiritual and elusive essence which resembles the spirit of the angels: his soul. The soul is bonded to man by something that bridges these two opposites, namely: his breath of life, body heat, blood, veins, nerves and arteries; [all of which have both physical and spiritual qualities]. Then God gave man flesh, bones, muscles, skin, hair and nails to protect these delicate organs, and shield them from injury.

GOD'S KINDNESS TO THE FETUS AND THE NEWBORN BABY

At the beginning of a human's existence, God appointed the mother's body to serve as a couch for the fetus, settling it in a well-protected place, where no hand can touch it, shielding it from heat and cold, where food is ready for it. There, the fetus grows and develops, moves about and eats effortlessly. The larger it grows, the more nourishment it receives, until it reaches full term. The baby then leaves the womb through a narrow passage without any skill or effort on its part, but only by the power of the wise, merciful, and gracious One who shows compassion to His creatures, as He said to Iyov, "*Do you know the season when the mountain goats give birth? Can you mark the time when the gazelles calve? Can you count the months as they come to term? Do you know the moment they give birth?*" (Iyov 39:1,2).

Except for taste and touch, a newborn infant's senses are underdeveloped. God provides for it food from its mother's breast. The blood that nourished it in the womb is now converted to sweet milk, which flows like a gushing spring when needed. The milk is not so abundant that it is too heavy for the mother or that it flows without suction. Nor is it too meager to tire the baby when it suckles. God's grace is also evident in the way He constructed the opening of the nipple like the eye of a needle; not so wide that the milk flows without suction, causing the baby to choke, nor so narrow that the baby would have to exert itself while nursing.

PARENTAL LOVE AND CARE

The baby then matures, to see and hear. God causes his parents to love him and have compassion on him, so that raising him is not a burden. They are more concerned with his food and drink than with their own, and the chores of raising him—like bathing and diapering him, as well as the need to guide him patiently and protect him from harm, even against his will—seem effortless to them.

The infant then becomes a child, yet his parents do not tire of him, nor are they annoyed by the many things he wants, and by the fact that he shows little appreciation for all they do for him. Their concern about him grows stronger until he grows into adolescence and has learned to speak correctly and sensibly.

As his senses and intelligence mature, he becomes smarter and more knowledgeable. With his physical senses he understands how the world functions, and with his mind he grasps the complexities of abstract ideas. As the wise Shlomoh said, *"For Hashem grants wisdom; from His mouth come knowledge and understanding"* (*Mishlei* 2:6).

It is a great kindness that a young child does not have the capacity to distinguish between good and bad. If he could think clearly, he would realize how capable adults are, going wherever they please, and caring for their cleanliness. Realizing that he was the opposite of an adult, [because he cannot walk and he wallows in his own excrement] he would die from anguish and distress.

Another wondrous thing is the fact that babies cry. [At first glance you might think that crying was harmful to a baby,] but according to the great physicians, it is actually good for babies. There is a fluid in the baby's brain that causes sickness if it remained there. The fluid is forced out of the brain by the [vibrations caused by the] baby's crying, thus saving the baby from disease. Another sign of God's kindness lies in the fact that a child's baby teeth fall out gradually, one after another, not all at the same time. That way the child continues to eat normally while his permanent teeth are coming in.

As the child grows, he occasionally suffers from sicknesses and has painful accidents. This is God's way of teaching him that life is a challenge and not to expect tranquility in this world, for if he trusts in this world, he will be controlled by his impulses like the dumb and senseless animals, as it says, *"Don't be like a senseless horse or mule which does not understand"* (Tehillim 32:9).

The Wonders of the Human Anatomy

Reflect on the functions of the organs of the body, and how each organ is helpful to man: the hands enable him to give and take, the feet to walk, the eyes to see, the ears to hear, the nose to smell, the tongue to speak, the mouth to eat, the teeth to chew, the stomach to digest, the liver to purify the blood [by removing toxic substances], the intestines to process waste, and the bowels and bladder to temporarily store waste. Reflect on the heart, the seat of the life-force, and on the brain which is the center of your spiritual faculties, the source of all emotions, and the hub of the central nervous system. Think how perfectly the womb preserves the fetus, and how all the other organs serve [to foster your well-being], and you will find that there is more we do not know about the organs than we do.

Think about the natural processes by which food is distributed to every part of the body. The wisdom you observe will inspire you to thank the Creator and praise Him, as David said, *"All my limbs will say, 'Hashem, who is like You?'"* (Tehillim 35:10). Food passes into the stomach through [the esophagus], a long, straight tube without any twists. The stomach then grinds the food more thoroughly than the teeth have done. The food is carried into the liver through thin connecting veins that act as a strainer, preventing anything coarse from entering the liver. The liver converts the food into blood, distributing it through the body through tubes created specifically for this purpose. The waste matter is eliminated through channels made for that purpose. Green bile goes to the gall bladder, black bile goes to the spleen, while fluids and juices flow to the lungs, and the refuse of the blood passes into the bladder.

Consider the wisdom of the Creator manifest in the composition of your body; how He set the organs in the right places to receive the waste matter, so that it can not spread in the body causing you sickness.

Then think about the formation of your vocal chords and the instruments of speech. The trachea is hollow for the production of sound; the tongue, the lips, and the teeth are designed for the clear articulation of consonants and vowels. And these organs have other uses too: air enters the lungs through the windpipe; the tongue enables you to taste savory dishes, and helps you swallow food and drink. The teeth chew solid food, and the lips serve to keep liquids in your mouth and to swallow the desired quantity. As far as the other organs are concerned, the purpose of some is known, of others, unknown.

Then, ponder the four forces of the body and their functions. The "receiving force" receives the food and pushes it downward through the esophagus and into the stomach;[9] the "retentive force" keeps the food in the stomach until nature takes its course; the "digestive force" absorbs the food and extracts the finer elements which it separates from the waste matter and distributes throughout the body; the "excretory force" expels the waste matter remaining in the body after the digestive process has drawn from the food all that the body needs.

Notice how these forces are arranged to serve the body's needs

---

[9.] Even in a head-down position solid food or liquids reach the stomach through peristaltic waves—the rhythmic muscular contractions of the esophagus.

most efficiently. The body is like a king's court with servants and officers in charge of running the royal household. One officer [the "receiving force"] is responsible for receiving the supplies and delivering them to the king's warehouse. The next [the "retentive force"] has the job of storing the supplies until they are ready to be used. The third [the "digestive force"] processes the supplies and doles them out to the servants. And the fourth [the "excretory force"] sweeps and cleans the palace and takes out the refuse.

The Wonders of the Human Mind

Consider the powers of the soul [i.e. the mind] and how helpful they are to you. These include thought, memory, the ability to forget, shame, reason and speech. Imagine your life without one of these powers. How difficult it would be if you were unable to remember what you owned and what you owed, what you took and what you gave, what you saw and what you heard, what you said and what others said to you, who did you a favor and who harmed you, who helped you and who hurt you. You would be unable to recognize a road you traveled many times before, nor remember a subject of study you learned your whole life. Experience would not help, you would not be able to decide what to do now or in the future. [Without memory] you virtually would lose your humanity.

But forgetting also has advantages. If you could not forget, you would always be depressed; nothing in the world would make you happy, and you would never enjoy yourself because you would always think of the great disasters of the world, [wondering when misfortune would strike you]. You could never rest from your worries nor come to conclusions. So you see that man was granted both memory and the ability to forget—two conflicting qualities—and each of them has its benefits.

THE FEELING OF SHAME

The feeling of shame is singular to man; How noble and beneficial it is! If not for this feeling, people would not welcome strangers into their homes, keep their word, do favors, act kindly, nor shrink from doing harm in any way. In fact, people keep many *mitzvos* only out of shame. Many people would not honor their parents— much less other people—if not for the feeling of shame; they would not return something entrusted to them for safekeeping, nor would they refrain from sinning. Whoever does any of the deplorable things mentioned above, does so only after shaking off his feelings of shame. As it says, *"They do not feel shame, and they cannot be made to blush" (Yirmeyah 6:15)*, and *"The wrongdoer knows no shame" (Tzefanyah 3:5)*.

While man has an innate tendency to be ashamed of other people, he shows no such shame before God Who constantly observes him. The reason [we have no ingrained pangs of conscience when we transgress against God] is, so that we should not feel compelled to serve God, in which case our merit would be diminished. [For if God's Presence were plain for everyone to see, we would have no choice but to serve Him. But the merit of such "forced" service is not as great as free-willed service.] Nevertheless, we are required to feel shame before God as a result of reflection [on His exaltedness and kindness], realizing that it is our a duty to serve Him, and knowing that He takes measure of our revealed and hidden actions. As it says, *"Be embarrassed and ashamed of your ways, O House of Israel" (Yechezkel 36:32)*.

THE HUMAN INTELLECT

God's greatest gift to us is our intellect and power of discernment which set us apart from the animals. There is no need to explain how important intelligence and discernment are for our physical well-being and the stable conduct of our daily affairs. This is obvious to anyone except one who lost his comprehension due to brain injury.

You can achieve a great many things by using your intellect. [Through reasoning] you to know that there is a wise, everlasting Creator, Who is the One and Only, the Almighty, Who is not bound by time and space, and is above all human qualities and beyond all human understanding, Who is merciful, kind and good, Who is like nothing else, and like Whom nothing else exists.

Your intellect helps you understand God's wisdom, power and compassion that pervade the world. It makes you aware that you are obliged to serve God because of His goodness toward mankind as a whole and toward each person individually. Through reason you come to believe in God's truthful Torah, given to Moshe His prophet. Because you have an intellect you are held responsible for your actions, and God can be exacting with you. Conversely, someone who has lost his mind loses all human qualities, so that the concepts of *mitzvos,* reward and punishment do not apply to him.

Intellect enables you draw logical inferences from things you see, like the movement of a shadow [across a sun dial which shows you what time it is], and how tiny drops of water have worn away a hard rock. [You deduce that the drops have eroded the rock over a long period of time.] With your intellect you can tell the difference between truth and falsehood, between the perfect and the imperfect, between good and evil, between the desirable, the possible and the objectionable. Through your intellect you are able to make other creatures work for you, [like a horse for you to ride, a donkey to carry burdens, an ox for plowing,] you can fix the positions of the stars and calculate their distances [from the earth and from each other] and their orbits, understand mathematical equations, geometric theorems and the rules of logic that apply in the science of reasoning, and other arts and sciences too numerous to mention.

The same goes for all other human dispositions and emotions: just like the intellect, they are perfect in the way they benefit us.

The Gift of Speech and the Art of Writing

How good has God been to you by giving you the ability to speak and to arrange words into meaningful sentences! By conversing with others you can express yourself and understand other people. The tongue is the heart's quill and the mind's messenger. Without speech there can be no social contact between people, and we would be no better than animals. A person's speech is a measurement of his intelligence. Through speech covenants are made between people, and between God and those who revere Him. Through verbal confession a person can repent of his missteps and ask forgiveness for his transgressions. A person's speech reveals his status. Man, so the saying goes, is "heart and tongue." Speech is what makes you human, since in essence you are a living, speaking and mortal being. It is your ability to speak that sets you apart from animals.

How wonderful is the alphabet and the art of writing! Thanks to the written word, the deeds and happenings of the dead and the living can be recorded for future generations. By writing letters you can stay in touch with people in faraway places and find out how your relatives in distant countries are getting along. A letter can cheer up the depressed, save a life or protect people from danger. Through the written word the various sciences are stored in books, and the novel ideas of thinkers are recorded and published. With it you are able to record business transactions, loans, purchases, marriages and divorces; there are simply too many examples to mention.

God's Wisdom is Manifest in the Human Anatomy

One of the greatest benefits God bestowed on you are your hands and fingers, with which you can draw, write, embroider, kindle fire, and perform precision work, which other creatures having no need for them, cannot do.

I can safely say that there is not one organ that does not exhibit in its structure, form and combination with other organs, the marks of divine wisdom to a thinking person. Each attests to God's love for you. Galen[10] already explained this in detail, in his book *"The Function of the Organs"*. Were I to elaborate on even one organ like he did, this book would be a massive, oversize volume. What we have said should suffice to give food for thought to whomever God has inspired to choose the right way.

SIGNS OF GOD'S WISDOM IN THE ANIMAL WORLD

If you study animal behavior and the way animals acquire their food, you cannot help but notice the signs of wisdom in them. That is why the Scriptures constantly refer to animals when mentioning God's wonders, as when God said to Iyov, *"Who provides food for the raven, when his young cry out to Hashem, helpless without food?"* (Iyov 38:41) and, *"He gives the animals their food, to young ravens that cry out for it"* (Tehillim 147:9). There are many such verses.

EVIDENCE OF GOD'S WISDOM IN CELESTIAL BODIES

So too, when you explore the motion and brightness of the stars you will find signs of God's indescribable power and wisdom. As David said, *"The heavens declare the glory of Hashem the firmament tells of His handiwork"* (Tehillim 19:2), *"When I behold Your heavens, the work of Your fingers, the moon and the stars that You have set in place"* (Tehillim 8:4).

A most impressive sight among the creations of God, which can be seen all the time, is the celestial sphere. Wherever on earth a person stands, he sees a hemisphere encircling the earth. Looking at it thoughtfully he realizes, that He Who created it with His will, has infinite power, wisdom and greatness.

---

[10] Greek physician, one of the most distinguished doctors of antiquity. He is often mentioned by the Rambam in his medical books.

Looking at the ruins of imposing historic structures we marvel at the genius of the ancients who erected those [fortresses, palaces and pyramids] and admire the physical strength and self-regard they must have had, to build such mighty fortresses. If such a relatively puny and insignificant edifice, which is only slightly better than we can build, evokes such wonderment in us, how much more must we marvel at He Who created the heavens, the earth and everything in it, effortlessly and with ease, without toil or fatigue, out of nothing, and impelled by nothing other than His will and desire. As it says, *"By the word of Hashem the heavens were made, by the breath of His mouth, all their host"* (Tehillim 33:6).

EVERYTHING IN CREATION BENEFITS MAN

The more you ponder the wisdom of God apparent in creation, the more you realize that, aside from attesting to the divinity and oneness of the Creator, all created things are there for the benefit of man. In some cases the benefit is obvious, in others it is not. The benefits of light are obvious, but it is not clear how we benefit from darkness, for in fact people become lethargic and slow down in the dark. Yet, were it not for the darkness of night, people and animals would collapse from toiling and rushing round the clock. Also thanks to the night, one day is set apart from the next, and we become aware of periods of time that we would not otherwise be aware of, like how long or short a person has lived.

If time were always the same, [and days were not separated by nights,] there could be no time-related mitzvos, like Shabbos, Yamim Tovim and fasts; people could not make appointments to meet at a set time, most things associated with time would be unknown to us, and not a single living creature would digest his food properly, [because digestion mainly takes place during the night].

But because man needs light at night to do some work and to visit and take care of the sick, God gave us, in place of daylight, the light of fire, which we can kindle or put out at will.

Another of God's wonders is that the sky is a deep blue, almost black color, which is precisely the color that strengthens our eyesight. If the sky were white, it would harm and weaken our eyes. In fact, you can find signs of God's wisdom in each and every created thing.

ANIMALS INSTINCTIVELY FEAR MAN

Among the many good things God did for man, was to instill fear of man in animals that would otherwise harm him. As it says, *"There shall be a fear and dread of you instilled in all the wild beasts of the earth, and all the birds of the sky, in all that will walk the land, and in all the fish of the sea. I have placed them in your hand"* *(Bereishis 9:2)*. That is why a baby is safe from a cat, a mouse or any such animal, while a corpse is not. As our Sages phrased it, "A newborn baby need not be protected from mice, whereas the corpse of Og, the king of Bashan [who was a giant], needs to be protected from mice. As it says, *'There shall be a fear and dread of you instilled in all the wild beasts of the earth'"* (Shabbos 151b).

THE MARVEL OF MOTION

All forms of life—from the highest to the lowest, from the smallest to the biggest—have motion. It is the invisible factor that keeps all of creation running perfectly. Although none of our senses perceive [the essence of motion], its existence can be inferred by the movement of things the senses can perceive. [Just like our senses cannot perceive the concept of time, but we infer it from the apparent motion of the sun in the sky.] Without motion, nothing in the world could come into being or be obliterated. As a matter of fact, a philosopher once said that most of nature is in a state of constant motion.

Once you understand the mystery of motion and its physical and spiritual aspects, you will realize that it is one of the wonders of divine wisdom, and you will recognize in it the Creator's great compassion for His creatures. You will realize that your movements and changes—great or small, physical or spiritual—are connected to God's will and desire, with the exception of your choices between good and evil which He placed in your domain, [so that you can be rewarded for your good deeds and punished for your transgressions].

Direct your attention to every move you make, remembering that you are connected to God's will. You will feel a sense of shame before Him at all times, be in awe of Him, accept His judgments, and submit to His decrees. As a result, you will win His favor, and everything will turn out to your benefit. As it says, *"He who trusts in Hashem is surrounded with kindness"* (Tehillim 32:10).

A Blessing in Disguise

Bear in mind the final outcome of adversities. You will discover that many unpleasant things that happen turn out to be advantageous, and vice versa. For example, the story is told of a group of travelers who slept at night next to a wall. A passing dog urinated on one of them, and he got up to wash himself. As soon as he distanced himself from the others, the wall collapsed, crushing them to death. He alone was spared. Things like that and the opposite [where perceived good things turn out to be harmful] happen very often.

The Gift of Rain

God's greatest gift to all living creatures and plant life is rain. It falls only in its proper time [but during the harvest season when the grain must dry in the field it does not rain], as it says, *"Can any of the false gods of the nations give rain? Can the skies, of themselves, give showers? Only You can, Hashem our God! So we hope in You, for only You made all these things" (Yirmeyah 14:22)*, and, *"They have not said to themselves, 'Let us revere Hashem our God, Who gives the rain—early and late rain—in season, Who keeps [it dry] for our benefit the weeks appointed for harvest'" (ibid. 5:24)*. Hashem's providence that is evident through rain is stressed in the verse, *"Who performs great deeds which cannot be fathomed, wondrous things without number; Who gives rain to the earth and sends water over the fields; Who raises the lowly, so that the dejected are uplifted in salvation" (Iyov 5:9)*.

ONE SEED CAN PRODUCE A PILE OF GRAIN

The way food grows from seeds is extraordinary. A single kernel— if it was not ruined [by hail or drought]—can produce a thousand or more seeds. It has been said that one single grain of wheat yields three hundred ears, each containing over twenty kernels. We have also seen huge trees evolve from a single seed or shoot, where each tree produced seeds in a greater ratio than the wheat we mentioned.

May the wise and gracious One, Who causes such huge quantities to emerge from such small and frail sources, be praised. As it says, *"By Him actions are measured" (1 Shmuel 2:3)*.

NOURISHMENT FOR ALL LIVING THINGS

The ways in which each species of animal is fed are too numerous to mention. An astute person reflecting on them recognizes the wisdom of the Creator's plan. As David phrased it, *"All of them look to You to give them their food when it is due. Give it to them, they gather it up; open Your hand, they are well satisfied" (Tehillim 104:27)*, and, *"You open Your hand, and satisfy the desire of every living thing" (ibid. 145:16)*. With God's help I will explain this better in the Gate of Trust.

THE GIVING OF THE TORAH

But the greatest good God has bestowed on man, and the strongest proof of His existence, is the Torah that was given to Moshe His prophet, and the signs he performed, the changes in the normal course of events he brought about, and the awesome miracles he displayed in order to cause people to believe in God and His prophet. As it says, *"Israel saw the great hand that Hashem inflicted on Egypt; and the people revered Hashem, and they had faith in Hashem and in Moshe His servant"* (Shemos 14:31), *"You have been shown in order to know that Hashem, He is the God! There is none beside Him!"* (Devarim 4:35), and, *"From heaven He caused you to see His voice in order to teach you, and on earth He showed you His great fire, and you heard His words from the midst of fire"* (ibid. v. 36).

Should anyone in our day and age want to see something to match [those miracles], all he need do is look at the survival of the Jewish people in exile among the nations, and see how well we are doing economically despite the fact that we share neither their religious beliefs nor their way of life, as they well know. Our standard of living is almost the same as theirs, and in times of war and political upheaval it may even be better than theirs. It is also clear that their middle and lower classes have to work harder than ours. This is exactly as our Creator promised when He said, *"But despite all this, even when they are in their enemies' land, I will not grow disgusted with them or tired of them, so that I would destroy them and break My covenant with them, since I am Hashem their God"* (Vayikra 26:44), and Ezra said, *"For we are slaves and our God has not forsaken us in our servitude"* (Ezra 5:9), and, *"Had not Hashem been with us when men rose up against us"* (Tehillim 124:2). In the next gate, "The Gate of Service to God" I hope, with God's help, to elaborate on the great favor God did in giving us His Torah.

THE ESTABLISHMENT OF GOVERNMENT

All people agree on the need to appoint a king, submitting to him, obeying his commandments and decrees and respecting him. He, in turn, protects them, cares for them, judges them fairly, and governs them for their own good, so they will not suffer or be defeated by an enemy. For if [they had no king] and everyone cared only for himself worrying about protecting his own rights, people would never agree to [make sacrifices for the common good] like building a tower or a fortified wall around the city, and society would be in chaos.

If the ruler observes the laws of ethics and governs the people justly, his government will be stable and lasting. As it says, *"Kindness and truth protect a king" (Mishlei 20:27),* and as our Sages said, "Pray for the welfare of the government, for if people would not fear it, a person would swallow his neighbor alive" (Avos 3:2).

ECONOMICS

Divine wisdom and goodness is seen in the fact that [instead of bartering,] people use gold and silver as a medium of exchange for goods and services. Furthermore, people have an innate drive to accumulate gold and silver to improve their lot, although, these metals themselves do not do them any good. If you are hungry or thirsty, you cannot eat or drink gold and silver, if you have pain, gold and silver will not bring you relief, since silver and gold are only rarely used for medicinal purposes.

A remarkable sign of Divine wisdom can be seen in the uneven distribution of silver and gold among people. A few people have an abundance of money, while most people have only small amounts of it. If everyone had a lot of money, they would not be able to buy anything with it; [nobody would want to sell anything since he had enough money of his own]. Gold and silver are of little value in one respect [i.e. they have no intrinsic worth], and of great value in another [because if you have money you can buy anything you want]. This is also part of the plan of Divine wisdom.

BASIC AND SECONDARY NEEDS

Study the things that are essential for the survival and upkeep of the body throughout life. You will find that the more something is needed to sustain life, the more abundant it is in nature; the more something is needed, the more readily available it is. Whatever we can do without, is scarce and hard to come by. For example, since it is impossible to live without air for more than a brief moment, God filled the atmosphere with it and made it readily available.

People also need water, but they can exist without it for a longer period of time. Therefore, God spread water over the surface of the earth and gathered it in specific locations. However, water is not as widespread as air; it is more readily available to some than to others, air is there for everyone, and one can get as much air as he wants, at all times, no matter where he is. But people who live far from water may even have to pay for it.

Food is also a basic necessity, but we can do without it or find a substitute for it more easily than we can in the case of air and water. That's why food is harder to get hold of and more scarce than water. Still there is plenty of it, and no one has to do without.

The same goes for clothing made of fur, wool, linen or cotton. Substitutes for these materials are more easily found than for food, you need only replace your clothing after a long time, and you do not need much clothing. Therefore clothing materials are more scarce than food, and they are available only at certain times.

There is very little need for precious stones, gold and silver. They are of limited use, and are valuable only because people agreed to attach value to them. The precious material held by the masses, amounts to less than the quantity of food in the pantry of a single individual. This is because people can do without these things.

Praised be the Creator Who is wise, compassionate and merciful to His servants, Who watches over them in goodness and promotes their best interests. There is no God but Him! As God said to Yonah the prophet, "*You cared about the kikayon plant, which you did not work for and which you did not grow, which appeared overnight and which perished overnight. And I should not care about Nineveh, that great city!*" *(Yonah 4:10)*, and, "*God is good to all, and His mercy is upon all His works*" *(Tehillim 145:9)*.

CHAPTER SIX

WHAT DETERS US FROM REFLECTING, AND THE RESULTS OF CONTEMPLATION

———— ◈ ————

Those things which we mentioned in the First Gate as standing in the way of accepting God's Oneness also prevent us from reflecting [on the signs of God's wisdom in creation]. This is besides the three factors mentioned at the beginning of this Gate.[11]

Another impediment [to reflection] is arrogance in the face of God's kindness. The fool thinks he deserves God's kindness, and expects more of it. That is why he does not reflect on the goodness of the Creator, feeling no obligation to thank and praise Him. The wise Shlomoh said about such a person, *"Every arrogant person is an abomination to Hashem" (Mishlei 16:5).*

As a result of reflection you will recognize the good things God has done for you, and you will serve Him. You will meditate constantly on the signs of God's wisdom, regardless of whether you perceive them through your senses or by reason. Inevitably you will discover new signs of God's wisdom each day. As David said, *"Day to day utters speech" (Tehillim 19:3)* [which the Malbim interprets: Each day brings to light more and more of the Divine wisdom in Creation.]

[11.] (1) The relentless pursuit of physical pleasures, (2) taking God's favors for granted and (3) failing to believe that suffering is ultimately for one's own good.

God's Wisdom and Power are Unfathomable

Know that the things touched on in this Gate are but a fraction of what you can gather from the many mysteries of God's wisdom through your own intellect. Many secrets will be revealed to you when you approach your studies with a pure heart and soul. After having grasped all you can of these mysteries, realize, that what you understand of God's wisdom and might, is nothing compared to His actual wisdom and might; we see only the things that were created for our benefit, not the full range of God's infinite power. Your fear of Him and His awesome power should be in accordance with His true power, not as you imagine it to be.

Parable of the Boy in the King's Prison

A child was born in the king's prison, knowing nothing of the outside world. The king pitied him and ordered that he be provided with the best of everything, until he would grow up and be able to understand. Day after day, a messenger of the king brought him everything he needed, like candles, food, drink and clothing. The messenger explained that he was a servant of the king, and that the prison, its equipment and all the food belonged to the king. In light of this, he urged the child to give thanks to the king and praise him.

The boy said, "I give praise to the master of this prison for making me his servant, for singling me out for all his benevolence, and for taking care of me."

Replied the messenger, "Don't say that! You are mistaken [in calling the king 'master of this prison']! The king does not rule only over this prison, he governs an empire that is infinitely greater than this prison. And you are not his only servant, he has a multitude of subjects. The goodness and kindness he has bestowed on you is nothing compared to what he has done for other people, and his caring for you vanishes into nothingness when you compare it to the way he has looked after others."

The boy countered, "I don't know what you are talking about, because I can judge the attributes of the king only by what I myself have experienced of his goodness and power." To which the messenger retorted, "You should say, 'I praise the exalted King, Whose sovereignty is boundless and Whose goodness and kindness is immeasurable. I am negligible compared to his many legions of servants, and as opposed to his power my person is trivial.'"

Now, for the first time, the boy began to understand the king's attributes. Awestruck by the king's grandeur, and recognizing his own unimportance against the king's eminence, he appreciated the king's generosity all the more.

Think of this parable, when you look at the celestial expanse that surrounds the earth. We cannot even understand all there is in a small patch here on earth, much less the earth in its entirety and space beyond, [just as the boy in the prison could not perceive the magnificence of the king].

Reflect on this parable, and figure from it how great and omnipotent God really is. Then you will realize how good and kind He has been to you, and you will appreciate that He watches over you although you are just one among the myriad of His creatures.

Treat His Torah, His mitzvos and His statutes with reverence. Think how respectful you act toward a person who is wealthier and more esteemed than you. The higher his status is compared to yours, and the less he needs you, the more you appreciate his favors, the more seriously you take his orders and warnings, and the harder you try to please him. Take this to heart, and with God's help you will be successful.

May God count us among those who serve Him and who recognize His goodness, mercy and kindness. Amen.

This concludes the Second Gate.

"*With my voice I call out to Hashem, and He answered me*" (*Tehillim 3:5*).

DUTIES OF THE HEART
GATE THREE

———◦(◉)◦———

The Gate of Service to God

INTRODUCTION

Our Obligation to Serve God

━━━━◖◗━━━━

A person who understands the obligation to believe in God's oneness and to reflect on His goodness to mankind as we explained in the last two gates, should reciprocate by committing himself to serving God. Common sense tells you that someone who receives a favor should repay his benefactor.

The Obligation to be Grateful

We will explain the various ways people are good to one another, and how one should express his gratitude for favors received. Taking this one step further, we will draw the inference [that if we must be thankful to people who help us], surely we must thank and praise God for His kindness and great goodness.

It is accepted fact that you must thank someone for his intention to help you, even if through circumstances beyond his control, he was unable to carry out his intention of helping you. On the other hand, if someone did you a favor without intention of helping you, you do not owe him any gratitude.

When you think about it, you find that there are five ways people are kind to one another. There is the kindness a father displays to his child; the kindness a master shows his servant; the kindness a rich man offers to the poor in order to earn a reward in the hereafter; the kindness people display toward one another in the hope of gaining respect or a material reward; and the kindness a strong person displays to a weak one because he feels sorry for him.

Now let us consider the motives of the aforementioned people to see whether each is acting selflessly, [and accordingly, how great is the obligation of the one being helped to be thankful to his benefactor].

Let us begin with the kindness a father bestows on his child. A father has his own interest in mind when he helps his child, because the child is an integral part of him, and because of the high hopes he has for him, [so when the father helps his child he is really helping himself]. This is obvious, because a father is more concerned for the needs of his children than his own needs when it comes to food, drink, clothing, and safety. He gladly puts up with toil and trouble to make things easy for them, because of his innate feeling of compassion for his children. Nevertheless, both the Torah and common sense demand that the child is obliged to serve, honor, and respect his parents. As it says, *"Honor your father and your mother" (Shemos 20:12), "Every man: Your mother and father shall you revere" (Vayikra 19:3) "My son, heed the discipline of your father, and do not forsake the instruction of your mother" (Mishlei 1:8)*, and *"A son will honor his father, and a servant his master" (Malachi 1:6)*. [A son is required to honor his father] even though the father is driven by a natural impulse to be kind to him and is only acting as an agent passing on God's goodness to his son.

A master is kind to his servant in order to increase his own wealth; for he needs the servant's services. Thus he has only his self-interest in mind. Nevertheless, the servant is obliged by God to serve and be grateful to his master, As it says, *"A son will honor his father, and a servant his master"* *(ibid.)*.

A rich man who acts kindly to the poor, in order to earn a heavenly reward, is like a merchant looking forward to reaping a huge profit in the future on the basis of a trivial investment. The rich man is investing for his soul in the World to Come by giving a paltry amount to the poor from the wealth God entrusted to him for the purpose of helping the deserving. And yet, it is universally accepted that a poor man is expected to thank and praise the rich man, although the rich man has in mind the glory of his soul in the hereafter. As it says, *"The blessings of the forlorn would come to me"* (*Iyov 29:13*) and, *"Did I ever see a forlorn person without a garment, or was there ever a destitute person without clothing, whose loins would not bless me when he warmed himself by the shearings of my sheep?"* (*Iyov 31:20*).

Those who show kindness to each other for honor, praise or financial reward, are like a person who deposits an object or money with a friend [for him to use], because he thinks that his investments are more secure under his friend's management. Although the person who did the favor had only his own interest in mind, as we mentioned, still he deserves to be thanked and praised, as the wise Shlomoh said, *"Many court the presence of a patron, and all befriend a man with gifts"* (*Mishlei 19:6*), and, *"A man's gift broadens access for him and leads him before the great"* (*ibid. 18:16*).

One who acts kindly to the underprivileged because his heart goes out to them, is really acting for himself, trying to soften the pain he feels because of his compassion. He is like a person who is trying to relieve a pain that was inflicted on him, with that which God in His goodness gave him. Nevertheless, he should be praised, as Iyov said, *"Did I ever see a forlorn person without a garment, or was there ever a destitute person without clothing, whose loins would not bless me, who would not warm himself from the shearings of my sheep?"* (*Iyov 31:19*).

Although a person acts kindly toward others primarily for selfish reasons—to be rewarded either in this world or the next, to soothe his pain, or to insure his investments—he is still entitled to praise, gratitude, love, respect and reward. This is despite the fact that he did the favor with property on loan to him [from God] and was compelled by his deep rooted nature.

When we consider that people are not kind and generous all the time, and their piety is tainted with self-interest or a wish to avoid harm, we realize how great is our obligation to serve, praise and thank God, Who created the good and the people who dispense the good, Whose goodness is infinite, continuous and never-ending, and Who doesn't give for selfish reasons or out of a wish to avoid harm, but as a gift and an act of kindness to all mankind.

Every person who is kind to his neighbor in any of the ways we have mentioned is only superior to him on the surface [in that he is wealthier or more learned than his neighbor], but in their humanity and their essence they are quite similar. In fact, they closely resemble each other in physique, figure, anatomy, nature, and disposition, and they fall victim to the same diseases and accidents. Yet, the one who receives the favor is expected to perform service to his benefactor.

Were the one who received the favor physically decrepit, then he is even more indebted to his benefactor. And if the benefactor was more perfect than anyone, and the recipient of the favor was more impaired than anyone, common sense tells you that the recipient's indebtedness is infinitely greater.

Taking this analogy one step further, we find that the Creator is exalted above everything that exists in the universe, and above anything that can be perceived by the senses or the mind, as we explained in the First Gate of this work. At the same time, if we compare man to the rest of the animal kingdom, we find man to be the most inferior and the weakest of all creatures, in three aspects:

One: In terms of early development, the young of other creatures are stronger, more able to endure pain, and better able to care for themselves without bothering their parents than humans.

Two: In terms of the filth of his body, it is noticeable when a human has not washed for a few days, [whereas animals stay clean even when they do not wash]. Also, the odor emitted by a human corpse is more offensive than that of a dead animal, and human feces and other waste matter are more loathsome than the excrements of animals.

Three: If a human suffers a head injury, and loses his power to speak and think—the faculties by which God made him superior to the other creatures—he becomes more foolish and corrupt than they, to the point that he is liable to harm himself or commit suicide. Furthermore most animals know instinctively what is good for them, and how to find food, which cannot be said of many a learned man, much less of a person who cannot think straight.

One who is firmly convinced of God's magnificence, His awesome power, wisdom, and absolute sovereignty, should set these glorious Divine attributes against man's weakness and inadequacy—how he never reaches perfection, how manifold his basic needs are [like food, clothing, and the like], and how incapable he is of satisfying them. He will realize that God intentionally created man with deficiencies, lacking the ways and means to survive, which he can obtain only by arduous labor. He was created with these inadequacies because God has compassion on him and wants him to reflect on his [helpless] condition [and thereby recognize God's kindness toward him]. As a result, he will commit himself to serving God, so that he will be rewarded in the World to Come; the purpose for which he was created in the first place. We already explained in [the Gate of Reflection], the Second Gate of this book, a person's obligation to praise and thank God constantly for all He has done.

Should some fool argue against our obligations to the Creator, let him reflect and delve into the matter, and he will admit the truth. The sleeper will awake, the negligent will be aroused, the fool will discern, and the thinker will come to understand clearly that it is our duty to serve God, based on the clarity of our proofs, the Scriptural substantiations we cite, and the truth of the miracles [that God performed for our ancestors at the Exodus and the Giving of the Torah]. As Moshe Rabbeinu said to those who neglected to take upon themselves to serve God, *"Is this the way you repay God, you ungrateful, unwise nation?" (Devarim 32:6).*

Man's obligation to commit himself to serving God in view of His unceasing goodness to him is hereby established.

We will now explain ten points pertaining to the theme of this Gate:

ONE: Awareness of the obligation to serve God and its particulars.

TWO: The necessity to be encouraged through both reason and the Torah.

THREE: The definition of Divine service, its various aspects and stages.

FOUR: The system of encouragement through the Torah; and the various levels people attain in Torah knowledge and comprehension.

FIVE: The system of encouragement by one's intellect, in question-and-answer form.

SIX: The Divine service that matches the favors received, and their subdivisions.

SEVEN: The minimum service to God.

EIGHT: The difference of opinion among the thinkers regarding the question of Divine compulsion and free will.

NINE: A brief discussion of the mystery of the creation of man

TEN: Using our character traits appropriately.

CHAPTER ONE

ENCOURAGING PEOPLE TO SERVE GOD AND THE WAYS TO DO IT

———◄◉►———

It is necessary to encourage people to serve God, because though you are obligated to serve God with your intellect and recognition, a long time goes by from the time [you are born when] you first benefitted from God's kindness to the time you are old enough to understand that you are obligated to repay Him by serving Him. Therefore you must be encouraged in your young years to do good deeds and to believe with perfect faith, otherwise you will be without faith until you are mature enough to think for yourself [and discover what your obligation is].

There are two kinds of encouragement. One is based on reason and is implanted in our minds from birth. The other is acquired from tradition, by studying the Torah that Moshe brought down, which teaches man how to serve God.

CHAPTER TWO

THE NEED FOR ENCOURAGEMENT THROUGH REASON AND TORAH

———❖———

We need both kinds of encouragement, because encouragement based on reason alone has three drawbacks and needs to be buttressed with Torah-based encouragement.

The first drawback, is that man was created with two components which are constantly at odds with each other—his soul and his body.

God implanted in man certain traits that arouse an appetite for things that fortify his body and give him the strength to procreate, so that the human race can exist. All living things have this desire for physical gratification. But God also introduced wisdom to man, which, when properly used, causes him to aspire to remove himself from this world. His physical desire has a head start, being within him from earliest childhood. This is an intense craving to which the child gets accustomed. The desire for sensual pleasure is stronger than his other faculties, including the intellect which, by the way, is the purpose of man's existence. Those sensual desires dim his eyes, and make his noble character traits gradually fade away. Therefore he needs outside help to overcome this deplorable lust for physical pleasure, and to stimulate his most noble quality, his power to think. The Torah is this outside help, which God presented through the prophets and His other messengers, teaching man how to serve Him.

The second drawback is, that the mind is ethereal and spiritual, emanating from the immaterial world above, and a stranger to this crass material world. Physical desires, on the other hand, are composed of both your natural instincts and a fusion of the basic elements [of fire and air, water and earth]. They are rooted in this world and are at home here. The food you eat energizes your desires, and physical gratification invigorates them. But the mind is a stranger in the physical world, with nothing there to support it. On the contrary, the whole physical world is arrayed against it. It is only natural that the mind becomes weakened and needs something to shake off the bonds of physical desire.

The Torah is the cure for this illness, which is, a disease of the soul and a sickness of his ethical character. This is why the Torah forbids certain foods, clothing, sexual relations, [illegal] acquisition of property, and actions that arouse our physical desire. This is also why the Torah commands us to do things that counteract physical desire, like prayer, fasting, charity, and kindness—to bolster the mind and to light up your life in this world and the World to Come. As David said, *"Your word is a lamp for my feet, and a light for my path" (Tehillim 119:105)*, *"For a commandment is a lamp, and the Torah is light" (Mishlei 6:23)*, and, *"And I perceived that wisdom excels folly as light excels darkness" (Koheles 2:13)*.

The third drawback is predicated on the fact that we indulge our desires while nourishing our body. We do this all the time, night and day, without letup, while we use our mind only now and then, when we want to restrain our desires. We know that the more often a limb or muscle is used, the stronger it becomes, and the less it is used, the weaker it gets. It follows that our physical desires become stronger because they are indulged all the time, while our minds become weaker because we seldom use them.

Therefore Torah was brought into our lives. It does not call for the involvement of our physical organs or our carnal desires, rather it uses our mind which is removed from desire. When your mind is engrossed in Torah study it becomes keen, pure and bright; it expels the shallowness that plagues your soul, ridding you of the ignorance that prevents you from seeing things in their true light and with the proper outlook. As it says, *"The Torah of Hashem is perfect, restoring the soul; the testimony of Hashem is trustworthy, making the simple one wise; the orders of Hashem are upright, gladdening the heart; the command of Hashem is clear, enlightening the eyes" (Tehillim 19:8,9).*

To summarize: It is our duty to encourage man to serve God by doing the mitzvos of the Torah—both the mitzvos we can understand and those we cannot understand—so that he reaches the point where he recognizes by his own reasoning that he must love God and be in awe of Him, for that is the purpose God created mankind.

CHAPTER THREE

THE DEFINITION OF DIVINE SERVICE

———— ◈ ————

S ervice means the submissive attitude a person who received a favor displays toward his benefactor by trying to return the favor to the best of his ability. There are two types of submission: one is prompted by fear of punishment and hope for reward; the other stems from an inner sense of duty that tells one to be submissive toward He who deserves to be exalted and praised.

The first kind of submissiveness to God is inspired by the Torah concept of reward and punishment in this world and the World to Come. The second kind, however, springs from a natural impulse that is ingrained in man from the moment his soul is joined with his body.

Both kinds of submission are commendable and lead to bliss in the World to Come. But submission induced by fear of punishment and hope of reward acquired from the Torah is a preparation and a stepping stone toward the second and higher kind of submission. This submission based on logical proofs, brings one closer to God and is more desirable for seven reasons:

THE ADVANTAGES OF SERVICE BASED ON REASON

One: When a person serves God because the Torah dictates it, he may do so sincerely for the sake of Heaven, or because his service is motivated by expectation of reward or fear of punishment, or he may serve Him in order to gain respect. But the service of God that is brought on by rational reasoning is devoted entirely to God, untarnished by hypocrisy, fraud, or self-importance. It is not based on the expectation of reward or fear of punishment, but on wisdom and the recognition of the fact that it is a person's duty to serve God.

Two: Since service of God based on the Torah command involves the expectation of reward or the fear of punishment, [a person will not serve God with single-minded dedication]. But service that stems from intellectual recognition of the duty to serve God, is offered in a spirit of total devotion and with fervent desire to worship God. The soul willingly serves God passionately when it understands that it will get back more [in spiritual elevation] than it gave, and that this pleases God.

Three: Although more good deeds are performed with the limbs through service based on the Torah command than service that springs from the heart, if a person serves God out of intellectual recognition, the ethical mitzvos he performs with his heart— namely the duties of the heart—outnumber many times the mitzvos he performs with his limbs.

Four: The service of God that is based on the Torah command is a starting point that leads to the service that comes from intellectual recognition. Intellectual recognition is like a seed, Torah observance is like tilling, plowing, and clearing the ground, and help from God is like rain that waters the ground, causing the seed eventually to produce fruit. So too, the aim of Torah-inspired service of God is to make service of the heart take root and grow into service of God, not for the sake of reward or for fear of punishment, but for His sake only. As our Sages warned us, *"Don't be like servants who serve their master for the sake of reward . . . and let the awe of Heaven be upon you" (Avos 1:3).*

Five: There are only a limited number of mitzvos, six hundred and thirteen in all, whereas the mitzvos of the intellect are almost infinite in number, for each day you discover more and more of them. The better you understand how good God is and how majestic is His dominion, the more humble and submissive you become. That is why David pleaded with God to prod him to do the duties of the heart, and to lift the veil of ignorance from his eyes. As it says, *"Unveil my eyes that I may perceive wonders from Your Torah" (Tehillim 119:18)*, *"Lead me on the path of Your commandments. Incline my heart toward Your testimonies" (ibid. v. 35,36)*. It says also, *"To every goal I have seen an end, but Your commandment is exceedingly broad" (ibid. v. 96)*, which means that we are obliged to serve God constantly because He showers goodness on us without end.

The story is told of certain ascetics who repented all their lives, because, as they gained new insight into God's greatness each day, they realized how imperfect their service had been in the past. As David put it, *"Day following day brings expressions of praise, and night following night bespeaks wisdom" (ibid. 19:3)*, *"My eyes shed streams of water, because they did not keep Your mitzvos" (ibid. 119:136)*.

Six: Service decreed by the Torah is easy to do and is accessible to anyone who wants to explore it. But service that stems from intellectual reasoning comes to a person only after a great deal of effort and only with the help of God, since the human mind by itself is unable to grasp it. That's why you find David continuously pleading with God in *Tehillim 119* to help him to attain it.

Seven: If you serve God only because the Torah says so, you cannot be sure that you will not stumble, because your lustful impulses are laying in ambush, waiting for the moment you become lax. But when your service is based on your own understanding, you can be sure that you will not stumble or go astray, for the soul is drawn to this service only after you have subdued your physical desires with the powers of your mind, which then uses them as it wishes. When you serve God out of inner conviction, you are assured not to stumble, and you are protected from error, as it says, *"No harm befalls the righteous" (Mishlei 12:21)*.

THE ADVANTAGES OF TORAH-INDUCED SERVICE

There are also seven reasons why inducement through Torah is necessary.

One: Since you are a blend of body and soul, you have conflicting traits. Sometimes you give in to your physical impulses, yielding to your sensual desires, and disconnecting yourself from sound reason. Then again, as a result of adversity, misfortune and misery, you may lean toward the higher world of the spirit, turning your back on the fleeting values of the material world.

Neither of these choices is desirable. Total commitment to the spiritual sphere would lead to chaos in the world, while unrestrained pursuit of physical pleasure would destroy mankind in this world and the next. So, in His compassion and great kindness the Creator showed man the way toward happiness and well-being in this world and the next. It is a way of life that follows the middle road between reason and desire. It is the teaching of the unfailing Torah. It fosters justice in public and private life, curbs your desires in this world, and safeguards your reward in the World to Come. As it says, *"Incline your ears and listen to the words of the wise, and set your heart to My knowledge. For it is pleasant if you guard them in your innards and establish all of them on your lips. Let your trust remain with Hashem; I have made this known to you today. Surely I have written for you [in the Torah] extremely noble things, with counsel and knowledge to teach you the veracity of true words, so that you may answer words of truth to those who send word to you"* (Mishlei 22:17-21).

Two: The intellectual urge to serve God does not in itself put you under the obligation to pray, fast, give charity and tithes, and be benevolent. Neither does it give you specific guidelines as to where, when and how to do these things and what is the punishment for failing to do them properly. There is a need for the standards and rules set by the Torah and the teachings of the prophets. Thanks to them we are able to accomplish what we must, in the service of God. As it says, *"God has made [the world] so that man should be in awe of Him"* (Koheles 3:14).

Three: Not everyone can convince himself intellectually to serve God. Some people are not as bright as others. But Torah-inspired service applies equally to all who are commanded to serve God, although some may understand it better than others, as we explained at the end of the First Gate.

A person who serves God out of intellectual conviction may do too little in some aspects and too much in other aspects, and his frame of mind may be affected by varying conditions [like health, distress or old age]. But Torah-inspired service never changes. It is the same for the child, the young adult, the elderly, the aged, the scholar and the fool, although the fervor and seriousness with which each of these groups perform a mitzvah may vary according to their level of understanding. The Torah says that its teaching applies to the entire people, stating, *"Gather together the people—the men, the women, and the small children, and your stranger who is in your cities, so that they will hear and so that they will learn" (Devarim 31:12)*, and, *"You shall read the Torah before all Israel, in their ears" (ibid. v. 11)*.

Four: Everyone agrees that your service to God should be in keeping with the amount of good God bestows on you. And everyone recognizes that in every generation there are times when a certain nation is singled out to receive more of God's goodness than any other nation. This nation, in turn, must stand out by offering greater service to God than any other nation. But we could never calculate by ourselves the great good God bestowed on us. We could never figure out on our own that God chose us by bringing us out of the land of Egypt, by dividing the Red Sea, and by doing other favors so well known they need not be mentioned. We could never comprehend by our own reckoning that God singled us out from the nations so that we should thank Him for these favors, and that He assured us of a reward, in this world and the next, that is generous and good beyond description.

All this [you cannot figure out by your own reasoning]; your only source for it is the Torah. As it says, *"You saw what I did in Egypt, carrying you on eagles' wings and bringing you to Me. Now if you obey Me and keep My covenant, you shall be My special treasure among all nations, because all the world is Mine. You will be a kingdom of priests and a holy nation" (Shemos 19:4-6).*

Five: Torah-inspired service is the stepping stone and path to service based on contemplation. Youngsters need teaching and guidance to hold their physical desires in check until their mind develops and matures. So too women, and men who are frivolous cannot be guided by reason, because their mind has only a very weak hold on them. They need a moderate plan for living, one they can cope with and understand. These are the mitzvos of the Torah which are performed with the promise of reward and the fear of punishment. A person who fulfills the mitzvos of the Torah can come to the level of the truly pious and is rewarded in this world and the next.

But if you soar from this level of service to the service that is induced by contemplation, you are ranked with the prophets and God's chosen ones, the saints. Your reward in this world will be the joy of the sweetness that comes from the service of God. As the prophet said, *"As soon as Your words come to me I devour them, for me Your word was the joy and gladness of my heart, for Your Name was proclaimed upon me, O Hashem, God of Legions" (Yirmeyah 15:16); "The righteous one will rejoice in Hashem and take refuge in Him, and all who are upright in heart will be glorified" (Tehillim 64:11),* and, *"Light is sown for the righteous, joy for the upright" (ibid. 97:11).*

Your reward in the World to Come will be to perceive the heavenly light that is beyond description and beyond comparison, as it says, *"If you walk in My paths and keep My charge, and you also administer My Temple, and you will also guard My courtyards, then I will let you walk among these [angels] who stand here" (Zechariah 3:7),* and, *"How abundant is the good that You have in store for those who fear You, that You have performed for those who take refuge in You in the presence of men" (Tehillim 31:20),* and, *No eye has ever seen, O God, -except for You—what [God] has prepared for those that trust in Him" (Yeshayah 64:3).*

Six: The Torah contains laws for which there is no rational explanation, [like the mitzvos of the red heifer, *shaatnez*, dietary laws etc.] which we nonetheless obey because they were revealed to us. The Torah also contains fundamental principles which we do understand. [The Torah mentions the mitzvos, like honoring parents, loving God, being kind to others] because Torah was given to the Jewish nation at a time that they were overwhelmed by their physical desires and too weak intellectually to understand many rational concepts. So the Torah spelled out the knowable mitzvos, so that the people should observe both the knowable and the inscrutable mitzvos equally. That way the intelligent among them would accept them because they understand their reasons in addition to the fact that the Torah decreed them. And the less than bright person who does not understand the reason for the rational mitzvos will accept them because the Torah requires it and will regard them as revealed mitzvos. And so everyone serves God in the best possible way, as it says, *"Its ways are ways of pleasantness and all its paths lead to peace"* (Mishlei 3:17).

Seven: The Torah was brought to us by [Moshe Rabbeinu], a human intermediary, who performed Divine signs and wonders that were seen and experienced by all with the same clarity. Since these miracles were undeniably true, the people accepted everything that Moshe said in the name of the Creator. We also have a deep-seated intellectual urge to serve God that was ingrained in us from birth.

Once we establish through intellectual argument and Torah based fact our obligation to serve God, think about all of God's blessings you received together with the world at large, and realize that this requires you to serve God by fulfilling all obligations your intellect demands. When you reflect on the kindnesses God bestowed on you by singling out the Jewish people from among all other nations, you will be convinced that you are required to fulfill also those mitzvos of the Torah that cannot be understood, which other nations do not observe. And finally, when you reflect on how good God has been to you by singling out your tribe from among the other tribes of your people, as in the case of *kohanim* and *levi'im*, recognize that you are obliged to observe the mitzvos God gave your tribe alone. There are twenty-four mitzvos that are performed by *kohanim* in response to the twenty-four gifts the *kohanim* receive [like various parts of the sacrifices, the *terumah* gift from the grain, the first-born of an animal and the five *shekels* of *pidyon haben*].

If God singles you out to grant you special favor, serve Him in an extraordinary way, thanking Him as best you can for the exceptional favor He has bestowed on you. As a result, the favor will continue and even increase and will bring you a reward in the World to Come. Don't be like the person about whom it says, "*I lavished silver and gold on her, but they used it for the Baal*" (Hoshea 2:10).

If a person neglects the service he should render for his personal favor, he is bound to ignore his service for the favor God has shown his family, he will then disregard the service he owes for the favors God has done for his people, and in the end he will turn his back on the Torah altogether. Once he does not accept the Torah, he will not accept the mitzvos dictated by reason. And when he rejects the mitzvos dictated by reason—although he understands them and his intellect tells him to fulfill them—he is no longer a human being. Even an animal knows what is right better than he does, as it says, "*An ox knows its owner, an ass its master's crib*"; *Israel does not know, My people does not comprehend*" (Yeshayah 1:3). He will become like the person about whom it says, "*For the wicked will perish, and the foes of Hashem are like the glory of fattened sheep: Consumed! In smoke they are consumed*" (Tehillim 37:20).

CHAPTER FOUR

Torah-Inspired Service, Its Divisions, and the Various Levels People Attain in Torah Knowledge and Comprehension

———◆———

Let me begin by saying that Torah-inspired service is the revelation of God through Moshe Rabbeinu in which He made known the service He wants us to perform, and for which He rewards us in this world and in the World to Come. This reward is an expression of God's kindness, generosity and goodness, [because we do not really deserve a reward for our service, since we owe Him infinite thanks for His bounties].

Three Categories of Human Actions

The Torah divides human actions into three categories: commandments, prohibitions, and the permissible.

The commandments fall into two categories. The first involve duties of the heart, like the sincere belief in God's Oneness, being wholehearted with Him, trusting Him, being submissive to His will, accepting His decrees [with love], believing in His prophets and His Torah, being in awe of Him, keeping His commandments, contemplating His miracles, reflecting on His goodness, and many others like these, too numerous to mention.

The second category of positive mitzvos includes duties of both the heart and the limbs, such as making your tongue reflect what is in your heart, [speaking with sincerity], reading and studying the Torah, praying, fasting, giving charity, resting on Shabbos and Yom Tov, fulfilling the mitzvos of *sukkah, lulav, tzitzis,* and the like.

The prohibitions, fall into two categories as well: those of the heart and those of the limbs.

Prohibitions involving the heart include worshipping a deity other than God, hypocrisy, yearning to do things that God has forbidden, arrogance, haughtiness, having disdain for others, scoffing at the prophets and the things they say in God's Name, despising good itself or good people, enjoying the company of evil people, being envious, rejoicing in the misfortune of others, crying out against the decrees of the Creator, and the like.

Prohibitions involving our limbs include the public worship of anything other than God, taking false oaths, lying, slandering, eating prohibited food, shedding blood, and many others.

Permitted things fall into three categories: basic needs, excesses, and less than the basic needs. Basic needs include essential things you cannot do without, like food and drink, clothing, shelter, the talking you have to do to run your daily life, your activities, your business, and your physical movements. All these you should engage in as much as necessary to maintain a suitable standard of living. As it says, *"Good is the man who is gracious and lends; who conducts his affairs with justice" (Tehillim 112:5)* [—meaning he follows the golden mean between excessiveness and frugality].

The second category of permitted things involves excessive acts which go beyond a person's basic needs. It includes eating and drinking excessively, which the wise Shlomoh warned against, saying, *"Do not be among those who guzzle wine, or glut themselves on meat" (Mishlei 23:20).* It also includes dressing flamboyantly, living in overly luxurious homes, and talking too much, because you can never be sure that you will not stumble [into slander or tale-bearing]. As the wise Shlomoh said, *"Where there is much talking there is no lack of transgressing" (Mishlei 10:19).* It also includes indulging in sexual relations to excess, about which it says, *"He who keeps company with harlots will lose his wealth" (Mishlei 29:3),* and *"Do not give your strength to women" (Mishlei 31:3).* And it says about a king, *"He must not have many wives" (Devarim 17:17).* Also included are people who overwork themselves in an effort to pile up possessions and accumulate wealth, about which it says, *"Do not toil to gain wealth, have the sense to desist" (Mishlei 23:4).* And it also says about the king, *"He shall not accumulate very much gold and silver" (Devarim 17:17).*

The extravagances supposedly give you pleasure but are actually bad for you, because they eventually cause you to do things the Creator warned you against and forbade you to do.

The third category of permitted things is called "less than the basic needs" where a person does not allow himself to fulfill even his most essential needs in the way of food, drink, conversation, earning a living, and the like.

This excessive frugality can be sparked by one of two motives. It can stem from piety or from worldly concerns. If your self-denial is rooted in piety and the desire to come closer to God, then your deeds are praiseworthy and you will be rewarded. As the wise Shlomoh said, *"Wise men are drawn to a house of mourning, and fools to a house of merrymaking" (Koheles 7:4).*

But if your penny-pinching is prompted by worldly considerations, by the desire to save money [by eating less and not buying decent clothes], or in order that people should praise you for being ascetic, that is disgraceful because you have swerved from the "golden mean" and abused your body, because of your fascination with material values. As a wise man once said, "Whoever abstains from the world because he loves the world is like one who tries to put out a fire with straw."

However curtailing your speech and sleep is inherently praise-worthy. It is good to curtail your speech because silence is good, as the wise Shlomoh said, *"Keep your mouth from being rash, and let not your heart be quick to utter a word before God; for God is in heaven, and you are on earth, that is why your words should be few" (Koheles 5:1).* It is also good to curtail your sleep, as it says, *"A bit more sleep, a bit more slumber, a bit more hugging yourself in bed,*

and poverty will come calling on you, and want, like an armed man"
(Mishlei 6:10,11).

It follows that all human activity, is either a command, a prohibition, or one that meets basic needs. Any deed that goes beyond the bounds of meeting a basic need—a deed that is either much more or much less than what is reasonably needed for survival—must necessarily be either a mitzvah, if it is done for the sake of Heaven, or a transgression, if it is not done for the sake of Heaven.

Exploring basic needs, we discover that earning a living can be considered a mitzvah. For it says in the story of Creation, *"God blessed them and God said to them, 'Be fruitful and multiply. Fill the land and conquer it'"* (Bereishis 1:28), which is followed by, *"God said, 'Behold, I have given you every seed bearing plant on the face of the earth . . . it shall be to you for food"* (ibid. v. 29). [Just as "be fruitful and multiply" is a command, so too,] earning a living to put food on the table is a command.

It is clear that all human activity must necessarily be either a mitzvah or a transgression. When someone does something, he is commanded to do, he is doing a good thing, and if he refrains from doing that same thing, he is remiss in his duty. If someone does something that is prohibited, he sins, while if he refrains, he is righteous, provided he refrains out of fear of God. As it says, *"Those who refrain from doing wrong are following in His ways"* (Tehillim 119:3) [the Redak explains: the fact that they have refrained from wrong is considered as if they had performed a mitzvah.] If someone does something that is permitted [but not a mitzvah] in the right and proper spirit, he is considered righteous too. As it says, *"Good is the man who is gracious and lends; he is gracious, compassionate and righteous"* (ibid. 112:5). If he oversteps the limits of his basic needs, [and lives lavishly,] he falls short, because he will end up doing things God has prohibited. If he denies himself necessities, although they are available to him, with the intention of training himself in the service of God or of controlling his desires in order to become closer to God, or to focus his thoughts on the World to Come, he is considered righteous, and is acting admirably. If he does not do this for the sake of Heaven, [but in order to gain fame or to save money,] then he falls short, and his conduct is deplorable.

All human actions are either good or bad. An intelligent person evaluates his actions in that light and weighs them before doing anything, selecting the good and discarding the others. As David said, *"I have considered my ways and returned to Your testimonies; I have hurried and not delayed to keep Your commandments"* *(Tehillim 119:59,60)*.

Furthermore the wise Shlomoh said, *"For God will judge every deed—even everything hidden—be it good or bad"* *(Koheles 12:14)*. Shlomoh puts down all human activities as either good or bad, which amounts to the same as our characterizations of "admirable" and "deplorable." We have amply explained that all human actions are either included in the commandments or prohibitions of the Torah.

TEN EDUCATIONAL LEVELS OF TORAH STUDENTS

The Torah is composed of words and subject matter which can be understood on ten levels.

The first level is comprised of people who study *Chumash* [the Five Books of the Torah] and are satisfied with merely reading the text without understanding it. They know neither the meaning of the words nor their correct pronunciation; they are like a donkey carrying a stack of books.

The second level is composed of people who concentrate on pronouncing the words correctly, and placing the accents on the proper syllables. They are students of punctuation and the *Masoretic* text.

The third level are people who recognize that the previous two levels are not enough. They learn the rules of vocalization and the cantillation marks [*trop, neginos*]. They also learn the conjugation of the words and the rules of grammar that govern nouns, verbs, conjunctions, absolute and construct forms of nouns, the use of the future tense to express the past, the use of an infinitive to express an imperative, complete and defective verbs, letters that are pronounced and letters that are mute, verbs with double letters, and the like.

The fourth level comprises people who explain the difficult words in *Tanach* according to the plain meaning of the text, and who determine which phrases are to be taken figuratively and which are meant literally. They research all synonyms and antonyms, words that are derived from other roots and those that are not, irregular verbs and nouns, adjectives and adverbs and the like.

The fifth level covers people who try to grasp the underlying themes of the Torah, understanding them in depth. They determine which phrases are metaphors, like the expressions that ascribe human qualities to God [such as "God saw, heard, spoke, dwells," "the mouth, the eyes, the hand of God"], and which are meant literally. They are the ones who explain the Scriptures according to their literal sense, but do not pay attention to traditional interpretations of the Sages.

The sixth level is composed of people who rely on the teachings of the Rabbis as expounded in the *Mishnah*, and who know some of the Torah obligations, commandments and laws, but they do not explore the Talmud [to learn the details and ramifications of the mitzvos].

The seventh level embraces people who recite the *Talmud* and read its decisions, but do not attempt to solve any Talmudic questions or unravel any of its complexities.

The eighth level is composed of people who make every effort to understand the statements of the Talmudic Sages, to clear up all doubts and find solutions to all difficulties. But they do so for fame and glory. They overlook the duties of the heart, and turn a blind eye to the things that undermine their proper conduct. They waste their time thinking up farfetched theoretical legal cases and deriving irrelevant, outlandish rulings from established legal decisions. They recall all the legal disagreements of the Sages, but they disregard matters of the soul upon which they are required to reflect.

They also ignore the fact that the Creator requires us to discover by ourselves logical proofs of His existence, to serve Him wholeheartedly and to do all the things we can understand intellectually which I will explain in this Gate.

The ninth level comprises people who do their utmost to know the duties of the heart and the limbs, as well as the things that hold us back from doing the right thing. They understand both the literal and mystical meaning of the Torah. They prove from Scriptural verses and through reason that the Oral Torah is true. After understanding the Torah's underlying principles, they arrange the laws, classifying the physical mitzvos according to when and where they should be observed. They are conscientious in fulfilling the mitzvos and urge others to do the same. They act truthfully, both in private and in public, following the truth, no matter what the outcome might be. The people who reached this level are the Sages of the Talmud, the *Geonim[1]*, and those who followed in their footsteps.

The tenth level is composed of people who inherited the wisdom of the Torah along with its interpretations and the inferences that should be drawn from its laws from the prophets. They include the Men of the Great Assembly[2] and those who received the tradition from them, namely the *Tannaim* who are the Sages of the Mishnah and Baraisa.

It states in *maseches Avos*, "Moshe received the Torah from Sinai and handed it down to Yehoshua; Yehoshua to the Elders; the Elders to the Prophets; and the Prophets handed it down to the Men of the Great Assembly."

The Men of the Great Assembly handed it down to Shimon Hatzaddik; Shimon Hatzaddik handed it down to Antigonus;

[1.] The *Geonim* are the Sages who lived after the close of the Talmudic period and who headed the yeshivos in Sura and Pumbedisa. The Era of the *Geonim* lasted from the end of the sixth to the middle of the eleventh century.

[2.] The Men of the Great Assembly (*Anshei Kenesses Hagedolah*) were the supreme legal authority in Eretz Yisrael after the return from the Babylonian exile under Ezra and Nechemiah.

Antigonus handed it down to Yose ben Yoezer and Yose ben
Yochanan of Yerushalayim; they handed it down to Yehoshua ben
Perachya and Nittai from Arbel, who handed it down to Yehudah
ben Tabbai and Shimon ben Shetach, and they handed it down to
Shemaya and Avtalyon, and from them it was handed down to
Shammai and Hillel.

It was then handed down to Rabbi Yochanan ben Zakkai, from
whom it was handed down to Rabbi Eliezer, Rabbi Yehoshua,
Rabbi Gamliel, Rabbi Eliezer ben Arach, Rabbi Yose Hakohen, and
Rabbi Shimon ben Nesanel. From them it was handed down to
Rabbi Akiva, Rabbi Elazar ben Azariah, Rabbi Tarfon, and Rabbi
Shimon ben Gamliel. From them it was handed down to Rabbi
Meir, Rabbi Yehudah, Rabbi Yose, Rabbi Shimon, and to Rabbi
Yehudah Hanasi, also known as Rabbeinu Hakadosh. It was he
who compiled the Mishnah, putting the Mishnayos in order, di-
viding them into chapters, and collecting them into tractates. The
Mishnah is a summary of the tradition we depend on [in interpret-
ing the laws of] our Torah.

Ten Reasons Why People Believe

There are ten level of people in regard to belief in the Torah and
why one serves God.

The first and lowest level are people who are attracted to foolishness and are overpowered by their desires, causing them to de-
spise the Torah. They consider the Torah a collection of senseless
tribal rituals like those of other nations and a set of customs designed to keep a tight rein on dimwitted people.

They think this way because their reason is overpowered by their
desires, and because they are coarse by nature. They don't accept
the yoke of Torah and aren't convinced by logic, because they want
to lead an unrestrained, wanton life. Shlomoh said about such people, *"The fool does not desire understanding; he wants to follow only
the impulse of his heart (Mishlei 18:2).*

The second level are people who do not deny the signs and miracles that were performed by the prophets, but doubt the authenticity of the Torah. Their ideas are similar to those of the previous level. They say that God wanted people to live a well-regulated and harmonious life, and therefore he encouraged prophets to guide them with ideas the prophet himself thought would do them good. God enabled the prophet to perform signs and miracles so that people would listen to him and accept his statutes. They do not believe in reward and punishment [for keeping the laws of the Torah].

At this point I will briefly respond to these views, by demonstrating the impossibility of their belief and by showing that, even assuming they were right, [and the laws of the Torah were the prophets own ideas], they are still obligated to observe the entire Torah, [and believe that there is Divine reward and punishment].

Their belief is impossible because the Creator is too exalted to change the laws of nature [and perform a miracle] for the sake of a self-styled "prophet" who would lie about God and say things in His name He never said—even if this impostor intended to direct the people to God with his lies. [Therefore, if they believe God performed miracles on behalf of a prophet, they must also accept his claim that it was God Who revealed to him the laws he was now giving to the people]. After all, it is no more miraculous for God to show a vision to a true prophet than to change the laws of nature [and perform a miracle].

Even could they clearly prove their belief [that the prophet made the laws of the Torah], it would still be logical to follow all the laws of the Torah. For God surely would not change the laws of nature or perform wonders through someone who does not recognize the right path. In addition, the person the Creator chose to teach us the right path and to guide us is worthy of our reliance. After all, we are required to rely on a king or ruler, as it says, *"Fear Hashem, my child, and the king" (Mishlei 24:21),* surely we have to rely on someone chosen by God through a sign.

Either way, the people who hold this belief are obliged to accept the Torah. The wise Shlomoh said about such people, *"O simple ones, learn to be clever! O fools, instruct your minds!" (Mishlei 8:5).*

The third level are people who are convinced of the truth of the Torah, but who believe that the Torah was given to us as a favor from God to refine our character and give us guidance in this world—not for reward and punishment in the World to Come. Because the Books of the Prophets speak very often about reward and punishment in this world, but do not mention reward and punishment in the World to Come, they make this mistake.

Rabbi Saadya Gaon proves the fallacy of this line of thinking in his commentary on *parashas Bechukosai (Vayikra 26:3)*. In fact, there are many clear indications of reward and punishment in the World to Come. For example, it says, *"For God will judge every deed—even everything hidden—whether good or evil" (Koheles 12:14); "And you will trample the wicked to a pulp, for they will be ashes under the soles of your feet on that day that I will bring about" (Malachi 3:21); "And you will come to see the difference between the righteous and the wicked, between him who serves God and him who does not serve Him" (ibid. 3:18); "They will go out and see the corpses of the men who rebelled against Me: their worms will not die, and their fire will not be extinguished, and they will be a horror to all mankind" (Yeshayah 66:24); "How abundant is the good that You have in store for those who fear You, that You have performed for those who take refuge in You" (Tehillim 31:20); "I will permit you to move among these [angels] who stand here" (Zechariah 3:7); "No eye had ever seen a god—except for You—that acted for those who trust in Him" (Yeshayah 64:3); "Many of those who sleep in the dust of the earth will awaken, some to eternal life, others to shame, to everlasting abhorrence" (Daniel 12:2);* and, *"Your righteous deeds will precede you, and the glory of Hashem will gather you in" (Yeshayah 58:8).* There are many more such verses, too numerous to mention.

The fourth level are people who firmly believe in the validity of the Torah and the truth of reward and punishment in the World to Come, but who have a taste for worldly delights.

They use the service of God as bait to capture material gains, [acting and dressing like deeply devout men, so that people will honor them, do favors for them and support them (*Marpe*

Lanefesh)]. They accept the Torah outwardly but not inwardly, with their tongues rather than with their hearts. It says about such people, *"With his mouth he speaks peace with his fellow, but in his heart he lies in ambush for him" (Yirmeyah 9:7)*; *"They honor me with their mouths and with their lips while their heart is far from Me" (Yeshayah 29:13).*

The fifth level comprises people who firmly believe in the validity of the Torah and the truth of reward and punishment in the World to Come, but they desire worldly pleasures. They accept the Torah and expect to receive a reward from God as well as honor and adulation in this world. This attitude comes under the heading of hypocrisy, and is a kind of hidden idolatry [because they are not serving God, rather they are serving themselves to receive reward].

The sixth level is composed of people who expect to receive a reward from the Creator in this world alone because they love the world and its delights, and do not understand the reward and the bliss of the World to Come.

The seventh level consists of people who firmly believe in all the above, but who expect to be rewarded for their service to God in this world and in the World to Come. They do not know what it means to serve God unselfishly, for His sake alone; or how to pay homage to Him, by glorifying and exalting Him in a fitting way. Our Sages had such people in mind when they warned, "Be not like servants who serve their master for the sake of receiving a reward; instead be like servants who serve their master not for the sake of receiving a reward. And let the awe of Heaven be upon you" (Avos 1:3).

The eighth level is composed of people who firmly believe in all the above, but who serve God because they are afraid that He will punish them in this world and the next [if they fail to serve Him]. We have already explained how deplorable these last two views are.

The ninth level embraces people who believe in the Torah and in reward and punishment in both worlds, who serve God for His sake alone in a way that befits him, but who are not on guard against things that stand in the way of this service [like pride and haughtiness]. As a result, the *yetzer hara* sneaks in, and they do not know where it came from. As it says, *"Dead flies putrefy the per-fumer's oil; a little folly outweighs wisdom and honor"* (Koheles 10:1). *"A single error destroys a great deal of good"* (ibid. 9:18).

A pious man once said to his disciples, "Were you free of sin, I would be afraid you would stumble over something worse than sin." His disciples asked, "But what can be worse than sin?" Replied the pious man, "Haughtiness and pride," as it says, *"Every haughty person is an abomination to Hashem"* (Mishlei 16:5).

The tenth level consists of people who firmly believe in the truth of Torah and in the principle of divine reward and punishment in both worlds. They are vigilant not to be negligent, and are always aware of how grateful they should be to the Creator for His great goodness and kindness, without regard to reward or punishment. They are eager to serve God for His sake alone, to exalt and praise Him because they know Him and recognize His magnificence.

This is the loftiest level for a Torah-observant Jew. It is the level attained by the prophets and the pious ones who committed themselves completely to God, made a covenant with Him [to be faithful to Him forever], tried to get close to Him, depended upon Him, dedicated their lives and the lives of their children as well as their possessions to Him, and who faithfully fulfilled all they took upon themselves. Scripture says about them, *"Bring in My devout ones, who made a covenant with Me over sacrifice"* (Tehillim 50:5).

We have set forth in this chapter the essence of Torah-inspired service, the various levels people attain in studying its wisdom, as well as the character traits of the various kinds of believers. There may well be grades and classes of students of Torah wisdom we have not mentioned, but we discussed the groups that are prevalent among the majority of our people.

Our exposition is very helpful for anyone searching for the correct path. After identifying the level he is closest to, he will be able to recognize the level above it and try to reach that higher level. He will also see the gap between his level and the ultimate level, and it will be easier for him to rise toward it step by step.

CHAPTER FIVE

THE SYSTEM OF ENCOURAGEMENT BY ONE'S INTELLECT IN QUESTION-AND-ANSWER FORM

——=◆=——

At this point it is fit to explain the system of encouragement by one's intellect in question-and-answer form. This is the best format to explain the subject at hand and I will continue with it until the end of this Gate.

Self-encouragement is actually God reminding you through your intellect to know God and to recognize the signs of His wisdom [that are evident in creation]. This reminder comes to you only after making the Torah the light of your path, and reaching intellectual maturity. You must be able to think clearly, yearning to fulfill His will, to rise to the level of the pious, and turn your thoughts away from worldly worries.

In order to achieve intellectual self-encouragement one must be fully aware of the values God has etched into the human mind. These include admiration for truth and contempt of lying, a preference for righteousness and an aversion to injustice, paying back with goodness and gratitude to those who do good, and retaliating against the wicked with evil and scorn; living on peaceful terms with everyone, and acting kindly to them; making the praise fit the good deed, the reward fit the righteous act, the punishment fit the crime; and forgiving offenders when they sincerely repent. Once you clearly understand these ideas, your mind will reach maturity, and your discernment will be sharp. If God is good to you and awakens in you the desire to serve Him, appreciate His favors. When you try to count His favors and grasp their magnitude you will find that you cannot do so, because they are so all-embracing, numerous, continuous and oft-repeated.

You will want to repay God for all the good He has done for you just as anyone wants to repay his benefactor. But when you realize that you cannot repay Him [because God's kindness is infinite], and that God does not need your favors in the first place, you feel humble, lowly and pitiful. Then if you ask yourself, "What can I do to draw closer to God as a token of gratitude for all His kindness?", your mind will show you the way.

DIALOGUE BETWEEN THE MIND AND THE SOUL

THE MIND: Is it clear to you that you owe thanks to your Creator for all His goodness, and that you belong to Him because of His many kindnesses and favors?

THE SOUL: Yes, it is clear.

THE MIND: Do you plan to repay the Creator in any way?

THE SOUL: Yes, I do.

THE MIND: How can you, if your longing for Him is so weak? Only someone who truly longs for health can tolerate bitter medicine; those who don't, refuse to take foul-tasting medication.

THE SOUL: My yearning is strong, and I am anxious to repay God as best I can. Please, keep prodding me, [and show me how I can repay Him].

THE MIND: If what you say is true, the medication may yet work for you. But if it is not true, you are only harming yourself. For a patient who lies to his doctor is deceiving himself. He wastes the doctor's time, and his sickness will get worse.

THE SOUL: How do I know whether my longing [to come closer to God] is real or not?

THE MIND: If your longing for God stems from a clear realization of your obligation to repay Him and your inability to fulfill it; if you recognize that failure to repay Him will be your undoing, and your efforts to repay Him will save you from punishment and bring you everlasting life, then your longing is real. If not, it is false.

THE SOUL: My desire had been weak and my longing a sham, because I was convinced to serve God from what I saw of past events, [how the righteous were rewarded and the wicked were punished], and I saw the truth through Torah. But then it came clear to me through my own reasoning. It was then that my longing [to come closer to God] became genuine and my desire [to show my gratitude to Him] became sincere.

THE REMEDY FOR THE SOUL

THE MIND: If what you say is true, give up the harmful food you are used to eating, and prepare to suffer the bitter taste of the medicine.

THE SOUL: What is the bad food you speak of?

THE MIND: It is the shameful character trait that has taken hold of you, and the inner forces that have nurtured this trait ever since your childhood.

THE SOUL: What is that character trait, and what are the inner forces that nurture it?

THE MIND: You have many vices, which are the result of two basic problems. The first is the love of pleasure you derive from eating, drinking, marital relations, and other bodily functions, which you acquired from your bad neighbor, the body. The second is love of power over others, arrogance, and jealousy, all of which tempt you to cut back on repaying the debt you owe your Benefactor. You acquired this quality from others while growing up.

THE SOUL: From what should I stay away from?

THE MIND: Overindulgence in drinking, dressing, sleeping, resting, relaxing, and the like, foster the first vice. Excessive socializing, currying favor, wanting praise, jealousy of the worldly possessions of others, pressuring others to turn their possessions over to you, having contempt for others, calling attention to others faults, and the like, foster the second vice.

Stay away from these bad qualities and you can reach the next stage on your way to recovery.

THE SOUL: It is hard to give up accustomed vices. Please teach me an easy way to get rid of them.

THE MIND: Any thinking person would gladly remove a limb that was spreading disease to other limbs. He realizes that he must choose the pain of surgery over death. You are in the same position. Weigh the benefits you accrue from your vices against the calamity you will suffer by continuing with them. Do that, and you will find it easy to give up these disgraceful traits.

THE SOUL: How will I benefit by giving them up, and how will I be hurt by continuing with them?

THE MIND: Your benefit from giving them up, will be peace of mind and tranquility in the murky darkness of this world. In this world all pleasures are mixed with sadness, and all enjoyment is short-lived. You will become mindful that your ultimate abode is in the World to Come, and to get there you must work hard. This path is one of the gates you must pass through to be successful [in this world] and gain life [in the World to Come].

Bad qualities bring constant sorrow about your unfulfilled worldly aspirations. Even if they are fulfilled, they turn out to be empty and fleeting, bound to pass on to someone else. You will have achieved nothing lasting in this world, and you will not enter the World to Come. You surely won't be able to satisfy your worldly desires, no matter how hard you try.

THE SOUL: I understand what you are saying. I hope, that the difficult task of dropping my vices will become easier. Please take me to the next step in the healing process and teach me what I need to know about the service of God.

THE SERVICE OF GOD

THE MIND: You must submit to the authority of the One Who is above you, just as you would expect your subordinate to bow to your authority, even though the two relationships are really not comparable, [because the difference of status between you and God is infinitely greater than that between you and your subordinate]. Act toward the One Who is above you like you would expect your subordinate to act towards you.

THE SOUL: Explain that to me, please.

THE MIND: Think of the favors God has bestowed on your community and on you personally. Imagine that you did these same favors for your servant. Act toward your Creator the way you would expect your servant to act toward you; what you consider wrong for your servant to do to you, consider wrong for you to do to the Creator.

THE SOUL: Please, explain this to me in greater detail.

THE RELATIONSHIP BETWEEN SERVANT AND MASTER

THE MIND: A servant whose master bestowed on him only a fraction of the good your Creator bestowed on you, would be expected to honor his master in word and deed, to be faithful to him and to revere him in his presence. As one of the pious men put it, "Do not rebel against your master while he is watching". You would expect the servant to be submissive to his master in deed and thought, to dress and act humbly, to honor him both in words and in his heart, to praise and thank him day and night, to recount all his good deeds to himself and to others, to pay homage to him in keeping with his eminence, to hurry to serve him happily and wholeheartedly because he loves him and because he wants to please him, and come as close as possible to fulfilling his will.

You would expect the servant to plead with his master to accept him, forgive him and love him. You would expect him to be afraid of being negligent in the service of his master; to comply with his wishes, to keep away from things his master has warned him against, and not to repeat past offenses. You would expect him to regard his master's kindnesses as great and abounding, downplaying his own deeds in light of what he should have done. Realizing how lowly he is compared to his master's greatness, he would often bow down and humbly prostrate himself before him.

He would trust his master to supply his needs, and he would be satisfied with whatever situation his master puts him in. If his master feeds him lavishly, he would thank him; and if the master were to leave him hungry, he would accept that. He would never suspect his master of judging him wrongly or unfairly. Whatever his master gave him would be enough, and he would accept his master's judgment when he punishes him.

He is also expected to show that he is his master's servant—by thinking only of his master, by gazing only at him, by listening to his words only, by eating only what his master offers him, by thinking only of his master's greatness, by being happy only when his master is satisfied with him, by being glad to serve him, by wanting only to please him, by hurrying to do his bidding, by refraining from disobeying him, by sitting only in his home, by firmly believing only in him, by reading only his books, by wearing only clothing that show his reverence for him, by sleeping only in a bed of love for him, by keeping only his image in mind, by awakening only to the sweet memory of him, by only being satisfied when he is with him, by fleeing from the opportunity to oppose his will, by grieving when he is angry, by fearing his outrage, by hoping for nothing but kindness from him, by being angry only when his master wants him to be angry, by being pleased only with those who do his master's will, by taking something only when his master allows him to, and giving only to those whom his master allows. The same would go for all his other activities as well; he would not move a foot or raise an eyelid except to fulfill his master's will.

The bad traits of the servant are the opposite of these good ones; there is no need to itemize them. I have put together and arranged enough examples for you to figure out the rest.

Now that we have set forth what masters, who are seldom kind to their servants, consider good service, it should be clear to you how much more you are required to repay God for all the good He has done to you.

CHAPTER SIX

THE OBLIGATION OF DIVINE SERVICE MATCHES THE FAVORS RECEIVED

———⫸⬦⫷———

T*HE SOUL:* [You compared the service to God with the service a servant must perform for his master.] I understand what you have said, and your explanation answered my questions. In what ways must I serve God more than a servant serves his master?

THE MIND: The amount of additional service you take upon yourself depends on the favor you received personally or as part of the people collectively. In general there are four levels of favor bestowed on man.

The first is the favor God bestows on mankind as a whole, creating man out of nothing, giving him life and all the goodness we mentioned in the Gate of Reflection. Since these favors are bestowed on all mankind equally, they are all equally obligated to serve the Creator by performing all logic-based commandments [such as, not stealing, not committing murder and the like, which were] observed by Adam, Chanoch, Noach and his sons, and Iyov and his friends, until the days of Moshe Rabbeinu.

If one commits himself to doing these commandments [not just because they make sense,] but in order to serve God, He will show him greater kindness than He bestows on others. God gives him a higher standing in this world and rewards him greatly in the World to Come, as he did to Avraham, to whom he said, "*Fear not*

Avram, I am your shield. Your reward is very great" (Bereishis 15:1).

But a person who rebels against God despite the kindness He has shown him, will slide from the lofty level of a thinking man to the lowly level of a dumb beast. His fate will be the same as the animals [who are fattened prior to slaughter]. As it says, *"The enemies of God are like the glory of fattened sheep: Consumed! In smoke they are consumed"* (Tehillim 37:20). And his fate in the next world will be the worst possible, as it says *"Your spirit is a fire that will consume you"* (Yeshayah 33:11).

The second level is the favor God bestows exclusively on a certain nation, as when he bestowed kindness on the children of Israel by taking us out of Egypt and bringing us to the land of Canaan. In return for this kindness He imposed on us—in addition to the logic-based service—the duty to fulfill the Torah-based mitzvos.

If you do these mitzvos intending to honor God, you will be singled out by Him for special favor, which will then obligate you to a yet higher degree of service than the rest of your nation or tribe. This was the case with the tribe of Levi, as it says, *"When Moshe said, 'Whoever is for God, join me!' All the Levites gathered around him"* (Shemos 32:26). God showed them special kindness, choosing Aharon and his sons from their midst to serve God at the site of His Glory. He commanded them to observe more mitzvos than the rest of the nation, and promised them a great reward in the World to Come.

But whoever rebels against the Creator will fall from both levels and be punished in two worlds. As the wise Shlomoh said, *"It will not be well with the wicked, and he will not long endure"* *"(Koheles 8:13).*

The third level of favor involves God's goodness to a particular family in a nation, like the Kohanim and the Leviim, or the descendants of the House of David. [In return for these favors, God imposed on them additional service], as outlined in the Torah. Regarding the additional service demanded of the House of David it says, *"O House of David, thus said Hashem: Administer justice diligently and save the robbed from the hand of an oppressor,"* (Yirmeyah 21:12).

One in this category who fulfills his obligations because he loves to do God's will, will be singled out by Him for a good life in this world and for a great reward in the World to Come. He will become either a leader of the community or a halachic authority, as it says about Pinchas, *"Pinchas arose and executed judgment, and the plague was halted. It was accounted to him as a righteous deed, for all generations, forever"* (Tehillim 106:30,31). And furthermore it says, *"But the Kohanim, the Levites, descendants of Zadok, who safeguarded the charge of My Sanctuary, when the children of Israel strayed from Me, let them draw near to Me to serve Me"* (Yechezkel 44:15).

If one in this category rebels against God, he will drop from his lofty status in this world and suffer a great deal in the hereafter, as you know from the rebellion of Korach and his party.

The fourth level of favor relates to the favor God bestows on a particular individual, by which he is singled out from the rest of his family, and from others. This may be a prophet or ruler chosen to lead the nation, or a sage to whom God granted wisdom, understanding and counsel. The more favors you receive, the more service you must render to God. Do so, and you will continuously enjoy in this world, both the all-inclusive goodness you share with the rest of the world and the goodness specifically set aside for you. As it says, *"Hashem has sworn to David, a truth from which He will never retreat, 'From the fruit of your issue I will place upon your throne. If your sons keep My covenant, and this, My testament, that I shall teach them, then their sons, too, forever and ever shall sit upon your throne'"* (Tehillim 132:11,12). About the reward in the World to Come it says, *"If not for my belief that I would enjoy the goodness of Hashem in the land of the living . . ."* (ibid. 27:13).

If a person who has been singled out for such kindness, rebels against God, he will fall from his unique level. God will be stern in holding him answerable in this world, as it says, *"This is exactly what Hashem meant when He said, 'I will be sanctified through those close to Me, and glorified before all the people.' Aharon remained silent"* (Vayikra 10:3). And as it says, *"You alone have I singled out of all the families of the earth; that is why will call you to account for all your iniquities" (Amos 3:2).* And his punishment in the World to Come will be very harrowing, as it says, *"For Hell has been prepared from yesterday, it has been readied even for the king; God has deepened and widened it; its inferno has much fire and wood, and the breath of Hashem is like a stream of sulfur burning within it"* (Yeshayah 30:33).

We must serve God according to the level of favor we receive. The more kindly the Creator treats you, the more obligated you are to serve Him. This can be proven by the way produce has to be tithed. It says, *"Take a tithe of all the seed crops that come forth in the field"* (Devarim 14:22). The person to whom God has given one hundred *kur* of produce is required to give ten *kur*, while the person who received ten *kur* has to give only one. If the first person were to set aside nine-and-a-half *kur*, and the second were to set aside one *kur*, the first person would be punished and the second rewarded [although the first gave much more than the second.]

Furthermore, a father has the duty to circumcise his son and teach him Torah, but these mitzvos do not apply to childless men. So too, a handicapped person is exempt from going to Yerushalayim on the three *regalim*—pilgrimage festivals—and a sick person is exempt from the mitzvos he cannot fulfill due to his illness. The fewer favors one receives, the less service is required. By the same token, a person whom the Creator has singled out for special kindness has to serve God and thank Him all the more.

The pious men of old worried when they received a special favor from God, for two reasons. Firstly, they feared they might not serve God sufficiently, thanking Him enough for the special favor they received; and then this shortcoming would bring them misfortune. As our father Yaakov said, *"I am unworthy of all the favors"* (Bereishis 32:11). Secondly, they worried that the favor they received might be God's reward for their service; if so, their reward in the World to Come would be reduced. As the early commentators expounded the verse, *"He rewards His enemies to their face [in this world], to destroy them [in the World to Come] (Devarim 7:10).*

SERVING GOD FOR THE RIGHT REASONS

THE SOUL: I am unable to fulfill my obligations to the Creator for the kindness He has shown me in common with all mankind, much less for the kindness He has shown specifically to me. When I want to repay God, I begin to think of the reward I will receive for serving Him, and with my thanks, I have in mind that He continue or even increase His generosity. I find myself, during my service, hoping for more, instead of serving Him for unselfish reasons, purely out of love of God.

How will I be able to serve Him for all the kindness He has shown me personally, when my intentions are far from pure? What is the minimum service I should offer, to deserve having these kindnesses continue?

THE MIND: You complain that you are anticipating God's favors to continue indefinitely. This attitude stems from three weaknesses in your character.

The first one is your self-love and desire for pleasure, which causes you to do nothing even service to God, except to acquire pleasure. I already warned you to stay clear of this trait, for only then do I have hope for your success.

Your second weakness is not understanding how kind the Creator has been to you. You assume that the only way to enjoy His kindness is by asking for it. In fact, God has been good to you in ways you know and don't know; and by asking for things, you show that you have forgotten Who it was that did all those good things for you in the first place. When you stop thinking this way, you will serve Him in the proper frame of mind and thank Him wholeheartedly. You will deserve to receive the good things for which you are hoping.

Your third weakness is that you do not realize how lowly you are, and how flawed is your behavior. You think you deserve the greatest of kindnesses, therefore you never stop asking for them. And as soon as kindness comes your way, you want something even more desirable. You forget that the Creator is entitled to the greatest possible service on your part. When you serve Him, you think you are doing Him a favor, when actually you rely on Him, and He does not need you at all.

Give up this foolish attitude. Realize that your Creator has your welfare in mind and knows better than you what is good for you and what is not. Accept each favor bestowed upon you and be sincerely and abundantly grateful to Him. You will no longer hope for reward for your service which stops you from appreciating the good that comes your way, and discourages you from repaying your debt to God.

[If you do away with these three shortcomings] you will doubtless receive the good things you deserve for serving God, even without hoping for and thinking about rewards.

CHAPTER SEVEN

THE MINIMUM SERVICE TO GOD

THE MIND: The minimum service you have to render to be assured of God's continued kindness has ten aspects:

One: Never use God's favors as a vehicle to rebel against Him [as the Israelites did when they made the golden calf from the mass of the Egyptian's gold that washed up from the Red Sea].

Two: Remember God's goodness by constantly talking about it and by frequently thanking and praising Him, in your thoughts and words.

Three: Never underestimate the goodness God bestowed on you.

Four: If God uses someone as an agent to bestow a favor on you, don't thank the person instead of the Creator. Make sure that you attribute to God the good things that happen to you.

Five: Don't brag about the gifts God has bestowed on you, and don't imagine that you acquired them through your own hard work and talents, or because you deserved it.

Six: Don't think God's bounty will continue only as long as you make the effort. [You should believe God's bounty will continue because He wills it, without regard of any effort on your part.]

Seven: Don't look down on a person who does not enjoy the same favors as you, nor consider yourself better than he in the eyes of God. It may well be that God is granting you these favors in order to test you, by either bringing to light any hidden evil tendencies you may harbor, or to tempt you to sin. If such is the case, the one who did not receive these favors is more loved by God than you.

Eight: Be completely honest with God, both in your convictions and your submissiveness to Him. Even if [after receiving favors], you can do nothing more than what you have done in the past, or you can show no more appreciation than what you have shown, continue what you were doing, directing your thoughts to God when you do. Surely do not detract from what you have been doing because of the goodness bestowed on you; do not let good fortune cause you to lessen your devotion to God.

Nine: Be more aware of people less fortunate than you, rather than the more fortunate [in order to be happy with your lot]. Be aware of people who are more devoted to God than you, encouraging yourself to attain their level. But do not pay attention to those who do less than you, to avoid becoming proud of yourself and lax in your service to God.

Ten: Because God does not express His anger at your failings, do not be misled into thinking that you are safe from God's wrath when you rebel.

We know from bygone days as well as from our own times, that all those favored with God's kindness who, nevertheless, rebelled against Him, did so for the ten abovementioned negative factors. This has been clearly spelled out in the books of the prophets throughout the ages.

If you are unable to serve God in accordance with the good bestowed on you, at least take upon yourself all we have mentioned for the sake of Heaven. Then you will deserve that the good meant for you will endure. And even then, there are two reasons why it might be taken away: either to wipe away some earlier transgression or to enable you to enjoy an even greater, more precious reward in the World to Come.

CHAPTER EIGHT

DIVINE COMPULSION VERSUS FREE WILL

———◦◉◦———

T*HE SOUL:*   Thanks to your efforts I am cured. You analyzed me and were kind enough to treat me. With your expertise you lifted the gloom of foolishness that enveloped me. But I am still tormented with one question that prevents Divine service. Cure me of this pain and my worst problem will be solved, and I will be nearly cured of all my ailments.

THE MIND: To what are you referring?

THE SOUL: I find in the Scriptures that everything, from mineral, vegetable, animal to human being is subject to God's will, predetermination, command, and compulsion. For it says, *"Whatever Hashem wished He did, in heaven and on earth" (Tehillim 135:6); "Hashem brings death and gives life, He lowers to the grave and raises up. Hashem impoverishes and makes rich, He humbles and He elevates" (1 Shmuel 2:6,7); "Whose decree was ever fulfilled, unless the Lord willed it? Is it not at the word of the Most High that evil and good befall?" (Eichah 3:37,38); "I form light and create darkness, I make peace and create evil" (Yeshayah 45:7); "If Hashem will not build the house, in vain do its builders labor on it; if Hashem will not guard the city, in vain is the watchman vigilant" (Tehillim 127:1); "It is in vain for you who rise early, who sit up late, who eat the bread of sorrows, for indeed, He gives His beloved ones restful sleep" (Tehillim 127:2).*

There are many other such verses, and they seem to teach us that God created man and other living things only to populate the world, moving about only with His permission, authority and ability, and resting only when He ordains it. For it says, *"When He grants a person serenity, who can cause that person turmoil? (Iyov 34:29); "When You hide Your face, they are dismayed; when You retrieve their spirit, they perish, and to their dust they return" (Tehillim 104:29).* All the ancient thinkers seem to agree on this.

Yet the Torah teaches us that man acts of his own free will, deciding himself to do whatever he wants; he acts willfully and by his own choice, which is why he is rewarded for his service and punished for his transgressions. As it says, *"See! Today I have set before you [a free choice] between life and good [on one side], and death and evil [on the other] (Devarim 30:15); "You must choose life!" (ibid. 19) "This [sin] comes from your hand" (Malachi 1:9); "For He repays the deeds of man" (Iyov 34:11); "A man's foolishness corrupts his way" (Mishlei 19:3).*

Our holy books—be it in the Torah itself, the mitzvos or our ethics—teach this outright. Reward for our service and punishment for our transgressions, teaches us that man's deeds are in his own hands, and that God's glory plays no part in our choices, whether good or evil, righteous or wicked.

I cannot reconcile these contradictory ideas. If there is a remedy for this disease, may God cure me of it with your help.

THE MIND: Reconciling these opposing thoughts is no more difficult than explaining the inconsistencies we find in our daily life. There seem to be times when we can accomplish what we set out to do, and times when we cannot. This is because God reigns over us, we are under His control, and He allows us to do the things He himself favors, and prevents us from doing the things He does not favor. I could show you instances of this in what we say, hear, and see. So too, reward and punishment come to a person on the basis of things he attempts to do in his service to God, or because of his rebellion against Him.

The great thinkers debated at length the question whether man acts under Divine compulsion or out of his own free will. Some said that man's actions are a result of his will, ability and strength; God left our actions to us and gave us control over them. He does not compel us to do anything. This being so, we are entitled to a reward [when we act righteously] or deserve punishment [when we choose to do evil].

Others hold that, like everything else, man's actions are in the hands of the Creator. They say that everything accomplished in this world, either by man or by inanimate objects, is accomplished only because the Creator permitted and decreed that it be accomplished—nothing can be done a hair's breadth more or less.

When asked, "How can someone who was compelled to act be rewarded or punished?" They said that we do not understand the workings of reward and punishment, but since we know that God is righteous and faithful in His testimony about reward and punishment, we believe that He will live up to what He said. Our minds are too weak to grasp the full range of God's wisdom, and His righteousness and kindness are too manifest for us to question.

Some reconcile both Divine compulsion and Divine justice. But they warn that anyone who delves deeply into these concepts is bound to stumble and sin regardless of how he explains it. Therefore, the correct approach is, to believe your actions are the result of free will and that you are rewarded and punished for our deeds. Thereby you will profit in both worlds. But trust that whatever God does, is for our own good, and firmly believe that all actions, movements, and good and bad fortune come about by the decree of God. [This is based on the principle, "Everything is in the hands of Heaven, except the fear of Heaven" (*Berachos 33b*). When it comes to the observance of mitzvos man has freedom of choice, and, is entitled to a reward. However all other things are in God's hands]. Accept that God can make endless claims against man [because man must admit that he can't fully understand] whereas man has no right to make claims against God.

This approach is closer to the truth than any of the previous ones. For our ignorance of God's ways, due to the weakness of our minds and the limitations of our understanding, is well known. Our ignorance is, in fact, a kindness from God, [for if these profound mysteries were revealed, we might misunderstand them, arriving at false conclusions, and be harmed by them.] Therefore those things are hidden from us, just as sunglasses filter out much of the sunlight to protect our eyes. If it would do us good to unravel these secrets, the Creator would reveal them to us.

Think of a person with poor vision. He cannot go into direct sunlight until he protects his eyes with a thin veil. The weaker his vision gets, the heavier a veil he will need, and the more his vision improves, the thinner the veil he needs.

[Don't be surprised that you cannot fathom God's ways,] because there are many amazing things, even in the physical world, that you would not believe existed unless you saw them with your eyes. If you never saw an astrolabe and someone described it to you explaining that with it you could calculate the movement of the spheres, the position of the stars, the changing seasons, the distance between two points [on earth or in the sky], and do many other things unfamiliar to you, you would not understand it or imagine what it looked like.

The same is true of a balance scale. If you did not see it with your eyes, you would never believe that a person could weigh something accurately with a scale [that does not have two trays suspended from even arms] but whose arms are uneven [like a balance scale used in a doctor's office]. And even more amazing, you can weigh many objects of different weights with one and the same stone [by moving the stone back and forth along the arm].

Something people encounter more often than a balance scale is the movement of the upper millstone which turns at a steady pace, driven by a minimal amount of water pressure. When you toss a pebble into a swift stream, it is not carried downstream—but sinks straight to the bottom. But the millstone which weighs much more than the pebble, is set into motion by the force of the water that is much weaker [than the current of the stream]. If someone told this to you and you had not seen it with your eyes, you would claim it false.

This is because we know so little about the fundamental properties of creation, and we understand so little about the causes and effects of things, their nature and their specific properties.

Someone so ignorant about things he deals with all the time [like the scale and the millstone], will never be aware of the hidden ways of the Creator regarding His foreknowledge and man's free will. As David says, *"My heart is not proud, O God, nor my look haughty, nor do I pursue matters too great and too wondrous for me"* (*Tehillim* 131:1), which is followed by a statement that touches on surrendering to God: *"I swear that I stilled and silenced my soul, like a suckling child is my soul"* (ibid. 131:2).

CHAPTER NINE

The Mystery of the Creation of Man

⸺◈⸺

T*HE SOUL:* You convinced me not to solve the problem [of Divine compulsion versus freedom of choice], explaining that it is too profound. But reveal the secret of my existence explaining why I was brought into this world. Clarify which of my actions are done under Divine compulsion and which through free will, so that I will avoid the fate of the legendary king who did not appreciate how fortunate he was.

A Parable

The citizens of an Indian island appointed a stranger to rule over them each year. When his year was over they would depose him and send him back to where he came from. One year they appointed as their ruler a fool who did not realize what would happen at the end of the year. [Thinking that he was their ruler for life,] he accumulated wealth, built palaces and fortifications and took nothing from the state. In fact, he even tried to bring his possessions, his wife and his children, in to the country.

When his year was over, the islanders sent him away empty-handed, taking away everything he had built or acquired in that year. He left with nothing. The fool regretted what he had done, moaning over all the trouble he had accumulating wealth, which ended up in someone else's hands.

Next, the people appointed a wise and understanding foreigner as their ruler. As soon as he was installed, he asked someone how they dealt with the previous ruler. The man revealed what would be done to him.

Upon hearing this, the wise ruler took everything of value out of the country and deposited all his possessions abroad. He paid no attention to the honor the people were lavishing on him. He was both happy and sad the entire time he was there. He was sad because he would have to leave soon, and he had not taken out many valuables. How much more he could accumulate, if he could only stay longer! At the same time he was happy because he knew that when he left, he would settle where he deposited his treasures, enjoying them forever, with peace of mind.

When his year came to an end he did not worry about leaving the people. He actually was anxious and happy to go, congratulating himself for his achievements and efforts, looking forward to enjoying a great fortune, honor and everlasting joy. He achieved happiness and attained his goals in both places.

CONTINUES THE SOUL: I am afraid that, like the fool, I will toil in this world and fail to receive reward in both worlds. Since God granted that you be my guide, please teach me about my situation and explain it to me. Tell me about the mystery of my self, and how I can improve.

THE MIND: You described your situation in this world quite accurately with that parable. Your situation is really like those rulers. You are a stranger in this world, and you will soon leave it. Do what the wise and understanding ruler did, and you will succeed. If you change from this course in any way, nothing I say will do you any good.

THE SOUL: If I was not interested in this, I would not have taken the trouble to explore the hidden aspects of my situation to begin with.

MAN'S PURPOSE IN THIS WORLD

THE MIND: The secret of your being in this world is as follows: God created you—[the soul]—along with all other spiritual beings out of nothingness. He wanted to elevate you above the level of [the angels, to reach the level of the souls of the righteous who are] His treasure, the chosen and pure ones, those closest to His glorious Light.

You will not be worthy of that until three things have come to pass: one, you remove the veil of foolishness that surrounds you, thereby enabling you to be enlightened by His wisdom; two, you must be tested to determine whether you will serve Him or rebel against Him; three, you will have to suffer hardship in this world to determine whether or not you bear the burden of serving Him. This will elevate you to the level of those exalted righteous who bore the burden of His service, and about whom it says, *"Bless Hashem, O His messengers; the strong warriors who do His bidding, to obey the voice of His word" (Tehillim 103:20).* Since these three things can not come about in a spiritual world, [God brought you down into this world].

For this purpose God, in His wisdom, created this world and all it contains—minerals, plant and animal life—in perfect order, for your benefit.

He chose a fully equipped palace for you, [for the human body which is the home of the soul is] made from the world's finest materials, and which resembles the world in its roots, branches, and features; [for the human body is a small-scale replica of the universe].

From this palace He opened five gates to the outside world: your eyes, ears, nose, tongue, and hands. He appointed five trusted gatekeepers to manage them: your five senses, sight, hearing, smell, taste and touch, which enable you to come in contact with the physical world.

He also appointed a hierarchy of four supervisors for the palace: the brain, the heart, the liver and the testicles. He also appointed four managers, namely: ingestion, retention, digestion and excretion. To keep the palace running smoothly, He made storehouses and dwelling places for the two galls, black and green; the white fluid; and the blood. He stationed servants throughout the palace area, both inside the palace and on the palace grounds, to serve and care for it. The inside servants are the intestines, veins, sinews, nerves, and arteries; the outside servants are the hands, feet, tongue, genitals, teeth, nails, and the like. He then prepared for you components that form a bridge between the spiritual and the physical: the blood, body heat, and life spirit. With His power and wisdom He anchored you securely in this palace and fastened you safely so that the three conditions we mentioned could be met. He prepared two advisors for your benefit and appointed two scribes [to record all your actions]. And he provided you with servants and attendants to take care of your needs in this world.

One of the two advisors is your [*yetzer tov*—good impulse, which is your] intellect which tells you God's will. The other [is your *yetzer hara*—evil impulse, which] tempts you to do things that anger God, your Creator.

One scribe records all the good things you do in private and in public, with your thoughts and your actions. It takes into account how you utilized your gatekeepers, supervisors, managers, servants, advisors, employees, and attendants. In the same way, the second, records your bad deeds.

The employees and attendants we mentioned are your emotions and character traits. These include happiness and worry, gladness and sorrow, memory and forgetfulness, wisdom and ignorance, courage and timidity, generosity and selfishness, righteousness and evil, bashfulness and insolence, hope and fear, love and hate, pleasure and pain, arrogance and humility, control and acquiescence, and many of the other traits within you.

The Creator instructed these gatekeepers, supervisors, managers, servants, advisors, employees and attendants to obey you and follow all your orders [until you die, which is] at a set time. There are special instances when they are not under your control, which was clearly stipulated when you were fused with your body. These are cases of Divine compulsion and Divine decree.

Man Is Judged According to His Intentions

God allowed you to use these traits for the well-being of your body, and in order to accomplish the things He gave you control over in this world, namely, the fulfillment of the mitzvos. These include mitzvos that make sense to you and mitzvos you cannot understand—and things that are permitted.

God said to you, "Don't be misled by the worldly pleasures I allowed you to enjoy in this world. Not one of them can do you good or harm, bring you delight or pain. They only affect your body in a physical sense, not your essential self.

"You do not need them! They are like the placenta to a newborn or an eggshell to a chick. [Although the placenta and the shell serve a need, it is not an integral part of the baby and the chick. So too, the body and, in fact, the whole world are not essential elements of the soul, and do not contribute anything to it. They are merely the means the soul uses to reach a higher spiritual level (*Tov Levanon*).] If you understand My intentions for [bringing you into this world] and that I want only the best for you; if you decide to serve Me rather than rebel against Me, using the things I gave you control over, I will raise you to the highest spiritual level, to be on equal footing with My chosen and elected ones. I will draw you close to Me in compassion, and clothe you in the radiance of My glory. But if you decide to rebel against Me, I will punish you severely and make you suffer long-term affliction.

"If you do not know how to use these things to serve Me, because you are too involved with your body—which I gave you in order to test you—then remember that I gave you your intellect, which is a wise and faithful adviser, in order to guide you when you are neglectful.

"Take its advice about everything. It will tell you how to use the things available to you in order to serve Me, and will turn your disgraceful qualities into praiseworthy ones, like the wise doctor who correctly uses harmful and even poisonous medicines as remedies to cure his patients.

"If you allow your intellect to gain the upper hand following its advice, the scribe who records your good deeds will record even your permitted actions [which are not mitzvos, like eating and drinking, since you are doing them for the sake of Heaven]. Your limbs and your senses will thereby be trained to help you serve Me.

"If you reject your intellect's advice and prefer the counsel of the other adviser [which is the *yetzer hara*], and make use of the things available to you as he advises, then your praiseworthy qualities will become disgraceful. You will be like the foolish doctor who, in his ignorance, kills patients with healthy medicines because he does not know how to use them. The scribe who records evil deeds, will then include all the permitted things you do, among your misdeeds.

"Your helpers, attendants, servants and everyone else you come in contact with, will agree with you, doing whatever you ask them to do [whether good or bad]. The choice is yours. See to it that your helpers be a source of happiness for you."

THE MIND CONTINUES: All this is based on Divine justice. For in your mind and heart you choose either to rebel against Him or serve Him. Your outward appearance and your inner nature are one and the same to Him, and He will repay you for all that He observes in you [according to your intentions, even if you were prevented from carrying out the good deed you had in mind]. He will repay you even for things hidden from others.

A human judge can only base his decision on the evidence before him, whether it be the testimony of witnesses or his own observation. If he knew what was in the minds of the litigants he would certainly base his decision on that. The Creator Who knows the obvious and the hidden equally well comes to a decision based on what He knows. As it says, *"The hidden things belong to Hashem, our God" (Devarim 29:28).*

When the Creator wants to spur you to repent or admonish you He commands one of His ministers to stop serving you, and that limb becomes ill. At times he will strike two, or all of your limbs, and you become sick and are in pain for a certain length of time.

When you respond by returning to Him, He commands the ministers to serve you again, healing your body, and bringing it back to its former health. As it says, *"Fools because of their sinful path and because of their iniquities, were afflicted. Their soul abhorred all food, and they reached the portals of death. Then they cried out to Hashem in their distress, He would save them from their straits. He sends His word and cures them"* (Tehillim 107:17-20).

When [your life in this world ends and] your days of trial and tribulation are over, the Creator commands all the gatekeepers, servants and employees to leave you, severing the connections between you and the body, and you return to your original state of being. As the wise Shlomoh said, *"And the dust returns to the ground as it was, and the spirit returns to God Who gave it"* (Koheles 12:7).

You are then shown the record of your deeds, thoughts, and desires, as well as what you occupied yourself with in life. That will be the basis of your reward.

You have already been warned about this by God's messengers, prophets and the faithful Torah. As the wise Shlomoh said, *"Incline your ear and hear the words of the wise; set your heart to My knowledge. For it is pleasant to keep them if you guard them in your innards . . . Surely, I have written for you [in the Torah] extremely noble things, with counsel and knowledge to teach you the veracity of the words, so that you may answer words of truth to those who send word to you"* (Mishlei 22:17-22).

CHAPTER TEN

Using Our Character Traits Appropriately

⎯⎯⎯⎯●⎯⎯⎯⎯

T*HE SOUL:*   I understood what you said, I ask you now to explain under what circumstances should I use my praiseworthy traits, and when should I use my disgraceful ones.

THE MIND: You have many contrasting character traits: for example, happiness and grief. Express happiness when you are experiencing lasting and permanent pleasure, without a tinge of sorrow or misfortune [which can happen only when you serve God and perform mitzvos]. Feel sad only when you run into permanent sorrow from which you cannot escape [which happens only when you transgress God's will].

There is fear and hope. Have fear when you are doing things that will bring you misfortune, and will inevitably be no good for you [namely, when you violate God's will. In all other cases trust in God Who only does what is good for you]. Be hopeful when fulfilling the mitzvos God commanded you to perform, preparing for your ultimate good, which no one can prevent and nothing can keep from you.

There is courage and timidity. Show courage against enemies of God. Fight and suffer any hardship to do the will of the Creator and the will of His pious ones. As it says, *"Because of Your sake we are killed all the time, we are considered sheep for slaughter"* (*Tehillim 44:23*), and *"Let the righteous one strike me with kindness and let him rebuke me" (ibid. 141:5)*. Express timidity when you meet people who love God, by not arguing with them and by not taking a stance against someone who reprimands you for your own good. As it says, *"Because your heart was soft and you humbled yourself before Hashem" (2 Melachim 22:19)*.

There is shame and impudence. Show shame when you rebel against the One Who does you favors, using these very favors to defy Him in His presence. Show shame when He is rebuking you with gentle and stern warnings [through sickness or misfortune] and through the words of His prophets. As it says, *"You Son of Man! Tell the House of Israel about the Temple, and let them be ashamed of their iniquities" (Yechezkel 43:10)*, *"I said, 'My God, I am embarrassed and ashamed to lift my face to You, my God" (Ezra 9:6)*. Be impudent against evil people, sinners, and those who argue with the truth, when you [stand up for the Torah and] urge people to act kindly or warn them against doing shameful things. Be impudent when you embarrass sinners and reproach children and adults, as it says, *"I made my face as hard as flint and knew that I would not be ashamed" (Yeshayah 50:7)*.

There is anger and graciousness. Express anger against people who depart from the ways of truth and justice. Be gracious when everything is done properly, when all is in its proper place and people act truthfully.

There is compassion and ruthlessness. Show compassion toward the needy, the poor, the sick, those condemned to death, those who do not know how to improve their lot, those who are clumsy, those who are imprisoned by enemies, those who have lost a great fortune, and those who regret and weep over past sins out of fear of Divine punishment. Be ruthless when you retaliate against the wicked and take revenge on the oppressors. As it says, *"Do not let your eyes pity him, do not show him any mercy, and do not try to cover up for him" (Devarim 13:9)*.

There is pride and humility. Express pride when you face atheists and people who reject God. Never be humble before such people, God forbid, giving them the impression that you accept their views and gravitate toward their perverse ideas. Show how much you oppose their way of thinking and how little you agree with them, just as Mordechai refused to bow down to Haman. Show humility when you encounter a pious, pure, God-fearing person, who is a Torah sage and is engaged in the service of God. Express humility toward someone who has been kind and generous to you, and to whom you owe a debt of gratitude.

All the more should you show humility toward the Creator, Whose kindnesses have been so great and numerous that you could never repay Him for them. Show humility by willingly accepting God's judgment upon yourself, as it says, *"When the time finally comes that their stubborn spirit is humbled, I will forgive their sins"* *(Vayikra 26:41)*.

There is love and hate. Express love when you are with someone who agrees with you about the service of God, as well as when you are with someone who will lead you toward ultimate happiness [in the World to Come]. Express hate toward someone who goes against God's will, and who leads you to do things that anger your Creator. As it says, *"Those who forsake the Torah praise the wicked, but the keepers of Torah contend with them"* *(Mishlei 28:4)*.

There is generosity and miserliness. Show generosity, by giving from your money and your knowledge to everyone who deserves it according to his need, as it says, *"Do not withhold good from one who deserves it when you have the power to give it to him"* *(ibid. 3:27)*, and, *"Let your springs gush forth"* *(ibid.5:16)*.

Be miserly with the heartless and the fools, as it says, *"One who chastises the scoffer acquires shame for himself, and he who rebukes the wicked acquires a blemish"* *(Mishlei 9:7)*, As our Sages put it, "Whoever does a favor for a person who does not appreciate it, is like someone casting a stone to the idol Mercury, [which was worshipped by throwing stones at it]."

And last, there is laziness and diligence. Be lazy in indulging your animal desires, those short-lived pleasures that bring in their wake nothing but shame in this world and punishment in the World to Come. Be diligent when you are enjoying spiritual delights, things favored by God, as David said, *"I hastened and I did not delay to keep Your commandments"* *(Tehillim 119:60)*.

[Concludes the author:] What I have mentioned in this Gate should be enough for one who has chosen the right path who searches for truth and pursues wisdom for its own sake.

May God in His mercy help us to reach the way to His service. Amen.

GLOSSARY

AVRAHAM - Abraham

BARAISA pl. *BARAISOS* - outside text, not included in the Mishnah

BEREISHIS - The Book of Genesis

DEVARIM - The Book of Deuteronomy

EICHA - The Book of Lamentations

GEMARA - Talmud

HASHEM - God

HOSHEA - The Book of Hosea

IYOV - Job

KOHANIM - Priests, descendants of Aaron

KOHELES - Ecclesiastes

LEVI'IM - from the tribe of Levi

LULAV - palm branch take on Sukkos

MASECHES - Tractate of

MELACHIM - The Book of Kings

MISHLEI - Proverbs

MISHNAH pl. *MISHNAYOS* - compilation of the oral tradition; it also refers to one paragraph of this compilation

MITZVAH pl. *MITZVOS* - commandment

MOSHE RABBEINU - Moses our Teacher

NOACH - Noah

OLAM HABA - The World to Come

PIDYON HABEN - Redemption of the first born

SHABBOS - The day of rest - Saturday

SHAATNEZ - The prohibition of wearing a garment of wool and linen

SHEMOS - The Book of Exodus

SHLOMOH - Solomon

SHMUEL - The Book of Samuel

SUKKAH - hut used on Sukkos

TANACH - Scriptures

TANNAIM - The Sages of the Mishnah

TEHILLIM - Psalms

TERUMAH pl. *TERUMOS* - contribution to the Kohein

TZITZIS - fringes worn on a four cornered garment

VAYIKRA - The Book of Leviticus

YAAKOV - Jacob

YAMIM TOVIM - Festivals

YECHEZKEL - Ezekiel

YEHOSHUA - Joshua

YESHAYAH - Isaiah

YIRMIYAH - Jeremiah